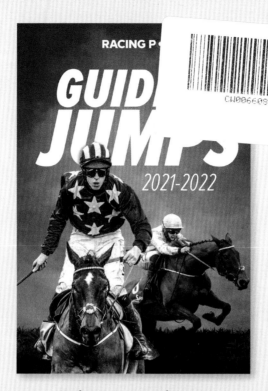

Edited and designed
by David Dew

Contributors

Richard Birch	Lawrie Kelsey
James Burn	Brian Sheerin
Tom Collins	Craig Thake
Ian Greensill	Nick Watts
Dylan Hill	Robbie Wilders
Paul Kealy	

Cover artwork by Duncan Olner

Inside artwork by Stefan Searle

Published in 2021 by Pitch Publishing on behalf of Racing Post, A2 Yeoman Gate, Yeoman Way, Worthing, Sussex, BN13 3QZ.

Copyright © Pitch Publishing and Racing Post, 2021. Every effort has been made to trace the copyright holders. Any oversight will be rectified in future editions at the earliest opportunity by the publisher.

ISBN: 978-1839500817

Printed by Buxton Press Ltd

NICKY HENDERSON

WINNERS IN LAST FOUR SEASONS 123, 130, 141, 140

Shishkin primed to take over top billing from the superstars

EMMA LAVELLE

Chasing could still happen for Paisley

OLIVER GREENALL

WINNERS IN LAST FOUR SEASONS 37, 12, 18, 11

Big-money purchases, prospering partnership and a festival dream

CHARLIE LONGSDON

WINNERS IN LAST FOUR SEASONS 31, 29, 36, 44

Garde's hurdles mark is too good to ignore

kelso-races.co.uk

LOWDOWN FROM THE TRAINERS

RACING POST EXPERTS

THIS SEASON'S KEY HORSES

HARRY FRY

WINNERS IN LAST FOUR SEASONS **31, 30, 47, 53**

Gunning to pick up the pace and kick on

THE building has finally stopped and now Harry Fry has started the rebuilding – of his career.

After moving from Seaborough in Dorset ten miles east to Higher Crockermoor, situated in 100 acres of picturesque rolling countryside, Fry has overseen the transformation of an old farm into a bespoke training establishment.

During the stable building over the last couple of years Fry's winners decreased to 30 and 31 from an average

Stable star: Metier (4) (below)

Ask Me Early: smart chaser could have comeback run over hurdles to protect his chase mark

" The Welsh National is an ideal target for Ask Me Early, who has already won twice at Chepstow and it's possible he'll have an entry in the Ladbrokes Trophy and the Welsh National Trial "

of 55 over the previous four seasons. The coronavirus pandemic hardly helped either.

So now, like a chippy that has reopened after a refurb, the team at Higher Crockermoor are "Frying again".

"We demolished an old farmyard and started from scratch basically, building on the old footprint," says Fry. "We have three American-style barns with plenty of ventilation and natural light.

Last season's solid base

"We have a two-furlong, deep-sand oval canter, and a four-and-a-half uphill gallop. So it was a big learning curve last year, getting builders out from under our feet, also getting to know the yard and getting into a routine, working out how best to use the gallops.

"We learned an awful lot last season and were delighted to get our first Grade 1 winner within six months of moving in during June.

"It was a good base to build on and now we're looking forward to a successful campaign. Hopefully, we've got a couple of horses that can take us to the big days. It's definitely a season when we have to deliver and get back to the heights we were at.

"We always strive to beat the previous season's tally and we'd like to get back to training 50 winners a year. We've 65 horses and capacity for 80.

"We're always looking to reinvest and replace, but it's about finding the right ones and not filling boxes for the sake of it.

"We've got some really nice horses to look forward to and 20 of those are unraced and include some nicely bred individuals."

If Fry unearths one as good as Rock On Ruby, whom he prepared in a satellite yard for trainer Paul Nicholls before victory in the 2012 Champion Hurdle, he'll be delighted.

He was a young man of 25 then, but nine seasons down the line he has further enhanced a reputation for saddling winners.

Leading the rebuilding process at Higher Crockermoor is **Metier**, winner of the Tolworth Hurdle at Sandown in January.

"He'll stay over hurdles and we're thinking of starting him in either the Greatwood [at Cheltenham in mid-November] or the Grade 2 Elite at Wincanton the week before," says Fry.

"We'll see which direction we go for the rest of the campaign from there. We think he's an exciting hurdler and there's plenty more to come yet.

"He was our first Grade 1 winner from the new yard, but it wasn't his true running in the Supreme at Cheltenham.

"He had an inflamed arytenoid cartilage, which makes up half the larynx and he couldn't breathe. That explains his below-par performance.

"We went into the spring with high hopes and when it didn't happen it was a relief when we were able to pinpoint the problem. It was frustrating but the main thing is he's made a full recovery.

"He's done well over the summer and we hope he can progress as a second-season hurdler, and it will be interesting to see him on slightly better ground at some point."

Welsh National target

The Midlands National was being lined up for **Ask Me Early** last season, but he didn't run his race at Sandown in February.

"We were able to diagnose and treat a kissing spine [where the vertebrae touch and cause pain]," says Fry. "He bounced back to form in the novice handicap chase at Uttoxeter on Midlands National day as we felt after Sandown we couldn't go for the big one.

"The Welsh National is an ideal target for Ask Me Early, who has already won twice at Chepstow and it's possible he'll have an entry in the Ladbrokes Trophy and the Welsh National Trial.

"He's exciting and, as he's never won over hurdles, his first run this season could be in a novice hurdle to help protect his mark."

After finishing second in both his Irish point-to-points two years ago **Boothill** was bought for £125,000 and has not disappointed connections.

He won his bumper at Kempton easily and followed up with an emphatic hurdles debut at Taunton where he jumped smoothly for Sean Bowen before coming clear for a near ten-length victory.

"He's lightly raced but talented. Last year he was on the sidelines with a splint after his winning debut over hurdles at Taunton and it settled down initially but then flared up again and it was just unfortunate timing," says Fry.

"He was back in full work by March/April, but the season and its main events were over. He's fully recovered and if we get a clear run with him we're looking forward to him going novice chasing.

"We've always thought of him as a chaser and hopefully he can make up for lost time over the bigger obstacles this winter. We have high hopes for him.

"We'll start him over two miles. He's never looked slow, but he'll dictate to us whether we go up to two and a half."

Promising mare for chases

Pure Bliss is another winning Irish pointer who has proved a shrewd purchase as well as being aptly named.

She won her bumper at Ffos Las impressively, followed up with two novice hurdle victories after wind surgery, then finished off last season by landing a 2m4f mares' handicap hurdle at the Punchestown Festival.

"She'll be going chasing this season as there's such an attractive range of choices in the programme book for mares over fences," says Fry.

"She's a big, strong mare who handles slow ground and is another novice chaser we're looking forward to. We think she can have a productive year over fences. She's certainly capable of getting black type."

If The Cap Fits is a Grade 1 and double Grade 2-winning hurdler who started off over fences last season but was switched back

■ Fry has an eyecatching five-year record at Exeter with 40 winners, a 33% strike-rate and profit of £63.99

" He won once, was second twice and third once in four starts. We'll be looking to mix and match over hurdles and fences again "

If The Cap Fits: didn't take particularly well to fences last season but will be given more chances to finesse his technique

to hurdles, a move that "didn't quite go to plan".

"Having said that, his chasing record was far from disgraceful," says Fry. "He won once, was second twice and third once in four starts. We'll be looking to mix and match over hurdles and fences again.

"He could start in the intermediate chase at Sandown in November, a race in which he finished runner-up last season."

Whitehotchillifili is a mare who loves it when "the mud's flying" as she proved when winning a Listed mares' hurdle at Sandown in January.

"She'll be targeting very similar races again this season and is definitely best when the ground is slow."

Phoenix Way is a lightly raced horse whom connections think has "a good prize in him this winter".

He won on debut over fences and was then highly tried in Grade 1 company. He could reappear at Newton Abbot in early October in an intermediate chase with a view to targeting the Paddy Power Gold Cup at the Cheltenham November meeting.

Veteran still going strong

Sir Ivan is an 11-year-old who did particularly well in veterans' chases last season, finishing third in the Veterans' Chase Series final at Sandown in January.

"He won at Newbury in March which qualifies him again for the final. He's struck up a fine partnership with our conditional, Lorcan Murtagh. He'll probably start out at Chepstow at the October meeting if ground conditions allow."

Momella won three times over fences, including a Listed mares' chase at Exeter. She'll be aimed again at similar mares' chases at Market Rasen in November, Newbury in December and a race she won at Exeter in early February. She's best when the ground is slow.

Master Debonair joined the Fry team last season and had only one start when unplaced in a Grade 3 hurdle at Aintree in April.

"He was a Listed bumper winner and Grade 2 novice hurdle winner and will go over fences this autumn.

"If we can get him back to the form of his early days we'll be pleased," says Fry.

Fortunes Melody is a highly promising import from France, where she won a Listed mares' race over hurdles and was subsequently placed three more times in Grade races over hurdles, all with plenty of cut in the ground.

"She was placed for us in her first two runs in the spring," says Fry. "She could have one more run over hurdles and then we'll probably look to use her four-year-old allowance over fences. She could be useful."

Revels Hill is a British point-to-point winner who won a handicap hurdle in April.

"He prefers better ground and will go novice chasing and should be ready by the middle of October."

Goudhurst Star has run only twice, winning a maiden hurdle at Warwick on his second start. "He's a chaser in the making but he should be progessive this winter over hurdles, particularly as we step him up in trip," says Fry.

Lady Adare won a bumper at Newcastle. She's been jumping particularly well at home and could develop into a useful novice hurdler.

One for the notebook

Make a particular note of **Might I**, who won an 18-runner bumper on debut at Warwick, then ran in a Listed bumper at Newbury but faded to finish fifth of 11.

"It was when my horses weren't on song and it wasn't his true running," stresses Fry. "He was the last off the bridle, but when push came to shove he couldn't see the race out.

"He's had a good summer and has had time to recover. He's schooled well, ticks all the boxes and is all set to go hurdling."

Ree Okka is a five-year-old who joined Fry after winning an Irish point-to-point.

"He jumps particularly well and that will be a real forte of his. We'll kick straight on over hurdles with him. He's by Getaway and from the family of Identity Thief."

HARRY FRY
CORSCOMBE, DORSET

Top to bottom: Master Debonair, Sir Ivan and Goudhurst Star

RECORD AROUND THE COURSES

	Total W-R	Per cent	Non-hcp Hdle	Non-hcp Chase	Hcp Hdle	Hcp Chase	N.H. Flat	£1 level stake
Exeter	40-121	33.1	21-53	8-18	4-26	4-11	3-13	+63.99
Wincanton	32-163	19.6	7-57	2-8	10-49	4-22	9-27	-2.82
Taunton	30-137	21.9	15-58	0-3	7-45	2-9	6-22	-34.84
Uttoxeter	24-90	26.7	5-18	1-10	6-21	8-26	4-15	+22.36
Ascot	20-86	23.3	12-23	1-7	4-24	3-23	0-9	-4.67
Newbury	19-95	20.0	6-25	2-7	2-25	3-21	6-17	-16.01
Kempton	18-97	18.6	6-27	1-6	6-24	4-26	1-14	-23.06
Newton Abbot	17-74	23.0	6-19	1-5	6-34	2-6	2-10	-12.19
Fontwell	14-60	23.3	4-20	1-4	6-20	3-6	0-10	-11.33
Cheltenham	14-124	11.3	6-33	0-12	3-41	3-29	2-9	-52.74
Plumpton	12-29	41.4	4-7	3-6	2-9	1-3	2-4	+23.23
Ludlow	11-49	22.4	4-14	1-3	2-10	2-13	2-9	-8.96
Warwick	11-61	18.0	4-21	3-9	2-10	1-5	1-16	-5.44
Southwell	10-34	29.4	3-12	0-0	2-7	3-9	2-6	+9.89
Doncaster	10-34	29.4	1-8	6-9	0-6	1-6	2-5	-1.46
Bangor	10-36	27.8	3-21	2-4	1-4	0-1	4-6	+9.46
Market Rasen	9-42	21.4	3-9	1-2	1-15	1-10	3-6	-4.42
Aintree	9-63	14.3	2-18	1-5	3-16	2-16	1-8	-9.27
Ffos Las	8-40	20.0	0-13	3-7	2-6	1-3	2-11	-6.07
Sandown	8-48	16.7	6-14	0-4	1-14	0-12	1-4	-4.63
Huntingdon	7-42	16.7	1-10	2-8	2-9	0-3	2-12	-18.48
Kempton (AW)	6-11	54.5	0-0	0-0	0-0	0-0	6-11	+66.25
Stratford	6-34	17.6	2-5	3-5	1-15	0-6	0-3	-18.20
Chepstow	5-49	10.2	1-16	0-2	1-11	3-11	0-9	-31.38
Haydock	4-22	18.2	1-4	0-0	3-13	0-5	0-0	+3.80
Towcester	3-5	60.0	0-1	0-0	1-1	0-0	2-3	+4.75
Leicester	3-9	33.3	1-4	1-1	0-1	1-3	0-0	+0.08
Wetherby	3-15	20.0	2-8	1-2	0-2	0-1	0-2	-5.75
Hereford	3-19	15.8	1-7	2-5	0-4	0-2	0-1	-6.55
Worcester	3-33	9.1	2-16	0-3	0-4	1-4	0-6	-25.30
Lingfield	2-8	25.0	2-3	0-0	0-4	0-1	0-0	-3.08
Fakenham	1-1	100.0	0-0	0-0	0-0	1-1	0-0	+1.25
Carlisle	1-2	50.0	0-0	1-2	0-0	0-0	0-0	+3.00
Kelso	1-5	20.0	0-2	0-1	1-2	0-0	0-0	+0.50
Sedgefield	0-1	0.0	0-1	0-0	0-0	0-0	0-0	-1.00
Musselburgh	0-2	0.0	0-0	0-0	0-2	0-0	0-0	-2.00
Perth	0-3	0.0	0-1	0-1	0-1	0-0	0-0	-3.00
Ayr	0-4	0.0	0-0	0-0	0-2	0-2	0-0	-4.00
Lingfield (AW)	0-4	0.0	0-0	0-0	0-0	0-0	0-4	-4.00

"I think he'll like the better ground, so we won't run him all through winter in deep ground. He looks an exciting addition to the team. We'll see how he progresses but he looks a lovely horse in the making."

Whisky Express made a winning racecourse debut at Taunton in March despite showing significant signs of inexperience. "She's a tall, rangey mare. We might wait for the Listed mares bumper at the Cheltenham November meeting which we won last year with her half-sister Ishkhara Lady," says Fry.

Walk On High is by Walk In The Park out of Highland Retreat, who was Fry's first ever winner.

"It's nice to come full circle and have progeny from my first winner in the yard," says Fry. "He'll be ready to run in a bumper in November. He's ticked all the boxes at home so far, so let's hope that proves to be the case on the racetrack."

How Will I Know, second in an Irish point-to-point bumper, will start off in bumpers after which he's likely to go over hurdles for which he's schooled well.

On My Command won a bumper and was placed over hurdles. "Hopefully, it won't be long before she loses her maiden tag over hurdles and will prove progressive this winter," says Fry.

Interview by Lawrie Kelsey

11

OLIVER GREENALL

Big-money purchases, prospering partnership and a festival dream

First light on the gallops, where Oliver Greenall (above right) and Josh Guerriero have been making plans

WHEN a little TLC is added to **Zinc White** over the coming months the team at Stockton Hall Farm in Cheshire hope the formula will produce a triumph of planning next spring.

At £310,000, the three-year-old gelding is the most expensive member of the 75-strong team which Oliver Greenall and his assistant trainer and business partner Josh Guerriero are preparing for an assault on some of jumping's most prestigious prizes.

And for juvenile hurdlers the prizes don't come any bigger than the Triumph Hurdle at the Cheltenham Festival in March.

That is this season's ultimate target for Zinc White, rated 87 on the Flat after winning impressively for Ralph Beckett over

WINNERS IN LAST FOUR SEASONS **37, 12, 18, 11**

one mile six furlongs at Wetherby and Sandown.

"He was expensive but he has everything to be a hurdler," says Guerriero. "He jumps brilliantly, he's very athletic, and finds everything very easy. He wants a galloping track and soft ground, so he won't be running until the rain comes.

"He's done everything right so far on the track and at home, so we can't not have high hopes.

"He'll be aimed at the Grade 2 juvenile hurdle at the Cheltenham trials meeting in November and the Grade 1 Finale Juvenile Hurdle at Chepstow in January, and the long-term plan is the Triumph Hurdle.

"We could also look at those decent handicaps in early spring at the start of the Flat season."

'Immaculate' Herbiers

Guerriero says **Herbiers** is another to carry high hopes as the yard aims to beat last year's total of 37 winners, which it ought to achieve having already welcomed back 17, including two on the Flat.

The four-year-old French bumper winner has already won three times over hurdles in Britain, including valuable races at Ascot and Sandown to earn a mark of 130.

"He was fantastic last year," says Guerriero. "He'll start at Chepstow in a four-year-old handicap hurdle and the plan is to go to the Greatwood at Cheltenham in November.

"Then, depending on how he goes, we'll decide whether to stay over hurdles or go over fences with him. He's a big chasing type. We've schooled him over fences and he's immaculate."

Herbiers (left): has a long-term future as a chaser but will start off this season over hurdles

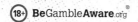
STAY AHEAD OF THE FIELD WITH
RACING POST MEMBERS' CLUB

ACCESS PREMIUM CONTENT AND FEATURES
FIND OUT MORE AT
RACINGPOST.COM/MEMBERS-CLUB

On the gallops: Greenall and Guerriero watch their future stars work at Stockton Hall Farm

Much of Stockton Hall's hopes for the new season rest with an intake of newcomers from the point-to-point field, and among them is **Jet Of Magic**.

"He's a big, imposing, chasing type who won a point-to-point bumper at Punchestown impressively on real heavy ground," says Guerriero. "He has no big targets. We'll start him off in two-mile novice hurdles in soft ground on a galloping track and take it from there. He'll stay all day."

Duke Of Deception finished a close third in an Irish point-to-point in late May behind two horses subsequently sold for six figures. He was in front at the last and just got beaten a length and a half and could prove to be a bargain at £48,000.

"He seems to have a lot of class," says Guerriero. "He'll start in a bumper, then go novice hurdling."

Emma Blue won her Irish point-to-point decisively and has been impressing since her move.

"She shows a lot of speed and class at home and has been schooling very well," says Guerriero.

"She'll probably start in a bumper at Uttoxeter in October because she shows so much speed and if she won there she'd probably go for a Listed mares' bumper at Cheltenham.

"If she won that I'd imagine we'd go for one of the championship bumpers. If not, she'll go novice hurdling."

Good Work is a five-year-old who came over from France where he was well regarded by his connections.

"I know they thought a lot of him as a four-year-old but he was big and backward," says Guerriero, who is confident the import will win over hurdles soon.

"He schools brilliantly. He's still a maiden, so we'll start him off in novice hurdles. He's rated 120, so he should be able to win a novice hurdle somewhere."

Adjournment was a decent British pointer last season and yet another considered to be an embryonic chaser. "He's a lovely, big, chasing type but we'll start him off in a bumper because he shows a lot of pace," says Guerriero. "He wants better ground, so we'll try and get him out early."

Monte Igueldo is another French import expected to hit the heights. "He's very exciting," says Guerriero. "He was second on his only start in France. He'll start off in a novice hurdle at somewhere like Wetherby in the middle of October. He seems to have a lot of ability and finds everything very easy. He goes in soft ground and could be anything."

Blackwell Bay 'a monster'

Yet another pointing the way to bumpers and novice hurdles is **Blackwell Bay**, who finished second in his only British point-to-point.

"He's a monster at 17 hands and bound to improve so much with a bit of time. He'll start off in a bumper at Ayr in October and then go novice hurdling. He's a three-mile chaser in the making."

Phil De Pail is another big staying type who has been placed in bumpers and is expected to "improve massively with time".

"He'll go over hurdles and will come into his own over a bit of a trip," says Guerriero. "He'll like soft ground and we'll probably start him off over two and a half on big galloping tracks."

Evander was a "star" for the yard last year, winning two chases.

Evander: winner of two handicap chases for the stable last season

"He'll start off in a novice hurdle at somewhere like Wetherby in the middle of October. He seems to have a lot of ability and finds everything very easy"

■ Kelso has been a lucky track for the Greenall stable. Three winners from just eight runners is a 38% strike-rate

"He's one of the highest-rated horses in the yard. We'll step him up to three miles and hope for more improvement. He'll probably be out at Sedgefield, where he's won previously."

Homme Public promised much after being second in both his French hurdle races and didn't let his new connections down when second first time out at Catterick, where he lost a shoe, then winning impressively at Market Rasen.

"We then went straight for the Fred Winter at Cheltenham but the ground had dried and he needs it soft," says Guerriero. "He was bang there two out but they quickened away from him and he finished 14th. He's on an attractive mark now of 124 and will definitely improve."

Brilliant jumper is promising

Dondiam, who won his only British point-to-point, has shown he has plenty of speed at home, so he'll be started off in a bumper, possibly at Bangor in late October.

"He's done loads of schooling and jumps brilliantly, so then he'll go over hurdles and, hopefully, he could be something nice."

Dooyork is another winning Irish point import for whom much is expected. She displays plenty of speed and class on the home gallop and could be introduced to British rules in a mares' bumper in October, maybe at Uttoxeter.

Ecossais has taken time to come to himself since coming over from France, but has never stopped improving.

"He's won three times and never been out of the first three in his last six races. He's a stable star," says Guerriero.

"We've got a three-and-a-half-mile race lined up at Haydock in November for him, then we'll aim him at those local Nationals at places like Sedgefield and Catterick, which will play to his strengths because he stays forever."

Make a note of the yard's popular 11-year-old **Late Romantic**, especially in hock-deep ground. The winner of three chases will be aimed at veterans' races again, including one at Haydock in December, which he won last year. "He's loving it and seems to get better every year," says Guerriero.

Vandemere is another Irish point-to-point winner "with a touch of class".

"He had a niggly leg problem but he's fine now and will go straight over hurdles," says Guerriero. "If we can keep him sound we could have a lot of fun with him. We could go somewhere decent with him, some of the good meetings."

Chris Cool is a big backward sort who ran much better than was expected in a bumper at Catterick where he was third, not beaten far. He's now strengthened up and will start off in two- or two-and-a-half-mile hurdle races in soft ground.

Three to follow

Two unraced newcomers for the notebook are **Ffree Pedro** by Yeats and **Hello My Love** by Shirocco.

And finally, a dark horse from Stockton Hall to follow is **Druk**, a three-year-old rated 75 on the Flat in Ireland, where he won once and was placed twice.

"He's a nice big horse, 16-2, and doesn't look like a three-year-old," says Guerriero.

"He'll prefer soft ground and will be running in juvenile hurdles. The long-term plan for him is the Fred Winter and we'll plan back from there."

Interview by Lawrie Kelsey

OLIVER GREENALL
MALPAS, CHESHIRE

RECORD AROUND THE COURSES

	Total W-R	Per cent	Non-hcp Hdle	Non-hcp Chase	Hcp Hdle	Hcp Chase	N.H. Flat	£1 level stake
Sedgefield	10-58	17.2	4-13	0-1	2-22	4-17	0-5	+11.15
Uttoxeter	10-133	7.5	1-37	0-0	6-69	3-21	0-6	-75.51
Southwell	9-50	18.0	2-10	0-0	2-20	5-18	0-2	-2.23
Doncaster	6-31	19.4	0-9	0-0	2-10	4-10	0-2	+21.50
Stratford	6-36	16.7	2-10	0-0	1-15	3-9	0-2	+13.08
Huntingdon	6-40	15.0	0-13	0-0	4-14	2-11	0-2	-13.05
Bangor	6-121	5.0	2-43	0-1	2-41	2-25	0-11	-96.15
Market Rasen	5-46	10.9	2-11	0-0	3-19	0-15	0-1	-1.63
Worcester	4-35	11.4	0-9	0-0	0-11	3-14	1-1	-15.14
Newcastle	4-36	11.1	1-4	0-0	3-15	0-13	0-4	-23.05
Kelso	3-8	37.5	0-0	0-0	0-3	3-4	0-1	+2.00
Hereford	3-21	14.3	2-13	0-1	1-6	0-1	0-0	+3.50
Cartmel	3-22	13.6	0-6	0-2	0-4	3-10	0-0	+10.50
Catterick	3-28	10.7	2-13	0-1	1-5	0-7	0-2	+18.00
Carlisle	3-37	8.1	0-11	0-0	0-13	3-8	0-5	-23.00
Wetherby	3-39	7.7	0-12	0-0	0-14	3-11	0-2	-22.50
Ludlow	3-56	5.4	1-31	0-6	0-12	2-5	0-2	-25.58
Ayr	2-13	15.4	0-2	0-0	2-5	0-5	0-1	-2.00
Exeter	2-17	11.8	1-4	0-0	1-13	0-0	0-0	-5.25
Haydock	2-18	11.1	1-3	0-0	0-9	1-6	0-0	-2.50
Ascot	1-1	100.0	0-0	0-0	1-1	0-0	0-0	+12.00
Taunton	1-7	14.3	0-0	0-0	1-6	0-1	0-0	+10.00
Sandown	1-7	14.3	0-0	0-1	1-4	0-2	0-0	+1.50
Wincanton	1-13	7.7	0-0	0-0	0-5	1-8	0-0	-8.50
Hexham	1-16	6.2	1-4	0-0	0-8	0-4	0-0	-13.75
Chepstow	1-19	5.3	0-6	0-0	0-7	1-5	0-1	-14.67
Lingfield	0-1	0.0	0-1	0-0	0-0	0-0	0-0	-1.00
Kempton	0-1	0.0	0-0	0-0	0-1	0-0	0-0	-1.00
Lingfield (AW)	0-1	0.0	0-0	0-0	0-0	0-0	0-1	-1.00
Musselburgh	0-6	0.0	0-2	0-0	0-3	0-1	0-0	-6.00
Towcester	0-6	0.0	0-0	0-0	0-4	0-2	0-0	-6.00
Cheltenham	0-6	0.0	0-0	0-1	0-2	0-2	0-1	-6.00
Newton Abbot	0-7	0.0	0-0	0-0	0-5	0-2	0-0	-7.00
Fontwell	0-8	0.0	0-0	0-0	0-2	0-6	0-0	-8.00
Newbury	0-8	0.0	0-5	0-0	0-1	0-1	0-1	-8.00
Aintree	0-9	0.0	0-2	0-3	0-2	0-2	0-0	-9.00
Ffos Las	0-10	0.0	0-0	0-0	0-4	0-6	0-0	-10.00
Leicester	0-11	0.0	0-3	0-1	0-5	0-2	0-0	-11.00
Perth	0-14	0.0	0-1	0-0	0-10	0-3	0-0	-14.00
Warwick	0-32	0.0	0-7	0-1	0-16	0-6	0-2	-32.00

Top to bottom: Ecossais, Late Romantic and (below left) Zinc White

NICKY HENDERSON

Shishkin primed to take over top billing from the superstars

SHISHKIN, named after the 19th century Russian landscape artist, looks a picture of health as he unknowingly begins the journey to help Nicky Henderson rewrite Cheltenham Festival history.

If last season's Arkle hero wins the Queen Mother Champion Chase it would give the master of Seven Barrows his seventh win in the race, one more than the two trainers with whom he's currently tied, Tom Dreaper and Paul Nicholls.

Henderson is hoping Shishkin, who also won the Supreme Novices' Hurdle the year before his Arkle victory, can join the stable's other old masters, Sprinter Sacre (2013, 2016) and Altior (2018, 2019) by landing the two-mile crown.

Bookmakers have him no higher than 2-1 to do just that but, if you consider the trainer's reaction at seeing the seven-year-

■ December is often a good month to back runners from the stable. Last year a 20% strike-rate equated to a profit of £18.46

WINNERS IN LAST FOUR SEASONS 103, 118, 141, 141

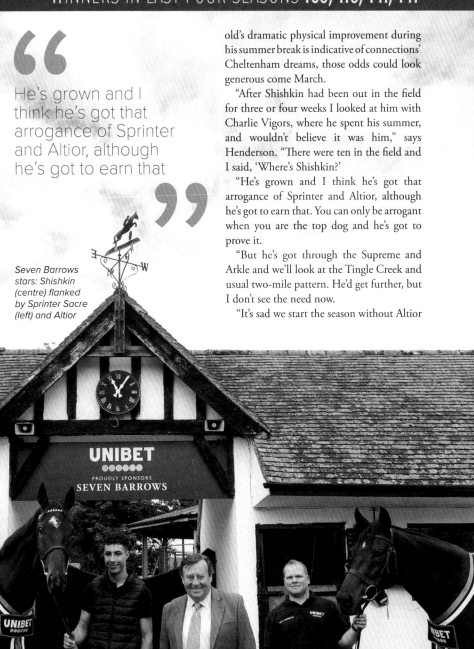

> He's grown and I think he's got that arrogance of Sprinter and Altior, although he's got to earn that

Seven Barrows stars: Shishkin (centre) flanked by Sprinter Sacre (left) and Altior

old's dramatic physical improvement during his summer break is indicative of connections' Cheltenham dreams, those odds could look generous come March.

"After Shishkin had been out in the field for three or four weeks I looked at him with Charlie Vigors, where he spent his summer, and wouldn't believe it was him," says Henderson. "There were ten in the field and I said, 'Where's Shishkin?'

"He's grown and I think he's got that arrogance of Sprinter and Altior, although he's got to earn that. You can only be arrogant when you are the top dog and he's got to prove it.

"But he's got through the Supreme and Arkle and we'll look at the Tingle Creek and usual two-mile pattern. He'd get further, but I don't see the need now.

"It's sad we start the season without Altior

and Santini [who has joined Polly Gundry], but it's unbelievable we could be in the middle of another [story] with Shishkin. After Sprinter and Altior it's almost too much to dream about, but we hope so."

Henderson is well aware how difficult it will be to win the Champion Chase against the likes of last year's first four home Put The Kettle On, Nube Negra, Chacun Pour Soi and Greaneteen as well as Energumene.

"The one thing about the two-mile division is it's going to be extremely hot, but Shishkin is going the right way and he's done phenomenally well over the summer," was Henderson's warning to other connections.

Shishkin's emergence as a leading novice was a high-water mark for Henderson last season, but lapping at his heels was **Chantry House**, who landed the Marsh Novices'

Chase at Cheltenham, then added Aintree's Mildmay Novices' Chase.

"If there were awards for which of our horses did best over the summer it would be between Shishkin and Chantry House," says Henderson.

"He was brilliant the first time over fences at Ascot but then he went to Cheltenham and was horrible behind Fusil Raffles – awful – but he'd got kissing spine [a condition in which the spaces between the vertebrae become so reduced they touch, causing pain and lameness].

"That meant surgery and within six weeks he won at Wetherby, but I had to get a race into him before Cheltenham. To have that surgery and get back was extraordinary; it worked wonders and he won at Aintree where we wanted to try three miles."

Champ looks fantastic now – unbelievable, and he's moving great

Champ (white cap): can be backed at 20-1 for the Gold Cup

He, too, is looking an impressive specimen after his summer break and Henderson is full of hope.

"He's grown and done brilliantly and could start in an intermediate chase at Sandown, which we've won with Might Bite and Santini, and we'll want to keep him and Champ apart as they're both owned by JP [McManus]."

More to come from Champ

Chantry House can be backed at 20-1 for the Cheltenham Gold Cup, in which Henderson believes **Champ** has unfinished business after he was pulled up in it in March.

"He's had considerable back surgery, which was the problem at Cheltenham," he says. "He jumped absolutely brilliantly at Newbury in the Game Spirit, but that triggered an old problem that Ger Kelly, JP's vet who had done surgery on Champ before, was always worried about and that there was a piece that needed to come out.

"I think at Newbury, Champ's exuberance probably created the problem and jarred this bit, which explains Cheltenham where he couldn't get off the ground.

"He looks fantastic now though, unbelievable, and he's moving great. My faith in him is very much intact because I'm more than confident Ger has done the job."

Champ is a general 20-1 chance for the Gold Cup, which Henderson has won with Long Run and Bobs Worth.

He is also hoping exciting chasers **Angels Breath** and **Allart** can fulfil their potential after serious injuries.

Angels Breath is held in the highest regard

but has been off since severing a tendon at Ascot in December 2019.

"He's back and could be anything, but there's a big 'but' with this," the trainer says. "He severed 40 per cent of his tendon and things are going well, but we've a hell of a way to go.

"It was a ferocious injury and the problem was not so much the 40 per cent of the tendon, but the damage done to the other 60 per cent that had the strain for the last two furlongs or so at Ascot.

"The 40 per cent has recovered and healed remarkably well. It will be worth it if we get him back because he's as good as any of my other chasers. He wants three miles on soft ground and would be in the same league as Champ and Chantry House if he can stand it."

Promising Allart improving

As for Allart, Henderson says: "He's quality and looked brilliant on his chasing debut at Ascot before falling at Haydock, after which we couldn't get him right. He hurt himself in his box on his holiday, and there were worries about his neck and brain.

"He's been to Newmarket to see Celia Marr, the vet who oversaw Sprinter Sacre. She's the neurological queen and he's back now, looking fabulous. He hasn't got to 100 per cent, but we think it's improving."

Other senior chasers to note are **Mister Fisher**, who could attempt a second win in the 2m4f Peterborough Chase, although Henderson is keen to explore three miles with him, while **Fusil Raffles**, who has grown into a "magnificent horse", is another under consideration for the Huntingdon highlight.

Henderson, lamenting the lack of a bona fide Randox Grand National contender among his string, is keen on **Caribean Boy**, who did well first time out last season but failed to build on it.

"He was fantastic at Newbury," says Henderson. "He didn't win again, but I probably ran him back too quickly, although I did think we saw something special at Newbury and the clock says that too. I don't

think he wants it bottomless and his trip is probably two miles four, maybe two six."

Leading the Seven Barrows hurdlers again will be **Epatante**, but Henderson (eight) and owner JP McManus (nine) know it will be difficult to improve their records in the Champion Hurdle with their 2020 winner.

Their heroine was dismissed easily in March by flying Irish mare Honeysuckle, who has never been beaten in 12 hurdles races and one point-to-point.

Henderson says: "She was disappointing last season. She was magnificent in the Fighting Fifth and we thought she was the Champion Hurdle winner, but she was beaten in the Christmas Hurdle, then finished third at Cheltenham.

"Honeysuckle was brilliant in the Champion and we weren't going to beat her, but we've always had to keep a close eye on Epatante's back. It's always been very tense and taut, so she had the same surgery as Champ, which we think and hope will make a big difference.

"I'm not in a month of Sundays going to say if she was right she'd have beaten Honeysuckle, but it was disappointing we couldn't give her a race."

Staying route for Buveur

Buveur D'Air, McManus's Champion Hurdle winner in 2017 and 2018, will not be entered in the race again. His route forward will be as a staying hurdler if he can return from injury.

"He suffered a freak leg injury and is at Martinstown, JP's stud in Ireland, having a lot of remedial work, but it would be fantastic if he could get back in time for another shot, but over further," says Henderson.

Buzz is also a staying hurdler to note, although the Cesarewitch at Newmarket will come first, providing the ground is suitably soft.

"After the Cesarewitch he'd probably be ready for the West Yorkshire Hurdle at Wetherby on Charlie Hall day [October 30]," Henderson says.

NICKY HENDERSON
UPPER LAMBOURN, BERKSHIRE

RECORD AROUND THE COURSES

	Total W-R	Per cent	Non-hcp Hdle	Non-hcp Chase	Hcp Hdle	Hcp Chase	N.H. Flat	£1 level stake
Kempton	125-468	26.7	49-164	31-72	23-116	9-63	13-53	+24.54
Newbury	98-441	22.2	52-155	11-32	15-115	8-92	12-47	-50.38
Cheltenham	98-729	13.4	37-219	31-115	17-218	9-154	4-23	-156.55
Sandown	74-311	23.8	31-84	17-48	21-114	3-54	2-11	+1.24
Ascot	68-316	21.5	28-107	16-48	10-91	10-48	4-22	-38.45
Doncaster	65-197	33.0	36-90	15-33	9-35	3-26	2-13	+21.10
Ludlow	60-219	27.4	29-97	6-16	2-31	6-31	17-44	-54.65
Huntingdon	59-191	30.9	32-83	13-27	4-33	4-11	6-37	-39.16
Aintree	55-304	18.1	22-92	12-40	12-76	7-68	2-28	-16.64
Market Rasen	44-149	29.5	20-42	2-10	7-47	5-22	10-28	+2.91
Warwick	43-170	25.3	19-72	5-13	7-29	4-11	8-45	-29.23
Southwell	42-129	32.6	17-47	3-9	2-27	1-9	19-37	-15.00
Uttoxeter	39-153	25.5	18-57	6-17	4-40	4-22	7-17	-40.81
Worcester	39-160	24.4	18-49	5-19	6-49	2-11	8-32	-10.95
Ffos Las	28-76	36.8	18-34	2-6	1-18	0-4	7-14	-11.20
Fontwell	27-83	32.5	11-29	7-13	5-15	1-5	3-21	-3.25
Fakenham	26-74	35.1	15-35	3-12	1-12	0-3	7-12	-21.12
Bangor	25-103	24.3	13-41	3-13	4-19	0-8	5-24	-31.85
Towcester	24-75	32.0	13-33	3-8	4-6	0-0	4-28	-6.16
Haydock	24-107	22.4	11-32	5-17	4-46	3-9	1-3	-21.96
Newton Abbot	23-65	35.4	11-22	2-6	5-25	2-6	3-6	+9.05
Taunton	23-79	29.1	13-33	2-4	5-29	1-6	2-7	-1.57
Stratford	20-97	20.6	2-18	3-8	10-39	3-18	2-14	-31.48
Plumpton	15-51	29.4	5-21	5-10	4-12	1-3	0-5	+3.18
Chepstow	15-76	19.7	9-34	2-7	1-15	0-11	3-9	-21.57
Wincanton	15-86	17.4	8-36	3-7	3-24	0-10	1-9	-32.37
Wetherby	14-36	38.9	7-12	5-10	0-7	0-4	2-3	-2.71
Hereford	13-32	40.6	9-18	1-3	2-5	0-0	1-6	-1.23
Newcastle	12-17	70.6	10-13	0-0	0-0	1-3	1-1	+5.63
Leicester	12-48	25.0	6-22	3-9	0-4	3-13	0-0	+3.11
Exeter	12-48	25.0	6-18	1-9	2-9	2-5	1-7	-4.44
Kelso	11-18	61.1	5-6	4-4	0-2	1-2	1-4	+7.67
Kempton (AW)	11-30	36.7	0-0	0-0	0-0	0-0	11-30	+6.00
Ayr	11-73	15.1	1-6	2-5	2-32	3-22	3-8	-27.45
Musselburgh	10-34	29.4	7-15	1-4	2-12	0-2	0-1	-10.47
Lingfield (AW)	8-40	20.0	0-0	0-0	0-0	0-0	8-40	-8.66
Hexham	6-15	40.0	1-2	1-2	1-6	1-2	2-3	+1.98
Lingfield	6-15	40.0	5-12	1-3	0-0	0-0	0-0	-0.92
Perth	6-31	19.4	3-9	0-2	0-8	3-10	0-2	-16.60
Catterick	3-11	27.3	0-3	3-5	0-1	0-1	0-1	-2.27
Sedgefield	2-2	100.0	2-2	0-0	0-0	0-0	0-0	+0.71
Carlisle	1-1	100.0	1-1	0-0	0-0	0-0	0-0	+0.91
Cartmel	1-2	50.0	0-0	1-1	0-1	0-0	0-0	+0.20
Wolverhampton (AW)	1-6	16.7	0-0	0-0	0-0	0-0	1-6	-4.27

Top to bottom: Epatante, Angels Breath and Caribean Boy

"**On The Blind Side** isn't a Grade 1 horse, but he was a star of last season. I ran him at Kempton and he was second after a fierce battle with McFabulous and they then put a race on a week later at Market Rasen and he won that. He loves small fields, but might be hard to place.

"I like **Captain Morgs**, who could have unfinished business over hurdles, and that applies to **Paros**. It took time for us to work him out and he started hanging right-handed, so we went to Musselburgh, which

is that way round, and he did it nicely. He's summered really well and retains plenty of potential as a hurdler."

Dusart is a Flemensfirth half-brother to late yard favourite Simonsig and promised much after landing a warm Newbury novice hurdle in November, but he missed most of the season before finishing third in the Top Novices' Hurdle at Aintree's Grand National meeting.

He looks a likely chaser but Henderson could give him more hurdling experience

27

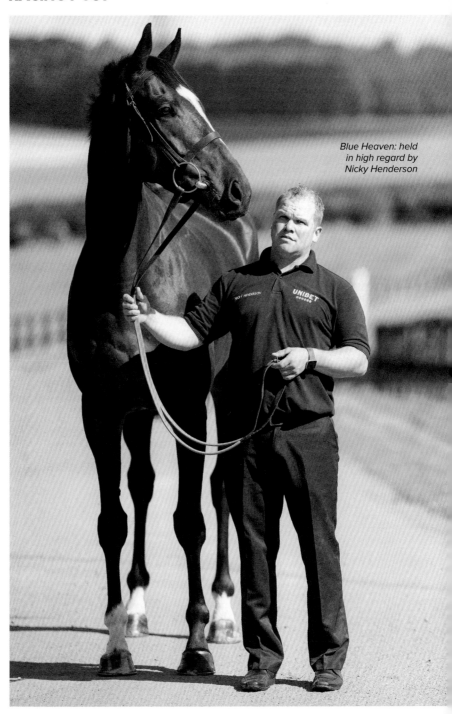

Blue Heaven: held in high regard by Nicky Henderson

before going down that route.

"He's only had two runs over hurdles, so could go either way, but he'll be very good," he says. "He wants two and a half miles and his run at Aintree was extraordinary because he was only half-ready after a freak accident during the season."

Gallyhill is in a similar class, but chasing is the plan for him, while Coral Cup second **Craigneiche** and the huge **Mister Coffey**, "who should be top class over fences", are hardened from handicap hurdles and worth following.

Other notable novice chasers to look out for are **Burrows Edge**, **Cascova**, **Emir Sacre**, from the family of Sprinter Sacre, **Fugitives Drift**, **Grand Mogul**, **Keen On**, **Mill Green** and **Steal A March**.

Henderson trains for The Queen and in 2022, her Platinum Jubilee year, he would be delighted to saddle a few winners for his royal owner.

"I'd say this is the nicest bunch [of mares] I've ever had for her," he says. "They include **Blue Heaven**, a filly I adore who didn't show her true running in a mares' bumper at Ludlow last time, but will put that right soon. There's also **Kincardine** and a youngster who hasn't run called **Wave The Wand**."

Three mares to follow

There are some well-regarded mares for other owners at Seven Barrows and Henderson selects a trio to follow.

"**Mind Sunday** is interesting, very interesting, and **Tweed Skirt** is very, very interesting. I like her a lot, while **Ahorsewithnoname** ran a great race at Newbury first time and then things went against her, but she's done fantastically over the summer."

The Irish domination of last season's Cheltenham Festival was a shock to British racing and many will be pinning their hopes on Henderson helping to halt a repeat of prizes being exported to Ireland.

Failure of the home side to pick up prizes was not helped when, for the first time since 1998, Henderson had no runners in the Supreme, Ballymore, Albert Bartlett and Triumph.

"It will be an awful disappointment if we have no runners again this season," he says. "Last year I was confident about the novice chasers and this year it's the novice hurdlers.

"I think this will be an exciting division for us and then next year I hope I'm talking about novice chasers again."

Jonbon looking 'magnificent'

One of those stirring the passions of the Seven Barrows team is Newbury bumper winner **Jonbon**, a brother to eight-time Grade 1 winner Douvan, who cost McManus £570,000 after landing his point-to-point.

"I've never been so frightened when I took him to Newbury because you know what everyone would have been like if he'd been beaten," says Henderson, "but I hadn't done much with him and he definitely wasn't wound up for it.

"He's come back looking magnificent. He's a big round ball with a great backside on him. There's a long way to go, but he's got that pace and I can't believe we'll start over further than two miles, although he could finish at two and a half and will be a chaser down the line."

I Am Maximus, who has not run since landing a Cheltenham bumper impressively last autumn, joins Jonbon as the yard's two outstanding novice hurdlers among "a very strong bunch".

"He could be anything," says Henderson, "and his form looks spectacular. He looks superb and has got all the speed in the world, so we'll start at two miles and see."

Finally, make a bold note of dual bumper winner **Firestep**, who has impressed everyone at Seven Barrows, not least Henderson's No 1 jockey Nico de Boinville.

"Nico is mad about him and his sister arrived recently after we bought her on the grounds that we think Firestep is going to be the bee's knees, in which case you need his little sister in your pocket."

Interview by James Burn

EMMA LAVELLE

Chasing could still happen for Paisley

HIGH-CLASS staying hurdler **Paisley Park**, the horse whose connections have always shied away from sending over fences, could go chasing this season.

"At this stage we wouldn't rule anything in or anything out. That would be wrong," says Emma Lavelle of her stable star.

"He's schooled over a fence and his schooling was very good, but we're a long way from saying that's the route we're going to go. This season we have lots of options."

Paisley Park, owned by Andrew Gemmell, hit the headlines when winning the 2019 Stayers' Hurdle at the Cheltenham Festival.

The following year he made headlines of a different sort when it was discovered he had an irregular heartbeat after finishing seventh in the same race in 2020.

In the week following his Cheltenham scare Paisley Park underwent a thorough check-up by vets at Newmarket's equine hospital and was given the all-clear.

His irregular heartbeat had sorted itself out and now the nine-year-old is working like the champion of old.

"He didn't have any heart issues last season and hopefully it's something that happened once and won't recur," says Lavelle.

The Cheltenham Stayers' Hurdle, in which

■ Backing Lavelle runners at 2m-2m1f is often profitable. A strike-rate of just 13% last term produced a profit of £33.37

WINNERS IN LAST FOUR SEASONS **32, 29, 35, 28**

31

> **I wouldn't rule out looking at a fence for him. I know we always said we wouldn't, but we'll see**

Pride and joy: Emma Lavelle and Barry Fenton with Paisley Park

he finished third last year, will be pencilled in lightly for Paisley Park's programme this season.

If that is the route connections choose, it could take in Newbury for the Grade 2 Long Distance Hurdle, the three-mile race at the end of November which he won in 2019 and was a narrow second last year.

"He's so well in himself at home that I think that's probably our option of choice, but I wouldn't rule out looking at a fence for him. I know we always said we wouldn't, but we'll see," says Lavelle.

Now Paisley Park is over his fibrillating heart worries, the only concern connections have is their star's homework.

"Our biggest problem with him as he's got older is he only does as much as he needs to at home," says Lavelle.

"Last season we missed the prep run on Trials Day and, although we took him for a racecourse gallop, it's not the same.

"Consequently, at Cheltenham he was probably a little race rusty not having run since Newbury. Although he ran a mighty race to finish third he lacked that match practice."

Paisley Park will be ridden by Aidan Coleman, his regular partner, but the rest of the yard's runners will be mainly partnered by Tom Bellamy.

Lavelle had been juggling the likes of Coleman, Adam Wedge, Ben Jones and Bellamy over the last few years, but was keen to bring in a regular rider to complete the team at Bonita Stables, the Wiltshire yard built in the 1890s and previously run by Sir Gordon Richards, Bob Turnell and Peter Makin.

She says: "I just wanted a bit of consistency

and to have someone who was able to get to know the horses well. We have some lovely horses and we wanted the right person and the consistency going on top of them. It's working well."

Rasher's National objective

Arguably the most exciting ride Bellamy can look forward to is the 2019 Ladbrokes Trophy winner **De Rasher Counter**, known as 'Streaky' at home.

He was ruled out of a repeat attempt last season with a tendon injury but he's back in training with the Grand National as his main target.

"His leg has been treated, he's had a long break and he looks absolutely fine now, so everything will be built around trying to make Aintree happen," says Lavelle.

"He's unlikely to be seen on the track until about Christmas time, then we'll get the races in him before the National."

Boreham Bill shot to prominence by winning the Listed Lanzarote Hurdle in January this year after an unsuccessful chasing campaign in the autumn, but ended the season with a disappointing 22nd of 26 in the Coral Cup.

"Cheltenham was a bit of a muddle for him after the Lanzarote because they had two false starts and he slightly lost his head," says Lavelle.

"He's quite a sensitive soul and it unsettled him from the get-go; that was definitely a non-event for him. He's had a lovely holiday, looks great and he's in a really good place mentally. I'm very happy with him.

"I'm not going to say he has any big targets. Bizarrely, even though he's shown a bit of a tendency to jump left, he seems to love it round Kempton. So there are a few nice races there, and I suppose it would be nice to win the Lanzarote again.

"I'll start him back over hurdles but I'm not ruling out going back over fences with him. He has his own technique, it would be true to say, and he's not always the most fluent over a fence, but he's still a novice over fences, which gives us some options."

Bright novice chase hope

Shang Tang finished three places in front of Boreham Bill in the Coral Cup but is best suited by two and a half miles on a flat track, says Lavelle.

"He's ready to start novice chasing this season and he'll be pretty exciting when he does.

"We'll get the first race out of the way and see that he jumps well, which we hope and expect him to, and if he does that we can look at some more interesting targets."

Manofthemountain delighted the yard by winning the Grade 2 Silver Trophy at Cheltenham in April and the team at Bonita has high expectations.

"He was an absolute star last season and once we confirmed that two and a half miles and decent ground were his ideal conditions, we had a fantastic time of it.

"He's a strong-travelling great jumper and is exciting. We'll probably have him ready for the two-and-a-half-mile handicap chase at Chepstow in October, then maybe look at the Grand Sefton [Aintree] as his second run.

"He doesn't want the ground too soft, so maybe he'll have a mid-season break and if everything goes to plan we'll look at the spring festivals."

Red Rookie won two bumpers impressively and a novice hurdle over two miles at Sandown before being stepped up to two and a half miles at Uttoxeter where he travelled well but didn't get home.

"He's a big, strapping, scopey chaser in the making and will go over fences this season. We'll start him over two miles and he definitely needs cut in the ground. He's a fair

performer and I'd be hopeful that with conditions to suit he could go a long way."

Eclair Surf won his last two starts over fences but is only now starting to fill his tall frame. He prefers soft ground and could develop into a Welsh Grand National type.

Butler can serve it up

One definitely for the shortlist is **Young Butler**, a half brother to Champion Chase winner Put The Kettle On.

On his only start to date, he finished fourth in a Newbury bumper after being kicked at the start.

"He's a lovely individual who's strengthened up a lot over the summer. He'll go novice hurdling and I think he should be a nice one."

Mumbo Jumbo finished a close second in a bumper at Newbury in January, with the rest well strung out.

"He's a big-striding, lovely individual who'll go novice hurdling this season. He only had one run because he deserved a bit more time to strengthen up."

Sam Barton was very impressive winning a novice hurdle at Doncaster in January before finishing fourth in the EBF final at Sandown.

"We were a bit unlucky in that the rain came that day and it got very soft," says Lavelle. "He's a horse who doesn't want it that soft and it took the edge off his speed.

"He's a typical Trevor Hemmings horse and it's always about jumping fences with him, so that's what he'll do this season. He's a real athlete. We like him a lot and he's got a bit of class about him."

Straight over hurdles

Wild Wilbur hasn't appeared in public yet. He was due to run in a bumper at the back end of last season but for various reasons didn't see the track.

"He's a lovely son of Presenting who is a relentless galloper. He'll probably go novice hurdling rather than the bumper route and will be a better-ground type of horse."

Top to bottom: Shang Tang, Red Rookie and Killer Clown

EMMA LAVELLE
MARLBOROUGH, WILTSHIRE

RECORD AROUND THE COURSES

	Total W-R	Per cent	Non-hcp Hdle	Non-hcp Chase	Hcp Hdle	Hcp Chase	N.H. Flat	£1 level stake
Wincanton	25-135	18.5	5-33	1-6	9-39	5-38	5-19	+44.08
Kempton	23-137	16.8	5-47	1-5	6-35	8-40	3-10	+99.34
Exeter	22-144	15.3	5-45	3-13	4-30	9-42	1-14	-31.97
Doncaster	20-77	26.0	5-20	0-2	5-17	7-26	3-12	+10.39
Worcester	19-98	19.4	4-23	1-4	4-26	10-36	0-9	+34.43
Newton Abbot	16-67	23.9	5-16	0-4	5-24	4-19	2-4	+61.50
Stratford	16-90	17.8	3-16	1-6	6-24	4-32	2-12	-4.78
Fontwell	14-94	14.9	5-27	1-4	5-24	2-29	1-10	+1.08
Taunton	13-72	18.1	2-19	0-2	7-24	4-21	0-6	-9.20
Uttoxeter	13-110	11.8	3-23	2-13	2-38	4-22	2-14	-47.64
Chepstow	12-93	12.9	7-34	1-5	2-19	1-23	1-12	-33.09
Market Rasen	11-63	17.5	2-5	0-1	5-22	3-27	1-8	+11.28
Sandown	9-64	14.1	3-9	0-3	2-27	3-21	1-4	-18.33
Haydock	8-39	20.5	2-7	0-5	4-21	1-5	1-1	+14.73
Plumpton	8-52	15.4	2-12	1-2	1-15	4-17	0-6	-17.38
Cheltenham	8-107	7.5	5-21	2-12	0-31	1-41	0-2	-68.13
Newbury	7-110	6.4	3-31	0-4	0-27	4-34	0-14	-71.77
Lingfield	6-23	26.1	3-14	1-2	0-1	2-6	0-0	+4.33
Huntingdon	6-69	8.7	3-16	1-6	2-20	0-14	0-13	-43.42
Warwick	6-92	6.5	2-26	0-6	2-22	2-20	0-18	-38.00
Leicester	5-17	29.4	3-6	1-1	0-1	1-9	0-0	-3.04
Hereford	5-29	17.2	3-13	0-0	1-6	1-5	0-5	-7.63
Southwell	5-34	14.7	2-11	0-0	1-12	1-7	1-4	-1.30
Ascot	5-72	6.9	3-17	1-5	0-18	1-26	0-6	-48.75
Ludlow	4-38	10.5	0-10	0-0	2-9	2-17	0-2	-16.50
Bangor	3-20	15.0	0-3	0-0	1-3	1-8	1-6	-1.75
Towcester	3-20	15.0	1-7	2-2	0-4	0-3	0-4	-8.17
Aintree	3-32	9.4	0-7	0-2	2-6	0-13	1-4	+3.50
Fakenham	2-9	22.2	1-3	0-0	0-0	1-6	0-0	-2.88
Lingfield (AW)	2-16	12.5	0-0	0-0	0-0	0-0	2-16	-6.00
Ffos Las	2-33	6.1	1-11	0-2	0-11	1-6	0-3	-26.25
Cartmel	1-1	100.0	0-0	0-0	1-1	0-0	0-0	+2.50
Kempton (AW)	1-10	10.0	0-0	0-0	0-0	0-0	1-10	+7.00
Kelso	0-1	0.0	0-0	0-0	0-0	0-1	0-0	-1.00
Ayr	0-3	0.0	0-0	0-0	0-1	0-2	0-0	-3.00
Newcastle	0-3	0.0	0-0	0-0	0-0	0-3	0-0	-3.00
Sedgefield	0-4	0.0	0-0	0-0	0-1	0-3	0-0	-4.00
Wetherby	0-6	0.0	0-2	0-0	0-2	0-2	0-0	-6.00

Jemima P is a "big, beautiful mare" who has taken time to fill her frame and be strong enough to do what connections thought she should do.

"She was a revelation when she went over fences and has won four of her last five races," says Lavelle. "She's a beautiful jumper and a great traveller but doesn't want the ground too soft. She'll hopefully contest some of the better mares' chases later in the season and should keep on improving.

"I wouldn't rule out Cheltenham but she's got to step up to another level first. She's already rated 142 and definitely going the right way."

Killer Clown was impressive winning a novice handicap chase at Kempton on Boxing Day, then finished second in the Grade 3 Greatwood Gold Cup chase at Newbury in March.

"He's a strong traveller and jumper. His target this side of Christmas will be the Old Roan at Aintree in October and we'll see what gives after that. He's a horse we like a lot and he's matured nicely. We're hoping this is his season."

Runswick Bay ran some decent races last year, including second to Bravemansgame at Exeter before winning at Taunton.

"He's an athletic horse, a really neat

jumper. He'll go over fences this season and novice handicap chases will be tailor-made for him," says Lavelle.

Top Dog raring to go

Much is expected of **Top Dog**, who is from the family of Altior, especially after he finished a close second in an Irish bumper.

"He's a real terrier – he just wants to get on with it. He won everywhere bar the line in his bumper. He'll handle a bit of cut in the ground and it'll be interesting to see how he does over here. We'll start him out in a bumper and it'll be nice to get a one by his name."

Although **Nollyador** has never run, he "looks the part".

"He's always been a natural athlete and has found everything easy that we've asked him.

"He's got a great temperament and a lovely way of going and has done everything right at home. It's now about what he does on the track. We'll have him schooled, see what the ground is like and take it from there."

Tedwin Hills, by Getaway out of a Presenting mare, is also unraced and a similar type to Nollyador.

"We took them both to Newbury for a racecourse gallop last backend and it was very difficult to split them; they are just two lovely horses.

"He'll start in a bumper and he's a horse we're very excited about."

Double Irish point-to-point winner **Wouldubewell** won first time out in a mares' hurdle race on soft ground at Uttoxeter in December before running "two lovely races finishing fourth and second".

On the schooling ground at Emma Lavelle's Bonita Racing Stables in Wiltshire

"She was marking time last season and is very much a chaser," says Lavelle. "I can't wait to see her over a fence. She wants soft ground and will be a staying mare. She will be absolutely dependent on what the weather does."

Hang In There has won two handicap hurdles and been beaten a head in two more in his last four outings.

"He's a proper little horse who is just a bundle of energy," says Lavelle. "When everything goes to plan he's a horse with a lot of ability and was impressive on his last start [at Stratford at the beginning of September].

"He loves the better ground and I think for the moment we'll stick to hurdling, but I wouldn't rule out seeing him over a fence in the spring."

Highly Prized has won nine times under rules and has been "a great servant" to his trainer.

"He's a genuine two-miler. We gave him one run over fences but he probably just didn't have the scope for it, and so, although he finished second, I'd say that will have been his only foray jumping the big ones.

"He'll come back over hurdles and I think there's a proper handicap in him."

Finally, one to note carefully is Lavelle's choice as her dark horse, **Eureka Creek**.

"She won a point-to-point in Ireland [in May] and seems to be very straightforward. She's a smashing jumper and a really hardy mare, the type you like to have on your side. She'll go straight over hurdles."

Interview by Lawrie Kelsey

Garde's hurdles mark is too good to ignore

ALMAZHAR GARDE may not be a champion but he holds a special place in Charlie Longsdon's heart after completing the trainer's full set last November.

His landmark victory at Kelso gave the Chipping Norton handler the unusual personal accolade of having trained a winner at every British jumps track.

Owned by Kate and Andrew Brooks, whose silks of light blue with red braces and white sleeves are well known to racing fans thanks to a stack of winners in the last few seasons, Almazhar Garde might be an old hand over fences with an unattractive mark of 139, but he is still a novice over hurdles.

And that could be the route Longsdon exploits with the gelding, who is still only six years old despite having run in 11 chases, four of which he's won.

"As he's a novice over hurdles, we might aim him at a few of the bigger novice races and see how far he can go," says Longsdon.

Almazhar Garde hasn't appeared over hurdles for two years but his rating of 126 looks far more attractive than his chasing mark.

"We probably ran him a couple of times too many in at the deep end over fences last season, so I might well go back down the novice hurdle route with him and run him in a couple of three-mile races at Kempton or Cheltenham."

Snow Leopardess, who had two years

Almazhar Garde: retains novice status over hurdles

■ Watch out for Tom Buckley riding for the stable. A 21% strike-rate gives a profit of £17.25

off to have a foal, thrilled connections by coming back last season to win a valuable chase at Haydock.

She then finished second in the Rowland Meyrick at Wetherby and fourth in the National Hunt Challenge Chase at the Cheltenham Festival to earn a glowing tribute from her trainer.

"She's been the most unbelievable mare and we're spoilt to have her," he says. "Although she won only one race last season, she ran consistently well in a few major races.

"There's no reason why she cannot go on from that this season. It will be tough with a handicap mark of 137, but she'll always put her best foot forward.

"We might well go down a similar route with her and go back to Haydock and then the Rowland Meyrick." Longsdon is also keeping open the option of jumping the Grand National fences in the Becher Chase [December 4] with the National itself a possibility if all went well.

Spring targets for Clouds

Beyond The Clouds has been ultra consistent so far this season, winning twice over fences and never being out of the first three in five outings.

"He's been running in muddly novice chases which has seen him beaten a couple of times carrying double penalties," says Longsdon. "He just wants a proper, true-run race on sounder ground, a decent strongly run handicap.

"He's going to Kelso in October for a 40-grand handicap and will then have one more run, somewhere like Cheltenham, and come back in the spring to be aimed at races like the Grand Annual or the Red Rum."

Castle Robin won two novice hurdles last season, including a good race at Cheltenham, before finishing sixth in the Lanzarote and third in a hot Grade 2 race at Doncaster.

"He ran third that day but to my mind he ran a bit flat. He'd probably had a hard race three weeks earlier in the Lanzarote.

"He's a proper, galloping horse and will be

a fun chaser this season, but he won't be ready until the ground softens up.

"He's rated 130 and looks well handicapped. I think chasing will be the making of him. I have no targets at this stage; he's just a horse I like. He's honest, loves his work and will be extremely exciting."

Juvenile hurdles plan

George Bancroft is a juvenile hurdler bought by JP McManus after winning on the Flat at Chepstow for Roger Varian.

Connections have high hopes for the son of fashionable jumping sire Australia, and was a rare winner on the Flat at Ripon for Longsdon in August.

"He's laid-back in his work and doesn't do more than he has to, but he's a progressive type and once he gets the hang of jumping I can see him being a better-than-fun type of juvenile hurdler," says Longsdon.

"He's taken to jumping very well. He has plenty of size and scope and he looks as if he'll stay two miles very well. There could even be another race on the Flat for him."

Glencassley won a bumper at Wetherby in March 2020 and was then sidelined with a small injury for most of last season, running only once when finishing a creditable sixth in a Grade 2 bumper at Aintree.

"I think he just needed the run but the jockey says he loved him. He then went and won a novice hurdle very easily at Southwell at the start of this season.

"The plan will be to win under a penalty and then step him up in class," says Longsdon. "He's from a proper staying family, so he'll want further than two miles and will probably end up staying three miles.

"He's a fine, big horse and will end up chasing but he could be a high-class novice hurdler this autumn."

Step up in trip on the agenda

Glen Forsa was bought in the spring out of Mick Channon's stable at the Tim Radford dispersal sale.

He had been strongly fancied for the 2019

CHARLIE LONGSDON
CHIPPING NORTON, OXFORDSHIRE

RECORD AROUND THE COURSES

	Total W-R	Per cent	Non-hcp Hdle	Non-hcp Chase	Hcp Hdle	Hcp Chase	N.H. Flat	£1 level stake
Uttoxeter	42-230	18.3	13-56	4-11	12-65	13-82	0-16	-36.42
Market Rasen	40-220	18.2	8-35	3-9	11-67	13-82	5-27	-77.26
Southwell	32-169	18.9	9-42	2-7	9-53	7-45	5-22	+0.92
Worcester	30-205	14.6	5-44	3-16	5-52	10-67	7-26	-24.02
Fontwell	28-148	18.9	9-31	1-4	5-44	9-49	4-20	-40.90
Huntingdon	28-217	12.9	6-54	4-13	7-74	9-52	2-24	-59.90
Stratford	27-141	19.1	4-31	2-8	11-43	6-47	4-12	+12.25
Warwick	22-187	11.8	6-55	2-11	4-51	7-49	3-21	-45.28
Bangor	21-120	17.5	7-28	3-12	3-28	6-38	2-14	-31.62
Wetherby	20-108	18.5	5-29	2-9	1-22	8-36	4-12	-16.80
Towcester	19-99	19.2	2-31	6-12	3-21	5-24	3-11	+7.36
Plumpton	15-94	16.0	5-32	0-2	2-23	7-32	1-5	-38.08
Ludlow	15-128	11.7	6-38	1-5	2-28	6-46	0-11	-37.80
Doncaster	15-147	10.2	3-46	0-7	4-34	7-53	1-7	-29.30
Kempton	14-125	11.2	2-20	1-5	3-38	8-56	0-6	-25.05
Carlisle	12-52	23.1	5-10	3-8	0-6	2-22	2-6	-24.33
Sandown	12-102	11.8	1-6	1-5	2-27	8-60	0-4	+20.00
Musselburgh	9-33	27.3	8-12	0-0	0-8	1-13	0-0	+19.21
Hereford	9-43	20.9	2-11	1-1	0-7	3-19	3-5	+48.60
Newton Abbot	8-42	19.0	2-5	1-3	1-13	4-18	0-3	+3.45
Haydock	7-67	10.4	1-4	1-2	3-22	1-34	1-5	-7.50
Chepstow	7-80	8.7	1-14	0-3	2-24	4-35	0-4	-45.02
Ascot	7-91	7.7	0-17	0-7	2-29	3-28	2-10	-14.50
Newbury	7-109	6.4	0-19	0-7	2-22	4-48	1-13	-62.63
Lingfield	6-34	17.6	1-12	1-3	1-5	3-14	0-0	+3.74
Aintree	6-93	6.5	2-19	0-3	3-28	1-31	0-12	-65.17
Leicester	5-47	10.6	0-16	2-4	0-4	3-23	0-0	-20.40
Wincanton	5-49	10.2	0-5	1-2	1-21	3-19	0-2	-6.50
Cartmel	4-11	36.4	0-1	0-0	1-3	3-7	0-0	+13.00
Hexham	4-16	25.0	1-6	2-3	1-1	0-4	0-2	-6.28
Sedgefield	4-21	19.0	0-5	1-3	1-4	2-7	0-2	-10.01
Fakenham	4-30	13.3	0-9	0-2	1-7	3-12	0-0	-18.16
Exeter	4-46	8.7	0-7	1-2	2-17	1-18	0-2	-16.13
Cheltenham	4-160	2.5	1-21	0-12	2-47	1-65	0-15	-130.00
Perth	3-13	23.1	0-0	1-2	0-4	2-7	0-0	+1.73
Newcastle	3-13	23.1	2-5	0-0	0-0	0-6	1-2	-4.75
Kempton (AW)	3-18	16.7	0-0	0-0	0-0	0-0	3-18	+2.50
Southwell (AW)	2-7	28.6	0-0	0-0	0-0	0-0	2-7	+2.50
Kelso	2-17	11.8	0-3	0-0	0-3	2-11	0-0	-7.25
Catterick	2-17	11.8	1-6	0-0	0-6	1-5	0-0	-10.46
Ffos Las	2-27	7.4	0-4	0-1	2-9	0-10	0-3	-12.50
Ayr	1-15	6.7	1-2	0-2	0-4	0-7	0-0	-13.90
Taunton	1-34	2.9	0-4	0-0	1-15	0-14	0-1	-29.00
Lingfield (AW)	0-7	0.0	0-0	0-0	0-0	0-0	0-7	-7.00

Top to bottom: Snow Leopardess, Castle Robin and Beyond The Clouds

Arkle, finished unplaced in last season's Grand Annual at Cheltenham and was then pulled up in the Topham.

He reached a mark of 154 over fences but is now down to 138, which looks an attractive mark.

"I think he wants a massive step up in trip. I'm keen to try him over three miles because from what I've seen at home so far he strikes me as not a speed horse. He's an out-and-out galloper and slowing everything down might suit him.

"If I'm right, he could be an exciting prospect with many of the decent staying chases to look forward to. In fact, I'd love to turn him into a Grand National horse.

"He could start out in the Sodexo over three miles at Ascot at the end of October and if he runs well there he could be a Hennessy or Grand National horse; but he'd have to stay the extra mile first."

Haas Boy is an unraced four-year-old by Diamond Boy "who does everything with a smile on his face".

Little Bruce: has Cheltenham's cross-country races on his agenda this season

"I like the way he goes. He's a fine-looking horse, jumps for fun and he's always eager to please.

"The plan is to have him ready to run in a bumper at Worcester in October, then we'll decide whether to stick to bumpers or go hurdling.

"I'm in no hurry with him. If he runs well in the bumper, as I'd like him to, we can set slightly loftier targets."

If I Say, who won a point-to-point bumper last season, is another Longsdon youngster with a promising future.

"I like the way she works. She's another one who just gets on with it and jumps for fun," he says.

"I'll run her in a bumper with the potential to go to Cheltenham for a Listed mares' bumper this autumn. She has a good attitude and is quick on her feet over hurdles."

Illegal Model is a big horse for whom soft ground is important.

"He had quite a tough season last year due to having to run in big handicaps with little experience," says Longsdon.

"The experience he gained will prove invaluable now that he'll go chasing. I think he'll turn out to be a good chaser and be aimed at some of the top staying chases later in the season. In time I can see him being a Welsh National horse," says his trainer.

Staying handicaps for Bruce

Little Bruce's first run for Longsdon after a move from Phil Kirby was "a fantastic" second in the Summer Cup at Uttoxeter at 66-1 at the end of June.

"He'll run in all the good staying chases and I can envisage him having another go at the cross-country races at Cheltenham this autumn, then we'll look at the veteran series come the new year," says Longsdon.

Lyrical Genius was bought after winning a British point-to-point in the spring

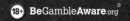

> " She's more than capable of winning off her mark of 130 and if we don't get some black type we'll have got it wrong "

and turned out for the summer.

"He's grown a lot and turned into a very good-looking horse," says Longsdon, who is taking a softly, softly approach with the son of Milan.

"I'm in no hurry with him and will wait until the ground softens, then run him in a bumper."

Moon set for return

Take special note of **Moon King**, a six-time Flat winner rated 91 for Ralph Beckett. He won a novice hurdle and an all-weather bumper for Longsdon before injuring a hind leg and spending time on the sidelines.

The five-year-old is back in training looking bigger and stronger after his long break, and to say his hurdling rating of 115 is attractive is a massive understatement.

Parramount is a half brother by Mount Nelson to Snow Leopardess, and won a bumper nicely at Stratford in March before running well in the Grade 2 Aintree bumper a month later.

"I think if things go his way he could be better than his half-sister," says Longsdon. "We might run him in a Listed bumper and, if he did, he'd run very well. If he didn't go down the bumper route I'd like to see him in the Grade 2 Winter Novices Hurdle at

Supremely Lucky: switched from Dan Skelton's yard and will be running over fences for Charlie Longsdon (inset)

Sandown in December, but not until he's proved he's good enough."

Black-type aim for Dalina

Saint Dalina won three times over hurdles which saw her rating rise from 101 to 130 since her handicap debut in the spring of 2020.

"She loves very soft ground, so we'll be running her in the depths of winter at somewhere like Ffos Las or Uttoxeter, and the priority will be to get some black type for her," says Longsdon.

"She's more than capable of winning off her mark of 130 and if we don't get some black type we'll have got it wrong."

The unraced **Stroll On By** is working very well and will go down the bumper route. "If he can win a bumper we can have some fun with him," says his trainer, who plans a different route for the ex-Dan Skelton chaser **Supremely Lucky**.

"He's an honest horse who gallops nicely and we'll stay chasing with him," says Longsdon.

Irish point-to-point winner **Tea For Free** won a bumper for Longsdon and will go novice hurdling, while **What About Time**, who won his only novice hurdle impressively, could be a "very nice horse" in time.
Interview by Lawrie Kelsey

OLLY MURPHY

OLLY MURPHY has itchy feet. Not that he wants to leave his Warren Chase base just to the north west of Stratford-upon-Avon.

It's just that he is an ambitious young trainer going places and no matter where he's standing, those itchy feet keep pointing towards Cheltenham, only 32 miles away.

In his fifth season as a trainer, Murphy has already saddled a Grade 1 winner and won prize-money nearing £2.5 million, but it's no surprise his major target each season is a Cheltenham Festival winner.

And the horse Murphy hopes could fulfil his festival ambition is . . . **Itchy Feet**.

As a six-year-old, he was 7-2 second favourite behind Faugheen, no less, to land the Marsh Novices' Chase at Cheltenham, but a blunder at the sixth fence shot Gavin Sheehan over his mount's head and the dream dissolved.

Itchy Feet missed Cheltenham last season but ended with a gallant third in the Grade 1 Marsh Chase at Aintree in April.

Just as he did last season, Murphy aims to start Itchy Feet's campaign in the Grade 2 Monet's Garden Old Roan Chase over 2m4f at Aintree on October 24.

Last season he finished third of 12 in a tactical race that ended in a sprint, which didn't suit Itchy Feet, who needs a trip nowadays.

Murphy will take it one race at a time and hasn't yet mapped out a programme for Itchy Feet.

"I wouldn't have a clue after Aintree, it's early days yet, but we'll have to mix it with the big boys this year, although I'm hoping he's capable of winning a big race," says Murphy.

Wherever he ends up, the 153-rated chaser will give followers a run for their money, and it could be at Cheltenham.

Another inmate who could end up going for top prizes is **Champagnesuperover**, but

Itchy Feet leads team high on quality

WINNERS IN LAST FOUR SEASONS **80, 67, 82, 47**

TOKYO Olympic eventing team gold medallist Laura Collett has joined Olly Murphy's team at Warren Chase stables in Warwickshire. "It's brilliant to have her on board," says Murphy. "To say she's a talented rider probably doesn't do her justice and I'm really happy to have her alongside us a couple or three days a week."

> We'll aim him at all the good two-and-a-half-mile Graded hurdles this season. He's had a little wind operation this summer and he's looking good. We're very hopeful

not over hurdles. He'll go novice chasing.

He was rated 137 last season after finishing seventh of 16 in the Albert Bartlett at the festival, then being pulled up in the Grade 1 Sefton Novices' Hurdle at Aintree.

"He had a good run in the Albert Bartlett where, but for a mistake at the last, he would have gone close. He was disappointing at Aintree where he ran flat.

"He'll go novice chasing this season. We'll start him off at two and a half and work on from that. He's schooled well and looks promising."

Following a year over fences for **Brewin'upastorm**, which included victories

at Carlisle and Taunton before unseating four out in the Arkle at Cheltenham, connections brought him back over hurdles early this year.

The move promptly reaped wins at Taunton and a Grade 2 at Fontwell before ending the season with a fifth in the Grade 1 Aintree Hurdle.

"We'll start him off in a two-and-a-half-mile conditions hurdle at Aintree at the end of October, then we'll aim him at all the good two-and-a-half-mile Graded hurdles this season," says Murphy.

"He's had a little wind operation this summer and he's looking good. We're very hopeful."

Brewin'upastorm: successful over fences in 2019, he was a dual winner back over hurdles last season and will follow that route again this time

Staying trips for Thomas

Thomas Darby has been tried over gradually increasing distances over the last three years until a run in the Coral Cup at Cheltenham over two miles and five furlongs in March finally persuaded Murphy to step him up to three miles for the first time.

That came at Aintree in the Grade 1 Ryanair Stayers' Hurdle where he was a revelation. He surprised everyone, including his delighted connections, by finishing third at 28-1.

"He ran a career-best at Aintree, so hopefully we seem to have found his best trip and we'll keep him at three miles all season in all those long-distance Graded races."

The eight-year-old will start his campaign off at Wetherby in the Grade 2 West Yorkshire Hurdle in late October and could end with a crack at the Stayers' Hurdle at Cheltenham next spring, a division which looks wide open this year, if all goes well.

The 130-rated hurdler **Allavina** is definitely one for the notebook judged on her trainer's comments.

"She could be a smart mare," he says. "She didn't do a lot wrong last season and this year she'll probably go jumping fences.

"She's one I'm really looking forward to and she could pick up a bit of black type."

The six-year-old mare won a bumper and three hurdles races before finding the competition too stiff in the Mares' Novices' Hurdle at Cheltenham, where she finished 13th of 15.

Restandbethankful is another who has done little wrong. In the last 12 months he has won three times and been runner-up twice in five outings.

His opening race of the season is likely to be a handicap hurdle at Chepstow's first meeting in October.

"He's had a little wind op and is working well," says Murphy.

Among his 115-strong string is an impressive bunch of novice hurdlers from whom Murphy not only hopes, but expects, a steady stream of winners.

'He's my star horse'

Among them is **Go Dante**, a super-smooth winner of a soft-ground bumper at Wincanton in March.

The Kayf Tara gelding thrashed 11 rivals by seven and a half lengths, never giving his jockey Aidan Coleman or his even-money backers a moment's worry.

"He's my star horse. He'll be a nice novice hurdler who'll be out in mid-October once the ground eases."

Washington is a similar type of horse, a dual bumper winner who'll have the same type of novice hurdle targets.

He won his debut race in November at Fakenham last year by 19 lengths and followed up with victory at Huntingdon in March.

OLLY MURPHY
STRATFORD-UPON-AVON, WARWICKSHIRE

RECORD AROUND THE COURSES

	Total W-R	Per cent	Non-hcp Hdle	Non-hcp Chase	Hcp Hdle	Hcp Chase	N.H. Flat	£1 level stake
Market Rasen	39-198	19.7	18-70	1-2	14-81	2-26	4-19	-54.12
Fakenham	31-139	22.3	13-56	0-2	11-50	5-21	2-10	-17.62
Uttoxeter	21-106	19.8	11-43	1-3	5-38	1-13	3-9	-7.27
Southwell	18-105	17.1	11-37	1-3	3-42	3-13	0-10	-56.94
Huntingdon	15-57	26.3	6-23	0-0	2-16	1-6	6-12	-10.92
Stratford	15-108	13.9	8-44	0-0	2-40	3-14	2-10	-59.07
Fontwell	13-52	25.0	6-18	0-2	2-18	2-8	3-6	-3.72
Perth	13-55	23.6	5-17	0-1	6-23	1-12	1-2	+11.79
Newton Abbot	10-29	34.5	5-11	0-0	2-10	2-3	1-5	+20.05
Ayr	8-34	23.5	4-9	1-4	0-10	0-7	3-4	-9.65
Taunton	8-45	17.8	3-25	1-1	2-14	2-4	0-1	-24.84
Bangor	8-66	12.1	3-25	1-3	1-19	3-13	0-6	-44.64
Wincanton	7-31	22.6	4-16	0-0	0-7	1-6	2-2	-9.27
Leicester	6-19	31.6	5-11	1-1	0-3	0-4	0-0	+26.20
Sedgefield	6-24	25.0	2-6	0-1	1-5	0-6	3-6	-9.57
Warwick	6-81	7.4	4-37	0-4	0-16	0-9	2-15	-18.33
Musselburgh	5-11	45.5	1-2	0-0	1-2	2-5	1-2	+5.85
Newcastle	5-24	20.8	3-10	0-0	0-4	1-3	1-7	-8.66
Worcester	5-32	15.6	3-10	0-1	2-16	0-4	0-1	-16.55
Ludlow	5-45	11.1	4-18	0-3	1-15	0-5	0-4	-35.96
Carlisle	4-15	26.7	2-6	1-4	0-2	0-0	1-3	-4.06
Doncaster	4-19	21.1	1-7	1-2	1-5	0-3	1-2	+20.07
Plumpton	4-23	17.4	2-9	0-0	1-10	1-4	0-0	-5.76
Kelso	4-23	17.4	1-7	0-1	2-10	1-5	0-0	-10.21
Hereford	4-31	12.9	0-10	1-2	2-13	0-2	1-4	+7.00
Chepstow	4-33	12.1	1-13	1-3	1-7	0-6	1-4	-8.00
Lingfield	3-10	30.0	0-1	1-1	2-5	0-3	0-0	+14.00
Catterick	3-14	21.4	2-8	0-1	1-4	0-1	0-0	-4.13
Ffos Las	3-15	20.0	0-3	1-1	0-5	1-2	1-4	-0.63
Haydock	3-16	18.7	0-6	0-1	2-7	0-1	1-1	-3.83
Lingfield (AW)	2-13	15.4	0-0	0-0	0-0	0-0	2-13	-6.30
Ascot	2-14	14.3	0-5	0-2	2-5	0-1	0-1	+5.00
Aintree	2-30	6.7	0-8	0-1	2-11	0-8	0-2	-19.67
Cheltenham	2-42	4.8	1-12	0-3	1-20	0-4	0-3	-31.50
Exeter	1-7	14.3	0-2	0-1	0-1	0-1	1-2	-3.50
Hexham	1-7	14.3	0-2	1-3	0-2	0-0	0-0	-4.90
Sandown	1-15	6.7	0-5	1-2	0-6	0-1	0-1	-7.00
Cartmel	1-16	6.2	1-6	0-0	0-8	0-2	0-0	-13.25
Kempton	1-22	4.5	1-10	0-3	0-7	0-2	0-0	-18.50
Wetherby	1-35	2.9	0-18	0-4	0-7	1-3	0-3	-32.50
Newcastle (AW)	0-1	0.0	0-0	0-0	0-0	0-0	0-1	-1.00
Towcester	0-10	0.0	0-1	0-2	0-6	0-1	0-0	-10.00
Newbury	0-26	0.0	0-15	0-0	0-5	0-1	0-5	-26.00

Allavina: could make the switch to fences this season

■ Jonjo O'Neill Jr has ridden for the stable only five times but rode three winners – a 60% strike-rate and £4.60 profit

"I'm hoping he can progress into a nice horse," was Murphy's guarded comment.

Moore Margaux is a well-regarded son of Flemensfirth who finished runner-up to a Dan Skelton hotpot in a Warwick novice hurdle in March. He is expected to carry plenty of stable confidence when he reappears this autumn and he too can be followed.

Novice hurdle prospect

Wolfspear was another to win on his racecourse debut, enhancing Murphy's reputation as an exponent of landing bumpers – he has an astonishing 24 per cent strike in the discipline.

Wolfspear beat First Street, a fancied

51

Copperless: Swinton Hurdle winner will head to Ffos Las for the Welsh Champion Hurdle

runner from the Nicky Henderson stable, by three lengths and looks "a nice novice hurdler".

Doctor Ken was a powerful winner of a Market Rasen bumper in March and is expected to make the transition to hurdling equally smoothly. He'll be "a lovely chaser in time", according to his trainer.

Bombs Away was "an unlucky loser" of a bumper at Southwell in May on his only start to date.

"He's been working very well and will be worthwhile following as a novice hurdler," says Murphy.

No Risk Des Flos, winner of two novice hurdles last season, will probably start off in hurdle races before jumping fences and looks to have a competitive rating.

"He could have a nice handicap mark," the trainer says knowingly.

Copperless, impressive winner of Haydock's Swinton Hurdle in May, will have the Welsh Champion Hurdle at Ffos Las on October 16 as his first target.

"He's working well and will go straight there without a prep race," says Murphy, who will form a programme for the son of Kayf Tara once the Ffos Las race is out of the way.

Lord Of Kerak was runner-up three times and a winner once over hurdles last season.

"He's had a small wind operation and could make a nice novice chaser," says the trainer.

After finishing just under three lengths third in his opening bumper at Newcastle in December, **Thunder Rock** reappeared in an Exeter bumper two months later and just held on to win.

He is expected to make "a nice novice hurdler" and be one of those who "rises to the top" of the Warren Chase group of young hurdlers this season.

Of the Warren Chase handicappers, make a note of **Mackelduff**. He was an 11-length winner of a maiden hurdle at Southwell in May and Murphy is confident the gelding's mark of 115 is exploitable.

Two bumper horses to follow are **Dominic's Fault** by Camelot and **Doctor Seb** by Dr Devious.

Finally, Murphy's dark horse for the season is **Duke Of Rockingham**, who has had a long break and summered well after finishing seventh of ten in a Newbury bumper last November.

The €130,000 Kayf Tara gelding has been given plenty of time to develop, is pleasing the Warren Chase team and is progressing nicely.

Interview by Lawrie Kelsey

NICKY RICHARDS

Greystoke maestro relishing chance of Takingrisks

THERE'S life in the old boy yet – and more victories judged on last season – so keep **Takingrisks** in mind when the veteran reappears.

The 12-year-old has won every year since he landed a point-to-point in Ireland in 2015, except the coronavirus pandemic lockdown year of 2020.

He's won nine of his 33 races under rules and one point-to-point and brought owner Frank Bird £294,698 in prize-money as well as a host of rich memories.

Little wonder the veteran chaser is one of the favourites at Nicky Richards' Rectory Farm Stables, Greystoke, five miles west of Penrith in the shadow of the Cumbrian fells, where the likes of chasing legends Playlord,

WINNERS IN LAST FOUR SEASONS **33, 34, 42, 29**

Takingrisks powers home to score at Doncaster last season for Nicky Richards (above)

Titus Oates, One Man, The Grey Monk and Monet's Garden have been trained.

He's still sprightly and enjoying life after a summer at grass following his exertions in the Grand National in April, when Sean Quinlan pulled him up before the 17th fence.

He'd earned his entry after winning the Listed Sky Bet Handicap Chase over three miles at Doncaster in January as well as a gutsy fourth in the Rehearsal Chase at Newcastle in November.

The Rehearsal was won by Takingrisks in 2019, the year he also landed the Scottish Grand National, and the Newcastle race is likely to be his target this season.

"He's a grand old horse," says Richards. "He'll take us on the journey. He's in the veteran stage now and if he's firing on all cylinders I've no doubt he'll pick up a good prize again this year."

Takingrisks has enjoyed a long summer break and according to Richards "he's done very well".

"He knows what to do when he's in a field – get fat – so he takes a bit of getting ready.

"He'll probably go to Ayr four weeks before the Rehearsal [for a 3m½f hurdle] and usually embarrasses everybody because he doesn't really like hurdling.

"That's been his prep race for the last three years. We usually put a young jockey on him just to give him a spin around."

Love set to conquer

Glittering Love is a staying handicap chaser who maintains his form well. He was consistent last season without winning, finishing second twice and never out of the first four in five outings.

"He didn't get his head in front, but I'll be fairly confident he'll get his head in front this year," says Richards.

"We need rain before we decide anything though. I'm getting a little held back with the schooling. You wouldn't believe the grass up here in the Lake District – it's firm. We had a little but it just kept the dust down."

When Glittering Love gets going in November the successful former pointer looks attractively weighted on a mark of 117 as he travels round the northern circuit again at tracks such as Ayr, Newcastle, Hexham and Kelso.

Ribble Valley has won five of his eight outings, two bumpers and three over hurdles, the last of which was a creditable third in last season's Fighting Fifth at Newcastle behind Epatante. He was injured that day, which kept him out for the rest of last season.

He'd already earned a fair reputation after demolishing a good field at Wetherby, earning a rating of 142.

He took that into a Grade 2 hurdle at Ascot where he was made odds-on favourite and, although acquitting himself well, was no match for the equally well-regarded Master Debonair.

"He's a classy horse and if all goes well he'll be back this season novice chasing and hopefully be there for one of the big spring meetings," says Richards.

"I wouldn't mind either Cheltenham or Aintree if he's proven to be good enough. He could even be an Arkle horse. He'll be out in the middle or end of November."

Exciting novice chaser

The ultra-consistent **Castle Rushen** has won three of his seven races, been second three times and third once.

Owned by Trevor Hemmings, Castle Rushen is described by Richards as "a beautiful big horse, a typical Mr Hemmings horse – and the right sort to go chasing with".

"He had a progressive sort of year last year, improving as the year was going on, looking like he was wanting further and further," says Richards. "We didn't want to put him up in distance too quickly though because he was still growing into his frame.

"The plan is to go novice chasing and hopefully get a nice bit of experience into him, and it'll be interesting to see where he takes us.

"If he goes up in grade he'll be away to the likes of Haydock, and that sort of place, and

NICKY RICHARDS
GREYSTOKE, CUMBRIA

RECORD AROUND THE COURSES

	Total W-R	Per cent	Non-hcp Hdle	Non-hcp Chase	Hcp Hdle	Hcp Chase	N.H. Flat	£1 level stake
Ayr	68-312	21.8	17-79	5-10	12-99	18-77	16-47	-44.28
Kelso	45-235	19.1	14-61	2-20	11-66	12-63	6-25	+0.25
Carlisle	44-173	25.4	12-44	3-19	14-50	9-44	6-16	+69.41
Perth	32-274	11.7	5-39	3-14	14-143	7-65	3-13	-82.00
Newcastle	29-146	19.9	9-36	1-4	4-33	6-46	9-27	-12.91
Hexham	26-93	28.0	9-33	3-6	7-23	7-25	0-6	+9.39
Musselburgh	17-114	14.9	3-18	0-3	10-70	1-10	3-13	-5.47
Sedgefield	15-61	24.6	5-20	2-5	4-17	3-10	1-9	+6.91
Doncaster	15-96	15.6	2-22	0-2	5-39	7-27	1-6	+42.25
Wetherby	14-78	17.9	2-11	2-7	5-28	4-22	1-10	+26.49
Market Rasen	13-87	14.9	0-13	1-6	11-47	0-13	1-8	-12.18
Bangor	8-54	14.8	0-8	0-2	3-31	5-11	0-2	-1.00
Cartmel	7-40	17.5	1-9	0-1	4-23	2-7	0-0	-6.42
Huntingdon	5-26	19.2	1-3	0-3	4-17	0-1	0-2	-9.15
Haydock	5-55	9.1	0-9	0-3	4-31	1-11	0-1	-16.75
Southwell	3-17	17.6	0-3	0-0	2-11	1-3	0-0	-1.00
Uttoxeter	3-27	11.1	0-1	0-1	2-17	0-7	1-1	-18.31
Newton Abbot	2-3	66.7	0-0	2-2	0-0	0-1	0-0	+0.33
Catterick	2-19	10.5	0-6	1-6	0-2	1-5	0-0	-8.50
Stratford	1-7	14.3	0-0	0-0	1-4	0-3	0-0	-4.90
Worcester	1-17	5.9	0-2	1-1	0-11	0-2	0-1	-11.00
Cheltenham	1-34	2.9	0-3	0-11	0-7	1-10	0-3	-24.00
Aintree	1-35	2.9	0-7	0-3	0-12	1-11	0-2	-30.50
Ffos Las	0-1	0.0	0-0	0-0	0-1	0-0	0-0	-1.00
Hereford	0-1	0.0	0-0	0-0	0-1	0-0	0-0	-1.00
Newcastle (AW)	0-1	0.0	0-0	0-0	0-0	0-0	0-1	-1.00
Warwick	0-2	0.0	0-0	0-0	0-0	0-2	0-0	-2.00
Fakenham	0-2	0.0	0-1	0-0	0-0	0-0	0-1	-2.00
Southwell (AW)	0-2	0.0	0-0	0-0	0-0	0-0	0-2	-2.00
Newbury	0-4	0.0	0-1	0-1	0-1	0-1	0-0	-4.00
Kempton	0-4	0.0	0-1	0-0	0-1	0-2	0-0	-4.00
Ludlow	0-5	0.0	0-0	0-1	0-3	0-1	0-0	-5.00
Sandown	0-7	0.0	0-0	0-0	0-2	0-4	0-1	-7.00
Ascot	0-10	0.0	0-1	0-2	0-3	0-4	0-0	-10.00

Top to bottom: Castle Rushen, Glittering Love, Marown and Ribble Valley

we can only hope he's good enough for Cheltenham or Aintree – but it's too early to talk about the Grand National. He hasn't jumped a fence in public yet, so you wouldn't want to be thinking that way yet."

A second Hemmings horse with a bright future is **Marown**, who was described by Richards in March after an impressive Wetherby novice chase victory as "a wonderful prospect".

He says: "Hopefully, he'll make a lovely handicapping horse. He's won a couple of novice chases and been Graded placed. We're on the journey and the dream's still alive. Where it ends, you never know with a big, lovely horse like him.

"He's a staying chaser in the making. We kept him at two and a half miles for most of the season just because he was growing into himself."

Richards reckons he has a nice team of novice hurdlers who did well in bumpers last

> He shows a good attitude and any horse who can win two bumpers has to be above average

season and leading the way is another Hemmings horse to watch out for, is **Famous Bridge.**

"He's a young horse who ran in an Irish point-to-point bumper at Punchestown where he finished third," says the trainer.

"He's another who is a big chasing type for the future but he will start over two and a half miles over hurdles.

"He looks an exciting chasing prospect who will want good to soft or soft ground."

Richards had "a fair team" of bumpers last season and reckons this year's intake could be equally as good, and in the "could be anything category" is **Crystal Glory**, who won both his point-to-points for Irish trainer Donnchadh Doyle and came across with a high reputation.

"I think he'll be a nice horse," says Richards. "He's a grand, big sort, so he'll go straight novice hurdling on a galloping track."

Champagne can flow

Everyday Champagne had his first outing at Ayr and was "an absolute embarrassment", according to his trainer. "I could have dug a hole and jumped in it. I ran two horses in the race and thought they'd both run nice races. It was very heavy and they could hardly pull their feet out of the ground."

He was made 5-4 favourite but was anchored by the heavy ground and finished a distant fourth.

"We got him home, freshened him up and took him to Perth, which wouldn't be his

Nells Son: dual bumper winner is a bright prospect for novice hurdles

place at all, but the owners are Perthshire people. He finished third but showed what he was all about – a future staying chaser, so I was pleased. He'll go novice hurdling when we get some good jumping ground."

Nells Son won both his bumpers last season and is another of the Richards bunch of tyros expected to make their mark over hurdles.

"He's a nice horse who will probably stay well. He'll want soft ground and be out in late November when we get some dig in the ground. He shows a good attitude and any horse who can win two bumpers has to be above average."

Release The Kraken ran well in two bumpers without winning, in the second

finishing runner-up at Hexham. "I thought he ran a grand race for a baby, staying all the way. He'll start in novice hurdles and should be a nice two-and-a-half or three-mile horse."

Novice hurdles beckon

Sauce Of Life was another newcomer to win both his bumpers last year. He had to dig deep to win at Market Rasen and battled well to the line.

"We'll keep to two miles with him on probably half-decent ground when he goes novice hurdling."

Snowy Clouds, bought out of the Trevor Hemmings dispersal sale, dead-heated in a point-to-point bumper and is another to add depth to Richards' powerful novice hurdling

59

Court Dreaming (11) could do well over extreme distances

brigade. "He's a big, likeable, strong horse who'll probably want two and a half miles when he goes novice hurdling."

Soft Risk is a big, strong French-bred horse who won a bumper very well at Ayr in May. "We'll start him at two miles and he'll guide us along and see what we'll be doing then."

'Bred and built for chasing'

Royal Arcade was a consistent novice hurdler last season, winning once and being placed twice in three outings at Richards' local Carlisle track.

"He may have a couple of runs over hurdles but he'll be getting a school over fences at the same time," says the trainer.

"He's bred and built for chasing and has never done anything wrong so far, so the dream's alive still.

"It's very hard with the novice chase handicapping system to get novice chasers educated nowadays, but, hopefully, he'll get a trouble-free preparation and then get a couple of trouble-free runs, so he could end up being a lovely handicap chaser for next season."

Court Dreaming is a consistent handicap chaser who is likely to go up in distance this year.

"It'll be interesting to see how he does because he could be quite useful in staying

■ Early spring is often a profitable time for the stable. In March 2020 there was a 41% strike-rate and profit of £17.93

chases over the more extreme distances as the season goes on," says Richards.

"I don't think he's quite big enough for the Grand National, to be honest, but he could be interesting in the races just below that sort of level."

Glorious Spirit won a mares' bumper at Uttoxeter in July, then landed her first race over hurdles at Sedgefield at the beginning of September.

"We're hoping she'll end up a useful staying hurdler as the season goes on," says Richards. "She'll want a bit of experience and then we might dip our toe in one or two of those better mares' hurdles."

Mayo Star, who won a couple of hurdle races last season but didn't fire when sent chasing, could be back over hurdles – and winning, according to his trainer.

Serious Ego is a consistent handicap hurdler who, predicts Richards, will offer members of his racing club "a lot of fun this season".

"He'll win more races and there are still shares to be had in him," says Richards. "He's a Saturday horse, although he won't be in the major races, he'll be on the undercard."

Finally, Richards offers ex-Gordon Elliott-trained **Smokey The Bandit** as his dark horse for the season in "lowish handicap hurdles".

Interview by Lawrie Kelsey

JAMIE SNOWDEN

Hardy can play part in hitting new record

AMONG the owners at Folly House will be two members of the Royal family. Zara Tindall, a new owner, has an unraced youngster by Telescope named Eye To The Sky, while Dark Motive is owned by the Duchess of Cornwall and Sir Chips Keswick.

WINNERS IN LAST FOUR SEASONS **23, 46, 31, 35**

JAMIE SNOWDEN has made a flying start to the jumps season and it could pay dividends to follow his runners for the rest of the campaign.

Towards the end of September his Lambourn yard had welcomed back 17 winners putting him well on course for a stab at beating his record of 46 and more than £375,000 prize-money two seasons ago.

Among the leading hopes of helping to achieve that goal is **Hardy Du Seuil**, a French four-year-old by Coastal Path.

"I'm really excited about him. He's a lovely horse," says the master of Folly House stables. "He finished second in a couple of French bumpers before winning a novice hurdle.

"He jumps his fences well, so we'll try to utilise that four-

Ga Law: brings up a hat-trick over fences last autumn with victory at Wincanton for Jamie Snowden (left)

year-old, weight-for-age allowance to go novice chasing this autumn."

The French import, who will handle cut in the ground, will be started over shorter trips starting in mid-October but will have his distances increased as he's from the family of prolific Grade 1 winner Silviniaco Conti, who excelled over longer trips, and Eglantine Du Seuil, who won the Mares' Novices' Hurdle at the 2019 Cheltenham Festival.

"It would be nice if he could follow in the footsteps of **Ga Law,** who utilised his four-year-old allowance last season to reach a rating of 150 after winning three times over fences, including a Grade 2 at Wincanton," says Snowden.

Ga Law was stepped up to Grade 1 in the Henry VIII Novices' Chase at Sandown but finished third behind Allmankind, who was considered good enough to tackle the Arkle at Cheltenham.

Snowden has already had a Cheltenham Festival winner with Present View in 2014 but has yet to saddle a Grade 1 winner, and that is his next target.

Hardy Du Seuil could follow a similar route to Ga Law but if he is not the horse to step up to Grade 1, perhaps the candidate among Snowden's string of 60 to do so could be the six-year-old mare **Anythingforlove**.

She won the Grade 2 Jane Seymour novice hurdle over two and a half miles at Sandown in February, one of two races at that level the stable had last season.

That was in heavy ground, so the presumption is she will stay further as she goes novice chasing.

"She should be a smart mare in that sphere," says Snowden. "I'm hoping she can step forward and progress again. She'll be out at Worcester in October."

Sefton the aim for Hogan's

In April, **Hogan's Height** became the yard's first runner in the Grand National, finishing a creditable 12th of the 40 starters.

"He was second of the British horses home, so without the Irish he'd have been second in the Grand National," says Snowden, tongue firmly in his cheek.

Three weeks earlier Hogan's Height had finished sixth in the cross-country race at the festival behind Irish and French runners, which, using Folly logic, would have handed him victory.

The gelding, now rated 139, has the Grand Sefton chase at Aintree in December pencilled in this season, a race he won two years ago, and then he'll go hunter chasing.

Thomas Macdonagh, a soft-ground-loving novice chase winner rated 131, will also go for the Grand Sefton, with the Bobby Renton at Wetherby in October chosen as a warm-up race.

"Those will be his early season targets and we'll decide where he goes after that. He's summered really well and we're very pleased with him."

Bright future for Kiltealy

Kiltealy Briggs was a twice-winning novice hurdler and a decent novice chaser last season, although he never won over fences, but hopes are high he will pay his way this season after a creditable ninth of 21 in the Grade 3 Paddy Power Plate at the Cheltenham Festival.

"He had an interrupted summer last year and ended up having colic on the back of running in the Albert Bartlett," says Snowden.

"He didn't really have a summer break, so he did well to run in his novice chases. He's done really well this time around. He's matured into a big, strong horse and I hope he can be a decent second-season novice chaser.

"He'll start off in a Listed chase at Chepstow and have all the decent novice chases as his targets later on."

Another Folly House favourite is **Stoney Mountain**, who will have a Grade 3 handicap hurdle at Haydock towards the end of November as an early season target, a race he won in 2019.

"We'll go back to Haydock for the same race and try to get him qualified for the Pertemps final at the festival. He's done it in

JAMIE SNOWDEN
UPPER LAMBOURN, BERKSHIRE

RECORD AROUND THE COURSES

	Total W-R	Per cent	Non-hcp Hdle	Non-hcp Chase	Hcp Hdle	Hcp Chase	N.H. Flat	£1 level stake
Fontwell	32-166	19.3	10-49	2-4	8-42	7-37	5-34	-8.11
Uttoxeter	17-103	16.5	4-24	0-6	3-31	8-31	2-11	+10.90
Worcester	16-105	15.2	5-36	3-6	1-22	7-33	0-8	-28.25
Ffos Las	13-56	23.2	6-19	0-2	4-19	2-10	1-6	+8.84
Newton Abbot	12-83	14.5	4-26	1-6	2-25	5-21	0-5	-42.67
Southwell	11-80	13.7	4-23	0-0	5-26	2-21	0-10	-14.93
Stratford	10-68	14.7	5-24	1-5	2-11	1-26	1-2	-33.99
Towcester	9-55	16.4	4-28	1-2	2-12	1-7	1-6	-12.95
Wincanton	9-83	10.8	1-27	1-5	1-22	5-25	1-4	-41.83
Catterick	8-17	47.1	3-6	2-2	0-4	2-3	1-2	+1.97
Wetherby	8-44	18.2	3-14	2-5	2-6	0-8	1-11	-3.84
Ludlow	8-51	15.7	3-16	1-2	1-16	1-6	2-11	-12.57
Market Rasen	8-76	10.5	3-25	1-4	0-20	2-15	2-12	-29.46
Huntingdon	8-88	9.1	2-35	1-6	1-17	2-20	2-10	-56.64
Sedgefield	7-35	20.0	5-16	0-0	0-6	1-8	1-5	+7.90
Chepstow	7-51	13.7	1-16	0-0	2-12	3-13	1-10	-4.01
Exeter	7-54	13.0	3-21	0-5	2-14	2-13	0-1	-15.00
Plumpton	7-88	8.0	3-31	1-3	0-20	2-24	1-10	-53.34
Haydock	6-19	31.6	1-5	1-2	1-3	3-8	0-1	+11.58
Hexham	6-23	26.1	4-10	0-2	0-4	0-4	2-3	-8.38
Lingfield	6-31	19.4	6-20	0-0	0-2	0-9	0-0	-6.71
Taunton	6-53	11.3	3-19	1-2	1-17	0-7	1-8	-9.93
Cheltenham	6-64	9.4	0-17	1-6	2-17	3-16	0-8	-1.50
Fakenham	5-28	17.9	1-9	0-1	2-5	2-10	0-3	-2.40
Bangor	5-54	9.3	2-10	0-7	0-13	1-18	2-6	-24.47
Hereford	4-25	16.0	0-7	0-1	1-8	3-7	0-2	-0.55
Kempton	4-27	14.8	1-8	0-2	1-9	2-8	0-0	-13.75
Kelso	3-6	50.0	2-2	0-1	1-1	0-2	0-0	+1.92
Carlisle	3-15	20.0	0-1	0-2	1-3	0-4	2-5	+3.62
Ascot	3-17	17.6	0-3	0-1	1-5	2-6	0-2	-3.50
Warwick	3-37	8.1	1-7	0-2	0-8	1-13	1-7	-27.22
Doncaster	2-28	7.1	0-9	0-1	1-13	0-2	1-3	-17.00
Perth	1-4	25.0	1-3	0-0	0-0	0-1	0-0	-2.39
Ayr	1-5	20.0	0-0	0-1	1-3	0-1	0-0	+12.00
Cartmel	1-15	6.7	0-3	0-1	0-4	1-7	0-0	-11.00
Leicester	1-16	6.2	0-3	0-3	1-3	0-7	0-0	-10.00
Aintree	1-23	4.3	0-5	0-2	0-6	1-7	0-3	-6.00
Sandown	1-25	4.0	1-4	0-8	0-5	0-6	0-2	-6.00
Newbury	1-40	2.5	0-13	0-1	0-11	1-8	0-7	-35.00
Musselburgh	0-1	0.0	0-0	0-0	0-1	0-0	0-0	-1.00
Southwell (AW)	0-1	0.0	0-0	0-0	0-0	0-0	0-1	-1.00
Kempton (AW)	0-2	0.0	0-0	0-0	0-0	0-0	0-2	-2.00
Newcastle	0-3	0.0	0-1	0-0	0-1	0-1	0-0	-3.00
Lingfield (AW)	0-6	0.0	0-0	0-0	0-0	0-0	0-6	-6.00

Top to bottom: Hogan's Height, Thomas Macdonagh and Kiltealy Briggs

the past and there's no reason why he can't do it again. He'll be out at Cheltenham at the end of October."

Up For Parol, twice a winner over hurdles at Wetherby and Ffos Las, has the Persian War at Chepstow in October as his first target before a possible career over fences.

"I'm sure he wants a trip on decent ground this side of Christmas, so we'll start him over two and a half and move from there. Whether he stays over hurdles this year or goes chasing depends on how he does in the Persian War."

Snowden was thinking that **Guinness Affair**, a ready winner of a Huntingdon bumper and two novice hurdles at Stratford and Fontwell, could progress into a Persian War horse, but has had second thoughts.

"This chap has been given an initial mark of 117, which I think is quite workable. So he might go down to Exeter for a two-mile-three handicap in early October and see where we are from there," he says.

Snowden is excited by Goffs Doncaster May purchase, **Git Maker**, a ten-length winning Irish pointer who was bought for £105,000 for the newly established sporting syndicate, Everest Racing Club.

"The club involves days out at golf, cricket, rugby and football. It's quite a fun set-up and shares are still available," says Snowden.

"It's an exclusive club bringing together like-minded people to enjoy the thrill of racing and sport in one package."

One for the long term

Another Goffs May purchase was **Super Survivor**, a close-up second on his only Irish point outing knocked down for £115,000.

"He's a big strapping chaser of the future. We'll start him off novice hurdling this season. He's a lovely type and will probably end up being a stayer and is one to follow."

Braveheart is a five-year-old gelding

bought for the Cherry Pickers syndicate, a group of members from Snowden's old regiment, the 11th Hussars, whose army nickname they have adopted.

"They want to win the Grand Military Gold Cup at Sandown," says Snowden, "although this season might be a bit optimistic. He goes very well at home and jumps well. We'll start him off in a bumper and take it from there."

The four-year-old filly **Viva Vamoos**, who finished second in a bumper at Southwell in March, is considered "a lovely sort" and a certain winner.

"She should be able to win a bumper this year before we start looking for a bit of black type," says Snowden.

Another reckoned to be a definite winner this season is **College Oak**, who landed a

Up For Parol (right): has the Persian War Hurdle at Chepstow as an early target

■ Sean Bowen is two winners from six rides for the stable – a 33% strike-rate that yields a profit of £15

College Oak (right): expected to win over fences this season

couple of hurdles last season, including a nice handicap at Ascot.

"He'll go novice handicap chasing this year and his first race will be at Fontwell in October over two and a half, but he'll stay further," says the trainer.

Dusky Days won a bumper in the spring and will head straight to novice hurdling. He'll start over two miles but is expected to stay longer distances.

Much is expected of **Datsalrightgino**, who has been placed in all four starts in bumpers. He's had a wind operation and will go novice hurdling. "He's a nice horse who works well," says Snowden.

Midnight Centurion is a similar type who has been runner-up twice in bumpers and will go juvenile hurdling this season, while **Cornicello**, a Flat winner in France who jumps well, will join him in the juvenile hurdling ranks.

Finally, two unraced four-year-old geldings to note are **Top Of The Bay**, "a lovely looker who is pleasing us" and **Valamix**, an Aga Khan-bred who is "a big scopey athletic sort".

"We have 60 in for the winter, which is up on previous years, and we've had 17 winners so far, which is a good start. So we're very hopeful."

Interview by Lawrie Kelsey

JOE TIZZARD

Ready to bounce back

THE father-and-son duo of Colin and Joe Tizzard could be in for a season tinged with a golden hue.

Their Venn Farm stables in 500 acres of prime arable land in the Blackmore Vale, two miles east of Sherborne in Dorset, houses a trio of talent who could all end up with Cheltenham Gold Cup on their agendas.

Veteran Native River, Lostintranslation and The Big Breakaway all begin the season with the Tizzards mentally pencilling in the festival's fourth race of the fourth day for each of them.

They are part of a 110-horsepower yard which has the potential to assuage the pain of last season's poor performance which brought a meagre 37 winners, the stable's lowest total for six years.

"It was a very disappointing season, without a shadow of doubt," says Joe *(right)*, who takes over the yard's licence from his father in October.

"Our bar is set high on the back of other years and last season the horses weren't performing to their best. We had some good days but there were some tough times as well.

"I think we had an underlying virus running through the yard. It was very difficult to put a finger on what it was

Native River leads
Lostintranslation on the
Tizzard gallops in Dorset

WINNERS IN LAST FOUR SEASONS **37, 61, 77, 79**

to the top table

exactly. They weren't coughing or anything, but certainly something wasn't right all last year.

"We've turned a corner, though, and we've had a good summer and the horses are running very well."

Spring campaign the plan

Lostintranslation will again have the Gold Cup as his main target but he will have to perform above his rating of 162 to have any chance after a season to forget.

"It was a difficult year with him last year; he was very disappointing; he couldn't even get round [in the Gold Cup], so we've been back to the drawing board with him.

"After he was third in the 2020 Gold Cup [beaten a length and a half by Al Boum Photo and Santini] we genuinely believed we had a horse capable of winning it last year.

"For whatever reason, it didn't happen. Whether he was being affected by a virus going around our yard more so than anything else, quite possibly."

None of the veterinary tests revealed a culprit, so the Tizzards are hoping a hobday operation in August to improve the gelding's breathing will translate into the form their star showed in spring of last year.

"We're in no rush to run him, so you'll not see him until the second part of the season. We'll give him every chance to fully recover from whatever it was.

"He'll tell us when he's ready to run, whether that's in the new year or we just give him one run before Cheltenham, we'll see.

"But we're definitely going to keep him for a spring campaign – and we definitely haven't lost faith in him, although it was a head-scratcher. The long break might just be the making of him."

Still top dog at Venn Farm stables is veteran **Native River**, now 11 and winner of the 2018 Gold Cup, third the year before and fourth in 2019 and 2021.

"He loves life. He's in great form and looks magnificent," says Joe. "As he's got older he's become ground dependent;

that's the key to him, simple as that.

"He wants soft ground now – it slows the rest down. On good ground or better he just lacks a gear.

"But there aren't stacks of options for him. There's the Many Clouds Chase in December at Aintree where he's run well for the last two years, there's the Cotswold Chase, and there's the option of going to Ireland for the Savills Chase over Christmas.

"We think he's still capable of winning one of those big races – we just need to get the conditions right for him.

"We had considered running him in a handicap but he'd have to give a lot of weight away all round and we don't want to abuse him. The condition races are often four or five runners, so we think that's the route we'll go down."

And another Gold Cup foray could come into the equation if the going were likely to be very soft or heavy.

'Bigger and stronger'

The Big Breakaway is the third of the Tizzards' golden triumvirate if he progresses the way they hope he will.

After finishing fourth in the Ballymore novice hurdle at the Cheltenham Festival in 2020 expectations were high.

He duly obliged on his chasing debut over an extended three miles at Cheltenham last November, winning impressively by ten lengths, then finished runner-up twice before a third place in the Brown Advisory Chase at the festival, "running a blinder" behind Monkfish.

"People questioned him last year, which I thought was a bit unfair on him. He's six now but he was only five and taking on horses a year older than him.

"He's had a very good summer and looks bigger and stronger than he's ever looked before and I think this year we'll have a lot of fun with him.

"He's rated 146 and only a winner once, so he can run in a graduation race to start with,

JOE TIZZARD
SHERBORNE, DORSET

RECORD AROUND THE COURSES

	Total W-R	Per cent	Non-hcp Hdle	Non-hcp Chase	Hcp Hdle	Hcp Chase	N.H. Flat	£1 level stake
Wincanton	69-499	13.8	14-106	2-16	15-135	34-190	4-52	-76.31
Exeter	55-349	15.8	12-86	16-42	12-88	14-110	1-23	-115.37
Newton Abbot	48-322	14.9	4-60	6-25	18-95	19-131	1-11	-45.52
Chepstow	38-327	11.6	14-86	6-18	2-61	16-129	0-33	-133.54
Fontwell	35-214	16.4	9-45	2-10	6-59	17-80	1-20	-83.13
Taunton	34-256	13.3	7-55	2-9	14-86	9-89	2-17	-40.62
Cheltenham	33-390	8.5	11-80	13-92	0-55	8-142	1-21	-165.97
Newbury	26-215	12.1	3-46	7-28	3-30	12-89	1-22	-87.32
Plumpton	22-146	15.1	7-51	1-6	5-29	9-52	0-8	-58.56
Kempton	18-135	13.3	5-24	6-32	2-24	2-44	3-11	+13.57
Aintree	17-116	14.7	5-27	6-20	0-16	6-51	0-2	+84.82
Ascot	16-131	12.2	5-25	4-27	1-20	5-47	1-12	-24.76
Uttoxeter	15-99	15.2	0-14	3-12	3-22	9-49	0-2	+9.07
Sandown	13-123	10.6	7-23	2-19	1-26	3-55	0-0	-68.46
Haydock	12-65	18.5	0-7	5-17	2-14	5-27	0-0	+1.03
Ffos Las	12-74	16.2	2-15	3-8	3-17	4-25	0-9	+6.23
Ludlow	8-59	13.6	3-10	0-2	2-11	2-30	1-6	-0.99
Huntingdon	6-30	20.0	0-6	1-3	2-7	3-11	0-3	-2.33
Hereford	6-54	11.1	1-9	0-2	1-17	4-22	0-4	-25.75
Warwick	6-89	6.7	2-18	1-10	2-27	1-27	0-7	-42.25
Newcastle	5-11	45.5	2-6	0-0	0-0	3-5	0-0	+29.50
Wetherby	4-24	16.7	1-4	1-7	1-3	1-10	0-0	-0.02
Lingfield	4-31	12.9	0-7	0-0	1-7	3-17	0-0	-17.50
Worcester	4-61	6.6	0-4	0-5	0-18	3-31	1-3	-43.75
Southwell	3-24	12.5	0-6	0-1	2-7	1-9	0-1	-4.00
Stratford	3-55	5.5	1-9	0-4	0-9	2-27	0-6	-29.25
Sedgefield	2-4	50.0	0-1	0-0	0-0	1-2	1-1	+7.91
Carlisle	2-11	18.2	0-1	1-4	0-1	1-5	0-0	-4.50
Market Rasen	2-15	13.3	1-3	0-1	1-5	0-5	0-1	-7.00
Bangor	2-19	10.5	1-4	0-2	0-3	0-6	1-4	-5.09
Towcester	1-6	16.7	1-3	0-0	0-1	0-0	0-2	-4.47
Fakenham	1-8	12.5	0-1	0-1	0-2	1-4	0-0	-4.75
Catterick	0-1	0.0	0-0	0-0	0-1	0-0	0-0	-1.00
Lingfield (AW)	0-1	0.0	0-0	0-0	0-0	0-0	0-1	-1.00
Kelso	0-2	0.0	0-0	0-1	0-1	0-0	0-0	-2.00
Perth	0-2	0.0	0-0	0-1	0-0	0-1	0-0	-2.00
Cartmel	0-2	0.0	0-0	0-0	0-1	0-1	0-0	-2.00
Kempton (AW)	0-2	0.0	0-0	0-0	0-0	0-0	0-2	-2.00
Leicester	0-6	0.0	0-0	0-1	0-1	0-4	0-0	-6.00
Doncaster	0-14	0.0	0-1	0-3	0-3	0-7	0-0	-14.00
Ayr	0-16	0.0	0-0	0-0	0-3	0-12	0-1	-16.00

Top to bottom: The Big Breakaway, Eldorado Allen and Native River

then we'll look at handicaps, whether that's two and a half round Cheltenham or something like the Ladbrokes, it'll be one of them. We think he's got the experience now and will be very competitive off his mark.

"We think we have another Gold Cup contender on our hands but he needs to go and win his handicaps off 146 for that to happen. If he keeps progressing, which I'm sure he will, we'll get him there."

Arkle runner-up **Eldorado Allen** will have the Ryanair Chase at the Cheltenham Festival as his major target and opening his programme will be a tilt at Exeter's Haldon Gold Cup on November 2.

The Grade 2 chase over two miles one and a half furlongs, a race won by chasing greats such as Best Mate, Edredon Bleu, Politologue and the Tizzards' own Cue Card, will begin the process of stepping him up in distance in preparation for two and a half miles at the festival.

"It'll be right up his street," says Joe. "If he won or ran well at Exeter we could look at something like the two- or two-and-a-half-mile handicap at Cheltenham in December, then take it from there."

In the Arkle, Eldorado Allen was no match for Shishkin, and then, when he ran in the Manifesto Novice Chase, it was clearly a race too many.

"When he got to Aintree he'd gone off the boil, as a lot of our horses had," says Joe, "but he's a talented horse. He's rated 151 and I think over a fence he's a little bit better than a handicapper. He's only a win in a good handicap away from taking him into those top races."

Big races on the cards

Fiddlerontheroof will have the Ladbrokes Trophy as his main target in the first half of the season.

"He was so consistent last year. I hope noone questions him because he was second a few times. I think he just came up against some very good horses. He ran extremely well all through the year."

One of his five runner-up berths came in the Brown Advisory Novice Chase at the Cheltenham Festival where he was beaten six and a half lengths by Monkfish with the Tizzards' stablemate The Big Breakaway in third.

"He'll go for the Colin Park Memorial Chase at Carlisle. Two and a half around there will be a lovely starting point, then we'll look for a nice handicap, possibly the Ladbrokes Trophy [3m2f] at the end of November."

That's a race the Tizzards won with Sizing Tennessee in 2018 and Native River in 2016.

"Fiddlerontheroof proved he got three miles last year as we stepped him up in trip and as a second-season chaser off 148, the Ladbrokes would be ideal for him. Although

Fiddlerontheroof (left): set to return at Carlisle before possible crack at the Ladbrokes Trophy

■ Watch out for Tizzard runners at Newcastle. Five winners from 16 runners is a 31% strike-rate and profit stands at £24.50

he's won on heavy, he's pretty versatile groundwise. He's back in training and looks superb. I couldn't be happier with him."

Oscar Elite joined the Tizzards last summer during lockdown and "didn't look much" until bolting up in his first couple of hurdles.

He ended the season by "running an absolute blinder" to be second in the Albert Bartlett at the festival and third in the Sefton novice hurdle at Aintree.

"He's run in three point-to-points, so he jumps well, but it's not set in stone that we go chasing with him; we might start him in something like the West Yorkshire Hurdle at Wetherby.

"What we don't want to do is find out he's a better chaser, so we'll school him over fences and make a plan from there.

"I like him. You can't fault his form and the way he jumps his hurdles I've got no doubt he'll jump fences well. And I think he's better than his rating of 139."

Welsh National aim

Copperhead began last season with a chasing mark of 148 but things didn't happen for him and he ended up having a "dreadful season".

"He was really sick after running in the Ladbrokes Trophy and pulled some muscles behind, but he looks very well again this year," says Joe.

"He was a fantastic horse the season before over fences and I think he could be really competitive in staying handicap chases, something like the Welsh National.

"He's rated 148, so he's no option but to run in races like that. We'd like to find a little race for him first to boost his confidence.

"If we scratch a line through last season, before that he was a progressive young chaser

" He's back in training and I couldn't be happier with him "

Mister Malarky: likely to continue paying his way in decent handicap company

who won the Reynoldstown at Ascot. He jumps well, he stays and he likes a bit of cut in the ground."

Irish point winner **Amarillo Sky** cost £280,000 but hardly looked worth the outlay in the first part of last season, nor was he showing much at home. In the spring, however, he turned the corner, winning nicely at Exeter.

"Then we tried him over the wrong trip at Aintree [2m4f] where he travelled well but didn't see it out," says Joe. "We ran back over two miles at Newton Abbot and he dotted up.

"We might start him in the Welsh Champion Hurdle, which is a limited handicap, and see where we go from there."

Another point winner sourced for the Tizzards by Ross Doyle, their man in Ireland, was **Killer Kane**, this time for £300,000.

He won an Exeter maiden hurdle on his third outing and will go straight into novice chases over two and a half miles this season.

"He's a nice young horse whom we think highly of," says Joe. "He's rated 129, but he's better than that. Hopefully, he can win a couple, then we can look for something bigger after Christmas."

Pose looks sure to strike

Striking A Pose is a British point winner who was "pretty clueless under rules" after arriving at Venn Farm.

"It took him a couple of runs to get the hang of the speed of races under rules. Then he won twice and was going well at Aintree until being brought down four out.

"He's ended up giving himself a nice mark and he could be very competitive."

The optimistically named **JPRone** is a store horse bought privately in Ireland and another sourced by Doyle.

"He's never run but he's a gorgeous-looking animal and we're looking forward to running him. We'll start him off in a bumper and then go novice hurdling. He's ticking all the right boxes."

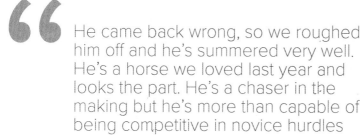

> He came back wrong, so we roughed him off and he's summered very well. He's a horse we loved last year and looks the part. He's a chaser in the making but he's more than capable of being competitive in novice hurdles

Sherborne, who finished second in a bumper last season, has come in from his summer break "looking an absolute picture". He will go novice hurdling and is expected to pay his way.

Autonomous Cloud won his first bumper despite being big and weak and was then "thrown into" a decent Newbury bumper in February but was tailed off.

"He came back wrong, so we roughed him off and he's summered very well. He's a horse we loved last year and looks the part. He's a chaser in the making but he's more than capable of being competitive in novice hurdles."

Patience can begin to pay off

There are big hopes for **Name In Lights**, another store horse bought two years ago in Ireland.

"He finished fourth in a bumper and is the most gorgeous-looking, old-fashioned type of horse. He's big and strong – he's 16-3," enthuses Joe.

"We've been patient with him and I'm sure it'll begin to pay off this season in novice hurdles."

Mister Malarky always wins a nice handicap each season and the owners are keen to run in the Ladbrokes Trophy, so a suitable prep race will be found for him. He was pulled up in last season's Grand National and could head back to Aintree.

But **Elegant Escape** is likely to be the Tizzards' main Grand National horse this season. He won the 2018 Welsh Grand National and was placed twice in the Ladbrokes Trophy and RSA Chase at Cheltenham.

He's been off with a tendon injury for a year but is back in training and being aimed at the 3m2f Becher Chase in December to give him experience over the National fences.

Three dark horses to follow are: **Numbers Man**, on a competitive mark of 104; **War Lord**, "a definite winner" in novice chases; and **Earth Business**.

Interview by Lawrie Kelsey

GALLOP WITH CONFIDENCE

EVAN WILLIAMS

Silver and Secret lead the way for Welsh wizard

Top-level strike: Silver Streak wins the Christmas Hurdle at Kempton for Evan Williams (left)

WINNERS IN LAST FOUR SEASONS 44, 49, 53, 52

IN A two-week spell either side of new year Evan Williams must have felt he'd reached the state of racing nirvana after hitting two of his major targets.

Silver Streak finally earned the first Grade 1 prize he'd been promising to do, the Christmas Hurdle at Kempton on Boxing Day, then Secret Reprieve won a delayed Welsh Grand National at Chepstow a fortnight later, the one race above all others Williams has yearned to win.

He is almost certain to let **Secret Reprieve** have a go at landing successive Welsh National victories, a feat achieved only once since the war when Peter Scudamore steered Bonanza Boy to triumph in 1988 and 1989.

The Martin Pipe-trained gelding carried only 10st 1lb in his first win when he was a seven-year-old, the same weight and age as Secret Reprieve, but a year later he humped 11st 11lb around Chepstow's undulations and 3m6½f.

The comparisons are there, but what weight will Secret Reprieve be allotted and will it deter Williams?

The answer is an emphatic no. "We'll try to get back there for a repeat in the same type of form as last season," he says.

"He handles Chepstow very well, but I don't know where we'll start him. There are plenty of options. He won the Welsh National trial last year in December but whether we'd wait that long to start him, I don't know.

"He can still run in a graduation chase,

which might be an option, but we'd like to start him in October or November and go from there."

And what about the Aintree Grand National, for which he so narrowly missed the cut last year when strongly fancied?

"I wouldn't say that is the ultimate target this year – that'll be further down the line – the aim is the Welsh National. Last year, because we'd had such a good run, I thought we'd roll the dice for Aintree.

"All we'll concentrate on is trying to get to the Welsh National in good form and we'll worry about anything else after that."

Williams' other stable star, **Silver Streak**, will follow the same path he has trodden for the last two seasons – the two-mile Listed hurdle at Kempton in late October, which he's won each time, up to Newcastle for the Fighting Fifth, back to Kempton for the Christmas Hurdle on Boxing Day, and finally the Champion Hurdle at the Cheltenham Festival.

The "lion-hearted" Streak, who looks "grand" after a long summer break, has an ideal attitude, according to his trainer.

"He's always got that grey head down trying his best," he says. "He's been the horse of a lifetime for us."

If truth be told, however, Silver Streak is a step down from the top rung of the hurdling ladder and unlikely to repeat his third in the 2019 Champion Hurdle, especially with a herd of Irish hotpots likely to line up.

"Cheltenham's not his track and the reality is he's not good enough to win a Champion Hurdle and probably not good enough to be placed in it again with the strength of the Irish horses.

"So we'll just worry about the races before Christmas and take it from there," was the candid assessment of the Welsh trainer.

Full of potential

The Welsh National is also a possibility for **No Rematch**, who is in the same William Rucker ownership as Secret Reprieve, although the Welsh National trial is the more

likely target rather than the big race itself.

The seven-year-old won a 2m7½f chase in heavy ground at Chepstow in February, which is his only experience of chasing.

"The concern with him is he's had only one run over fences. He's going to have to get a couple more races under his belt somewhere down the line, so it might be the wrong year for him," says Williams.

"I'm not worried about his experience – he jumps especially well, as you see from his debut there and he handles the track – it's his rating. He can't run in those kinds of races until he's had another two races over fences.

"It would be nearly impossible to get two runs into him before the Welsh National trial in early December, so I'm not going to try. He's a heavy horse and needs winter ground, so that's also against us in the first part of the season."

Star Gate is an Irish point winner who has made the transition to rules racing effortlessly, and looks to be a talented performer with a promising future.

He won two of his three hurdles races, including a Grade 2 in heavy ground at Sandown in December, before finishing second to Bravemansgame at Newbury later that month.

"I'd like to have him ready for when the real winter weather sets in," says Williams. "I don't want to run him before, so we won't rush him. He wants plenty of cut in the ground.

"He's a very good horse on his day. There are plenty of those conditions hurdles that cut up in the height of the winter, so we'll definitely keep that up our sleeves.

"We have to gain experience but we'll keep an open mind with him. We might go over fences, but we don't know what we'll do at this stage.

"He's only a four-year-old but because he was pleasing us last year we did push some high-class races together very quickly. So we've given him a long holiday just to make sure we haven't overdone him as a youngster."

EVAN WILLIAMS
LLANCARFAN, VALE OF GLAMORGAN

RECORD AROUND THE COURSES

	Total W-R	Per cent	Non-hcp Hdle	Non-hcp Chase	Hcp Hdle	Hcp Chase	N.H. Flat	£1 level stake
Ffos Las	91-687	13.2	22-149	3-22	32-236	26-238	8-42	-128.57
Ludlow	68-479	14.2	16-128	5-21	12-110	27-186	8-34	-165.99
Chepstow	52-394	13.2	16-97	1-9	15-125	19-144	1-19	+18.71
Newton Abbot	37-231	16.0	7-47	6-20	13-81	11-78	0-5	-70.64
Taunton	28-235	11.9	3-58	0-2	14-97	10-71	1-7	-56.05
Exeter	25-141	17.7	4-35	5-21	9-41	7-39	0-5	+15.87
Uttoxeter	25-236	10.6	7-57	1-9	7-87	9-73	1-10	-31.18
Sedgefield	22-88	25.0	5-14	1-3	3-26	12-43	1-2	+8.90
Worcester	21-183	11.5	6-51	1-8	8-55	5-67	1-2	-56.65
Stratford	16-147	10.9	4-36	1-6	2-31	9-66	0-8	-66.01
Hereford	16-182	8.8	3-49	4-7	3-61	6-57	0-8	-106.09
Fontwell	15-102	14.7	3-20	1-3	5-39	5-33	1-7	-34.71
Warwick	14-101	13.9	3-25	1-6	5-37	5-24	0-9	-4.92
Haydock	14-125	11.2	1-17	1-7	10-51	2-48	0-2	+18.75
Southwell	12-160	7.5	7-48	0-7	2-61	1-36	2-8	-67.40
Bangor	11-140	7.9	2-40	0-8	3-42	6-40	0-10	-86.13
Wincanton	10-77	13.0	1-19	1-1	3-24	4-27	1-6	-10.76
Cheltenham	10-160	6.2	2-28	2-14	1-58	5-57	0-3	-53.50
Carlisle	9-30	30.0	2-7	2-7	1-5	4-9	0-2	-0.22
Fakenham	9-51	17.6	1-10	4-7	1-13	3-19	0-2	-2.03
Leicester	6-40	15.0	1-12	1-1	1-10	3-17	0-0	-10.67
Huntingdon	6-42	14.3	3-9	0-4	1-12	1-13	1-4	-18.47
Plumpton	6-43	14.0	2-9	0-0	3-20	1-13	0-1	-12.72
Market Rasen	6-74	8.1	1-10	0-4	3-36	2-23	0-1	-38.50
Sandown	6-87	6.9	1-13	1-8	1-32	3-33	0-1	-36.75
Ayr	5-12	41.7	2-2	0-1	1-4	2-5	0-0	+19.96
Catterick	5-21	23.8	1-6	1-4	1-6	1-4	1-1	+4.62
Kempton	5-45	11.1	3-16	0-2	2-10	0-16	0-1	-20.25
Aintree	5-70	7.1	2-13	0-3	1-17	2-31	0-6	-36.50
Perth	4-17	23.5	1-1	1-2	1-3	1-11	0-0	+6.00
Lingfield	4-28	14.3	0-9	0-1	1-8	3-10	0-0	-10.00
Ascot	4-73	5.5	0-12	0-3	1-27	3-28	0-3	-40.00
Newbury	4-80	5.0	2-14	0-2	2-24	0-28	0-12	-42.01
Wetherby	3-19	15.8	1-5	1-5	0-0	1-9	0-0	-4.33
Towcester	3-20	15.0	0-9	0-0	3-8	0-3	0-0	+11.50
Doncaster	3-25	12.0	1-5	0-3	1-5	1-11	0-1	-9.25
Cartmel	3-34	8.8	0-4	0-4	1-13	2-13	0-0	-11.50
Musselburgh	2-3	66.7	0-0	1-1	1-1	0-1	0-0	+3.60
Hexham	1-3	33.3	1-1	0-0	0-1	0-1	0-0	+0.50
Kelso	0-3	0.0	0-2	0-1	0-0	0-0	0-0	-3.00
Lingfield (AW)	0-3	0.0	0-0	0-0	0-0	0-0	0-3	-3.00
Newcastle	0-11	0.0	0-3	0-1	0-3	0-4	0-0	-11.00

Top to bottom: Secret Reprieve, Coole Cody and Star Gate

Options open for Cody

Paddy Power Gold Cup winner **Coole Cody** might go for a repeat in November, but Williams is open to taking the ten-year-old in another direction.

"To win a Paddy Power with an older horse like him is almost job done. If we could get him back to another Paddy Power, that would be fantastic.

"To win those top handicaps is very difficult and to go back and do it again is just as difficult. He has a lower rating over

hurdles, so that might be something we explore, but there are plenty of options throughout the year, so we'll see."

Only The Bold won once and was placed three times in four outings last season.

"He was always in and out last year but when he won his maiden hurdle at Southwell he was quite pleasing."

He looks as though he could be well handicapped on a mark of 126, a point made by his trainer.

"He didn't have a hard time last season and

didn't go winning any penalties, so he could slot into a nice handicap. There are plenty of options for him."

Dans Le Vent had some very progressive form in decent handicaps at the backend of last season and was a shade unlucky not to win at Aintree in April after finishing eighth in the Coral Cup at the Cheltenham Festival.

"He's gone up in the weights and it will be tough for him to reproduce that form over hurdles off his current mark [134], but he has plenty of ability and could come good in one of those meaty handicaps down the line."

Bold Plan is a "funny little horse" but is more than capable of winning on his day, as he has done twice over hurdles and once over fences.

"It's very important he doesn't get to the front too soon in his races," says Williams, who could switch him between handicap hurdles and fences. "He could be up to winning a good pot."

Coconut Splash, who won his maiden hurdle at Wetherby, has yet to break his duck over fences, but he has nevertheless performed with credit, being placed each time in three outings.

"He's a horse we like, although he's probably been badly placed by his trainer, some would say. He got beaten by a couple of very nice horses, but it probably didn't hurt him not to win because he's still a novice for the coming season.

"He probably wants two and a half miles and will stay a good bit further in time. But he struck me as being rather babyish last year and a good summer of grass will have been a big help to him."

'Ability and a good attitude'

Fado Des Brosses won impressively over fences at Hereford in December and Williams thinks the handicapper was "hard enough on him because of that".

"He's a big rangy horse who does want plenty of cut in the ground, but those second-season novice chasers can improve quite a bit with a little time."

Williams thinks highly of him, claiming: "He's definitely a horse with plenty of ability and a good attitude."

Winds Of Fire has finished runner-up four times and won once in his last five starts over hurdles, and ran particularly well in defeat in his last race at Cheltenham.

Although beaten over six lengths into second, he had the rest of the field well strung out and the trainer feels there's much more to come from him.

"He could be one for fences, although he's not bred for chasing. He's a nice horse."

Champagne Rhythm has never raced outside Wales since joining Williams last October, winning once, finishing runner-up three times and third once in six outings at Chepstow and Ffos Las.

He's described by his trainer as "a very tricky customer unsuited to maidens and novices".

"He's got to be delivered literally yards from the post, otherwise he'll get beat," says Williams.

"He's a strong travelling horse and handicaps might suit him better. We'll find a nice handicap hurdle for him before we go chasing."

The four-year-old handicap at Chepstow's first meeting in October is a race which often sees a fancied Williams runner and **State Crown** could fill this year's bill.

"We've had a lot of luck in that handicap and he's a horse I was pretty keen to get a run under his belt before Chepstow.

"So we ran him at Newton Abbot [August 31] and he won. It was a Mickey Mouse race and he ran very fresh, but he's sure to come on for it. He'll be taking on a lot of horses who haven't run and he could just nick it."

Ballinsker is a horse Williams likes, despite a slightly disappointing season.

"Perhaps I'm guilty of liking him too much, but I still have faith in him. He's run some great races in defeat in some good races.

"I hope he can be a chaser because I do like

him and I think he has ability. He deserves a bit of luck down the line."

Deserves Large slice of luck

Esprit Du Large, winner of the Grade 1 Henry VIII Chase at Sandown in 2019, is a "smashing horse on his day" but is another who has been out of luck.

"He just hasn't got his act together as a second-season chaser. He fell in the Arkle last year and fell in good chases at Exeter and Chepstow when holding chances.

"He's definitely one with ability if we can just get his brain and legs working together. We'll start him off over hurdles this season."

Ex-Tom Mullins inmate **Canford Light** came from Ireland this summer in "smashing nick" and looks one to follow closely, as is a "left-field" choice **On The Quiet**, who has strengthened after a long break and could be well handicapped in low-key races.

Finally, make a note of **Golden Whisky**, who was progressive in his last two races, and **Supreme Escape** in staying handicap chases off a featherweight.

Interview by Lawrie Kelsey

In the last five years Williams has sent 13 runners to Ayr and six won. That 46% strike-rate delivered a profit of £21.83

Canford Light (left): intriguing arrival from Ireland

THE
EXPERTS

VIEW FROM IRELAND BRIAN SHEERIN

De Bromhead's wealth of quality for top races

WHO in their wildest dreams could have predicted the dizzying heights Henry de Bromhead would scale last season?

De Bromhead became the first trainer to win the Champion Hurdle, Champion Chase and Gold Cup at the Cheltenham Festival before signing off on his remarkable campaign by sending out Minella Times to land the Aintree Grand National.

Honeysuckle is the undoubted star of De Bromhead's all-conquering stable. Unbeaten in 12 starts under rules, she took her form to a new level by blowing her Champion Hurdle rivals to pieces at Cheltenham and connections have already gone on the record to say they will be resisting the temptation to send the superstar mare over fences this term.

Even in this early stage of the season, it's hard to see Honeysuckle being knocked off her perch and she can be expected to chart a similar path back towards the Champion Hurdle.

Triumph Hurdle winner **Quilixios** could be a nice addition for De Bromhead in this sphere and could step up in trip as the season progresses, while **Aspire Tower** and **Jason The Militant** will also win plenty of races.

Something of an unsung hero of Irish racing, **Put The Kettle On** proved her liking for Cheltenham by backing up her Arkle success with victory in the Champion Chase, and she can be expected to be kept on her travels this season.

De Bromhead crowned a glorious week in the Cotswolds when **Minella Indo** led home

stablemate **A Plus Tard** in the Gold Cup to crown a historic hat-trick in the Festival's Championship races.

It won't surprise many to see Minella Indo and A Plus Tard dominate the ante-post betting for the Gold Cup, while **Envoi Allen**, who underwent surgery for a chipped joint after pulling up at Punchestown, would enter the picture for the race if De Bromhead can rekindle his form.

We may have been denied the match between Shishkin and **Energumene** in the Arkle last term, with the latter ruled out of Cheltenham at the eleventh hour, but that will make the Champion Chase an even greater spectacle.

In blowing away his rivals at the Punchestown festival, Energumene did little to dissuade talk that he was capable of proving himself at Championship level and, along with **Chacun Pour Soi**, he rates as a hugely exciting Champion Chase contender for Willie Mullins this campaign.

Mullins does not appear to have an obvious Champion Hurdle contender at this juncture but that could change if **Ferny Hollow** is kept over hurdles.

Allaho, **Janidil**, **Franco De Port** and **Asterion Forlonge** are just a number of Mullins-trained horses who will come into the Ryanair picture, while **Al Boum Photo** will attempt to emulate Kauto Star by regaining his Gold Cup crown.

There was a time when Ireland struggled for Championship level horses but the quality is spread among a number of stables and Gavin Cromwell's **Flooring Porter** will be bidding to land back-to-back Stayers' Hurdles.

Gordon Elliott may be lacking championship horses but **Abacadabras** remains a top level hurdler, **Sire Du Berlais** will bid to go one better in the Stayers' Hurdle while it will be interesting to see in which direction National Hunt Chase winner **Galvin** goes.

Tiger Roll could yet equal Red Rum's record of three Grand Nationals and remains the star attraction at Cullentra House Stables.

If there is a horse who could surprise a few this season, perhaps the Joseph O'Brien-trained **Fakir D'Oudairies** is the one. He was wildly impressive in winning the Melling Chase and, while he was well held by Clan Des Obeaux in the Punchestown Gold Cup, he is open to plenty of improvement at the age of six and is lightly tried over staying trips.

APPRECIATE IT HEADS CLOSUTTON'S TEAM OF CLASSY NOVICE CHASERS

APPRECIATE IT was described as "Vautour-like" by Mullins after the Supreme Novices' Hurdle and he could have the world at his feet as he embarks over fences.

He went from strength to strength last term, winning three Grade 1s in an unbeaten novice hurdle campaign, and it will be fascinating to see what direction he goes over fences. He is already as short as 7-2 for the Arkle with most firms.

Blue Lord was in the process of running a big race behind Appreciate It before he fell and he should make up into a nice novice chaser.

Ferny Hollow, who beat Appreciate It in the 2019 Champion Bumper, would be a fascinating recruit to fences but the fact his novice hurdles campaign was cut short through injury might tempt Mullins to keep him to the smaller obstacles.

Another former Supreme winner,

Klassical Dream, confirmed himself back on track when producing a silky smooth victory in the Grade 1 Stayers' Hurdle at Punchestown off the back of a 487-day absence but it wouldn't be a surprise to see him come back in trip and be sent over fences this season.

All that talent and we still haven't discussed Grade 1 novice hurdle winners **Gaillard Du Mesnil** and **Galopin Des Champs**, who could also take high rank over fences.

Stattler was sent off 7-2 favourite for the Albert Bartlett and, while he could manage only fourth, he looks likely to make up into a decent staying chaser and may even be a National Hunt Chase horse in the making.

Mullins may have an enviable list of novice chasers but whatever he decides to aim at the Marsh Novices' Chase will need to be pretty special to thwart **Bob Olinger**, who De Bromhead has already confirmed will go chasing this season.

De Bromhead also has the option to send **Ballyadam** chasing this season and he would look tailor made for the Arkle.

Elliott may not have any household names to send over fences this season but that's not to say there aren't many classy prospects. Far from it, in fact.

One gets the impression **Farouk D'Alene** never quite got a clear run at last season despite beating Vanillier in a Grade 2 at Limerick but he remains an exciting staying chaser in the making.

Fury Road didn't quite make up into Grade 1 class as a staying hurdler but might well be up to that grade over fences while fellow Gigginstown-owned **Torygraph** is a relentless galloper.

There won't be many better second-season novices around than **Run Wild Fred**, who finished second in the Irish Grand National last season, while **The Bosses Oscar** could have a big day in him over fences.

Throw **Fakiera** and **Gars De Sceaux** into the mix and Elliott's novice chase hand is much stronger than it first appears.

Cromwell's **Vanillier** has already accounted

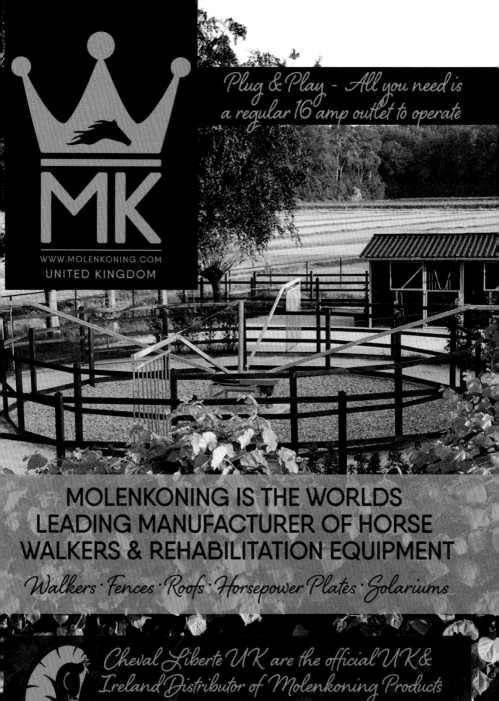

for Stattler, Torygraph and Fakiera in the Albert Bartlett and looks likely to make an even better chaser. **Gabynako** may not have been as good as Vanillier over hurdles but is another classy prospect Cromwell has to look forward to over fences this term.

John McConnell has done well with limited stock in recent seasons but Albert Bartlett third **Streets Of Doyen** could be a dark horse over fences this season, while Ronan McNally has a decision to make on whether his Grade 2 novice hurdle winner **Dreal Deal** stays over the smaller obstacles or tackles fences.

Gentlemansgame may have been a shade disappointing in the spring for Mouse Morris but could easily find the necessary improvement over fences to compete at the highest level.

Jessica Harrington's **Ashdale Bob** is also interesting while there could be a big payday in O'Brien's **Keskonrisk**.

MULLINS MASS OF FIREPOWER IN THE NOVICE HURDLE RANKS

LAST SEASON'S Champion Bumper provided a snapshot of what the future will hold for Mullins with **Sir Gerhard** leading home **Kilcruit** to provide the champion trainer with a one-two. Both are at the top of the ante-post novice hurdle markets for Cheltenham.

Away from the big two, Mullins has serious strength in depth in his novice hurdle brigade, backed up by the fact he won 44 individual bumpers last term.

Along with Sir Gerhard, Cheveley Park Stud sent Mullins **Classic Getaway** and **Grangeclare West** from Elliott's in the spring, with both confirming themselves classy prospects by winning bumpers before being put away for the summer.

Ramillies was highly tried after winning his bumper at Leopardstown and is likely to make up into a better jumper while **Dysart Dynamo** is also hugely exciting.

Dual bumper winner **Dark Raven**,

Thurles scorer **Deploy The Getaway**, Land Rover hero **Adamantly Chosen** and the mares **Brandy Love** and **Ashroe Diamond** are others to note from the Mullins camp.

It tends to be the case that, whatever wins a bumper for De Bromhead is usually blessed with plenty of ability, and this much is certainly true of **Journey With Me**.

An impressive winner between the flags at Ballindenisk, Journey With Me skated home to win the same point-to-point bumper at Gowran Park that De Bromhead has won with Minella Melody and Bob Olinger.

Fellow Robcour-owned **Grand Jury** could make up into a nice staying novice, while **Ballybough Native**, who fetched £195,000 after winning his bumper for Ian McCarthy, looks a nice addition to the stable.

There may be a giant Sir Gerhard-shaped hole in Cullentra House Stables but Elliott still has a huge amount of young talent to look forward to in this sphere.

Classy bumper performers **Chemical Energy** and **Weseekhimhere** have already made successful starts over hurdles but **Hollow Games** is the one who excites in this bracket.

Champion Bumper third **Three Stripe Life**, French recruit **Saint Felicien** and **Party Central** are others to note.

It's not all about the big stables and the Stuart Crawford-trained **O'Toole** could make a splash over hurdles this season while Cromwell's **Letsbeclearaboutit** should also do well over the winter.

Noel Meade's **Harry Alonzo** was no match for Letsbeclearaboutit in a winners' bumper at Fairyhouse but is a nice horse in his own right, while Joseph O'Brien's **Eric Bloodaxe** remains exciting for that he has been clearly difficult to keep right.

If there is a horse who could surprise a few this season, perhaps Arthur Moore's impressive Aintree bumper winner **Me Too Please**, could be the one. She would look an obvious type for the Mares' Novices' Hurdle, a race Peter Fahey's **Gypsy Island** could also be aimed towards.

ANTE-POST ANALYSIS NICK WATTS

Ferny Hollow catches the eye at around 12-1

CHAMPION HURDLE

Honeysuckle heads the market and you wouldn't want to start anywhere else given her unblemished 12-race win record. The only negative is her price which is short enough if you are taking a potshot at the race this far out.

One who could trouble the mare at a bigger price perhaps is **Ferny Hollow**. Plans for him remain unclear, but if staying over hurdles his credentials are potentially strong.

He beat Bob Olinger fair and square on his hurdles debut at Gowran Park before injury intervened (form that now looks very strong) while his Cheltenham bumper defeat of Appreciate It the previous season also looks extraordinarily good.

It's never easy to know how much ability a horse retains after suffering a season-ending injury so early in the campaign, but if Ferny Hollow is the same horse now as he was then, he could make a mockery of his current 12-1 odds and beat them all. Honeysuckle included.

CHAMPION CHASE

I'm not too bothered about this race in betting terms with the awesome **Shishkin** likely to win the race if his second season over fences goes as well as his first did. Nicky Henderson gave a very positive bulletin on him recently and wind surgery might well improve him further.

STAYERS' HURDLE

Klassical Dream looks a strong contender after a breathtaking display upped in trip at Punchestown last April when he hosed up in a three-mile Grade 1 hurdle without coming off the bridle.

It was his first outing for a long time, but you wouldn't have thought so to watch him through the race, as there were never any signs of rust and he simply outclassed his rivals. A first-time hood seemed to make a big difference, and as a three-time Grade 1 winner over two miles, he has speed to go with his now proven stamina. That's a huge asset in staying races, and although he is only 6-1 to win this, such is his ability that price might look big come March.

GOLD CUP

Monkfish headed the market at around 6-1 until he was ruled out for the season through injury. Minella Indo and A Plus Tard are now right up there in the betting, but then you have Al Boum Photo, who surely won't win another Gold Cup, and Envoi Allen who now has questions to answer despite what his committed disciples might tell you.

All of a sudden you are into horses who are 20-1 plus and two of them appeal.

The first is **Chantry House** who was a festival winner last season and who showed his staying potential when following up at Aintree over 3m1f – by quite some margin the longest trip he had tackled under rules.

> He made a great transition to chasing, improving dramatically when upped to extreme trips. This was particularly apparent in the Midlands National in March when lack of experience proved no barrier to success, as he showed tremendous resolution

Although the result of his Aintree win was in doubt until Espoir De Romay departed, Chantry House still looked dangerous and it is never a mean feat to win at two spring festivals – impressive or not.

Quite what route he takes this season is open to conjecture, but races like the Cotswold Chase could well be on his radar pre-festival.

The other interesting one is **Latest Exhibition** at 40-1. He got beaten by Monkfish a couple of times over fences last season, but he was only a neck off him in the 2020 Albert Bartlett, and if connections had rolled the dice and gone for the RSA last season it wouldn't have been surprising had he finally got the better of his old foe – who was lacklustre on the day.

Instead connections went for the Irish National where he ran a cracker to finish fifth under top weight. He will probably be seen in all the big Irish three-mile chases throughout the season and wouldn't need to improve that much to trouble the best in the division. He is solid, consistent and a big price.

GRAND NATIONAL

It took owner JP McManus a long time to win the Grand National. But after doing it in 2010 with Don't Push It, his runners provided him with the first and third places last season courtesy of Minella Times and Any Second Now.

They will undoubtedly be back for more this time, giving him a very strong hand, but to that mix you can also add **Time To Get Up**, who might possibly prove best of the trio in 2022.

The eight-year-old is very light on experience having run only seven times, and that is a concern, but in terms of ability and staying power he is without fault.

Second to Monkfish over hurdles when trained in Ireland, he made a great transition to chasing last season, improving dramatically when upped to extreme trips. This was particularly apparent in the Midlands National in March when lack of experience proved no barrier to success, as he showed tremendous resolution to wrest the prize from Mighty Thunder, who looked the likely victor for much of the home straight.

The value of the form was underlined when Mighty Thunder went on to win the Scottish National on his next start and it is hard to think of a horse better suited to the Aintree challenge than Jonjo O'Neill's charge.

On a mark of 144 – good enough to get in – don't expect to see too much of him in the winter months as it would make sense to try and keep him as close as possible to his current mark. But do have him in the forefront of your mind after the Aintree weights unveiling in February.

Time To Get Up: likely to prove another string to JP McManus's bow come Aintree in April

Annsam can win at a top track

IT IS highly unlikely there's a Cheltenham Gold Cup or Champion Hurdle winner among my ten to follow for the 2021-22 campaign, but a 7-2 winner at Fontwell returns exactly the same amount as a 7-2 scorer at the Festival, so here we go . . .

ANNSAM

On the face of it a 42-length Ludlow beginners' chase destruction of Fidelio Vallis appears to have ruined his handicap mark as the assessor hit him with a 12lb rise.

However, the runner-up is unbeaten in four subsequent starts, and Annsam remains a lightly raced six-year-old open to further improvement. He has the potential to win a valuable 2m4f handicap chase at a Grade 1 track on soft ground with Adam Wedge — who is very important to him — in the plate.

BAVINGTON BOB

Unbeaten in two starts over hurdles since switched to handicaps, and has the potential to develop into a useful staying chaser this term. His tendency to idle in front means that he begins the campaign on a mark of just 113 — only 8lb higher than when he won his first race at Carlisle — and there is plenty more to come as he steps up in trip. His trainer places her horses particularly well, and this six-year-old has stacks of physical scope to progress again after a summer break.

BENEVOLENTDICTATOR

Stamina-packed seven-year-old who remains at the right end of the weights on an official mark of 122. A race such as the Southern National at Fontwell looks a good starting point for this dual winner who could well progress into a Welsh National contender in due course. He's clearly suited by deep mud, and there was plenty of petrol in the tank at the finish of the Sussex National at Plumpton in January when he finished third.

BIG 'N BETTER

Has very few miles on the clock for a nine-year-old, and it's hard to get away from the suspicion he begins the 2021-22 campaign on an extremely favourable chase mark of 107 based on his Fontwell novice handicap chase success in May. The big horse jumped

Benevolentdictator: will be at home given a thorough test of stamina over fences

Cedar Hill (left) has the winning line in sight at his beloved Kelso

beautifully that day, and had all his rivals under maximum pressure five out before breezing 11 lengths clear. That combination of measured fencing and bold front-running should ensure he makes up into a 120-plus performer this season.

BURROWS DIAMOND

Six-year-old mare took time to come to hand last season, but signed off with two impressive wins in handicap hurdles at Newcastle and Sedgefield, and is bred to be much better than her current mark of 117. The manner in which she travelled through both those races was that of a rapid improver well ahead of her rating, and she's likely to take another significant step forward in terms of form when encountering fences this term. A galloping track suits.

CEDAR HILL

Kelso specialist, who simply loves jumping fences around the Borders circuit which favours the nippy type who can lie up close to the pace. The seven-year-old won three times at his beloved venue last season, and was arguably most unfortunate not to have added two more triumphs to his tally there when circumstances merely conspired against him. Obviously he'll find life tougher off a higher mark now, but his strong-travelling style suggests there's more in his locker.

GALLOW FORD

Dual point winner who got off the mark over hurdles when a comfortable Exeter scorer in April. The six-year-old carries the same colours as stable star Minellacelebration, and

it's not difficult envisaging this embryo chaser making rapid progress when switched to fences. He jumps hurdles well and races with lots of enthusiasm. Expect him to win plenty.

SOFT RISK

Put up one of the most impressive performances in a bumper seen all last season when barely coming out of cruise control to slam Fathers Advice by nine lengths at Ayr in May. Having the first race of his life, Soft Risk settled beautifully, travelled strongly throughout, and Brian Hughes barely needed to flex a muscle in the final two furlongs. The five-year-old son of My Risk will go novice hurdling this year – expect to see him at an early Carlisle meeting – and rates a most exciting prospect.

THE RUTLAND REBEL

Dual winner of staying handicaps on the Flat at Wolverhampton last winter, and is currently rated 70 in that sphere. With only four runs over hurdles behind him and a mark of just 80 to exploit, connections should have plenty of fun during the coming months in 3m events at places like Sedgefield, Hexham and Newcastle.

WHOA BLACK BETTY

Really likeable staying hurdler who scored at Musselburgh and Newcastle last season yet is still rated below 100. She's only six, remains lightly raced, and is from the family of Gala's Image, factors which all combine to suggest there are plenty more races to be won with her.

97

Profitable names to note – and when you should pay particularly close attention

IDIOMS are an undoubtedly overused colloquialism in British language. 'Don't beat around the bush', 'a blessing in disguise', 'take off your rose-tinted glasses' are just three examples of an extensive selection of common one-liners that have become stale in the English language. But what do they have to do with horseracing?

It is the last idiom – 'take off your rose-tinted glasses' that relates. You don't need to be overly accustomed to sports betting to realise that punters possess a high level of optimism. Such is the way that wagering works, you need rose-tinted glasses to have the desire to place money on a selection.

Should that selection win – whether the horse won hard-held on the bridle by 20 lengths or by outbobbing a long-time leader on the line – overwhelming joy will exude from the punter and cries of 'brilliant ride!' will be unleashed. The horse's role in the victory was evidently vital, so was the decision to wager, but it's the jockey who gets commended.

But should a selection lose, those rose-tinted glasses are nowhere to be found and it's generally the rider who gets the brunt of it, even if defeat was by no means their fault.

To become a jockey you need extreme talent and horsemanship – not everyone can do it, and those who can are predominantly on a similar level to each other. Given the over-exaggerated importance of pinpointing the best riders and avoiding the worst, those

who put added weight on those in the saddle need to find an edge that will allow them to keep those rose-tinted spectacles firmly on.

An obvious starting point is to find out whether you would make a profit by backing every single mount from one jockey over the course of a season. Looking back to last year, 71 out of 371 jumps riders in Great Britain returned a £1 level-stake profit. However, just 15 of those had a sample size greater than 100 mounts between January and December 2020.

Backing every single ride from one jockey is obviously flawed, as is judging success on profit over a season given bigger-priced winners can quickly swing the total, but Charlie Hammond (+£145.96) and Derek Fox (+£127.25) interestingly sit atop the standings. Tom Scudamore (+£87.22) and Bryony Frost (+£45.99) also feature high on the list.

If strike-rates are your thing, Harry Skelton (22 per cent) is the jockey to follow on last year's evidence. His 37 per cent record on favourites backs up his sublime consistency in the saddle, especially given that he partners more market leaders than most and therefore a fall in probability is assumed.

Nico de Boinville and Harry Cobden, both of whom recorded 21 per cent strike-rates, are the only other jockeys from a similarly large sample size to win on more than one in five of their rides. They also finished first and second for the 2019 season,

so look for continued success with strong backing from leading stables.

Those with a liking for De Boinville should pay attention to when he journeys up to Wetherby (7-15) or Fakenham (14-40). Similarly, Cobden has proved near untouchable at Musselburgh (10-19) and more often than not enjoys success at Wincanton (77-250).

Specifying three of the most renowned and successful jumps jockeys in the weighing room is hardly unveiling gravity-defying logic, so who else may turn a losing bet into a winning one on more than one occasion this upcoming season?

Rachael Blackmore has done more for the sport in regards to diversity over the last few years than anyone could have possibly imagined, inspiring girls and ladies to get into race riding. Charlotte Jones is just one who has excelled in the last two seasons and her sparkling connection with trainer Jimmy Moffatt has to be noted.

Despite gaining a handful of rides for outside yards, Jones has ridden all 33 career winners for Moffatt – 15 of which have come around the idiosyncratic and picturesque Cartmel. With a lack of southern challengers on a course that favours specialists, expect this left-field partnership to rack up further successes at the Cumbria venue.

Another burgeoning relationship is that between Fergal O'Brien, who has recently announced that he is joining forces with

trainer Graeme McPherson, and conditional rider Liam Harrison. The 5lb claimer is sure to see increased opportunities this year behind stable jockey Paddy Brennan and could thrive with a talented group of hurdlers set to make their mark.

Harrison has finished in the first four on 56 per cent (137-246) of his rides under rules and partnered Ask Dillon to win a competitive 3m handicap hurdle at Cheltenham last April. Already sitting on 17 victories this calendar year, he has a big future ahead of him and is situated with the right man in O'Brien.

The clearest way to differentiate jockeys is by becoming accustomed to their riding style. Should they significantly favour one type of riding – David Bass' aggressive front-running riding often sees him plunder staying chases, for example – then following that specific race type can produce long-term gains.

One of the most notable differences between chasing and hurdles strike-rates is provided by Sean Bowen, whose 20 per cent record and +£100.87 to a £1 level-stake difference over fences dwarfs his 15 per cent return (-£211.28) over hurdles.

With most of his rides coming for Peter Bowen, Harry Fry and Caroline Bailey, all of whom have a considerable string of chasers, stick to backing Bowen over fences. With one minute to post and Bowen on your side in a chase, those rose-tinted spectacles can return.

Charlotte Jones (leading) heads to another victory for Jimmy Moffatt at Cartmel

A dozen who can make it to the biggest stages

ALLAHO

Allaho was at the top of my list for last season, although it's fair to say things didn't quite go according to plan as I was hoping to see him excel over 3m. What we still don't know is whether he can be a top-class three-miler, as he wasn't in form when a distant fourth in the Savills, and his close RSA third the previous season doesn't look too shabby now considering runner-up Minella Indo won the Gold Cup. I would expect Willie Mullins to give him another chance at the trip, and I think he'll stay when he's right, but if that doesn't work he's going to be the one to beat in the Ryanair again.

BRAVEMANSGAME

It's possible Paul Nicholls was getting a shade carried away when comparing Bravemansgame with Denman last season, but it's also possible this embryonic chaser wasn't quite the finished article as a novice hurdler. This guy was made for fences, though, and it will be no surprise if he runs up a sequence in all the right races before heading back to the spring festivals with a serious shout of some more Grade 1 glory.

ESPOIR DE ROMAY

Rapidly developed into a high-class novice chaser last season, and was arguably unlucky not to bag a Grade 1 at Aintree on his final start. A new rating of 160 is not going to make things easy, but Espoir De Romay is normally a fine jumper and is fully effective at 2m4f, so don't be surprised if he follows Imperial Aura's 2020 early season route by running in the Colin Parker Memorial at Carlisle followed by the 1965 Chase at Ascot.

FAKIERA

Having finished second three times in a row in his first season over hurdles, Fakiera got off the mark at the first time of asking at Fairyhouse last season and then landed a Grade 3 when stepped up to 2m4f for the first time at Navan in November. Ante-post backers must have been feeling pretty happy when he joined the leaders at the second-last and seemingly going well in the Albert Bartlett at Cheltenham. However, Fakiera emptied pretty quickly after that, with temporary trainer Denise Foster at a loss to explain what happened. Not surprisingly, he hasn't run since, but any horse should be forgiven one flop and, still only six, Fakiera ought to have more in him. And for a horse who plied his trade mostly in Graded company last season, he doesn't look to have a bad handicap mark (144).

GAELIC WARRIOR

This is the first of two complete unknowns for the Willie Mullins stable, each of whom are in the ownership of Susannah Ricci. Gaelic Warrior is the only one with hurdles experience, having run three times at Auteuil in the spring, and improved with every run.

What the form is actually worth remains to be seen, but the French assessor puts him on 139, and it won't be much of a surprise if he continues to improve now he has moved to Mullins from Hector de Lageneste and Guillaume Macaire.

GALVIN

Galvin was always likely to get a trip and so it proved when he took the now 3m6f National Hunt Chase at Cheltenham for Ian Ferguson in March. That had been the plan for him since he finished second to Imperial Aura in the novice handicap chase at the 2020 Cheltenham Festival, and that plan came to fruition following four novice chase successes last summer and autumn. All roads now surely lead to the Grand National at Aintree and, while he will still only be eight then, that can no longer be seen as a disadvantage. While eight-year-olds averaged no more than one win a decade from Red Rum in 1973 to Bindaree in 2002, four of the last six winners have been that age and the other two were just nine. With easier fences and a shorter distance in recent years, it's becoming a young man's game, and Galvin makes plenty of appeal at 33-1 ante-post.

HAPPYGOLUCKY

Having finished a 25-1 fourth in the Martin Pipe Handicap Hurdle in 2020, Happygolucky was sent over fences in October and quickly developed into a useful performer, winning two of his first three starts. Given a break after that, he was sent off an incredibly well backed favourite for the Ultima at Cheltenham, and while he came up one place short when second to race regular Vintage Clouds, he certainly made no mistake when scoring by just under three lengths at Aintree in April. He could head

back to Aintree for the Grand National in the spring, but it wouldn't be a great surprise if he lined up first in the Ladbrokes Trophy at Newbury in November. He has run just five times over fences and just nine times in all, so there could easily be more to come.

HUBRISKO

Another Susannah Ricci project and this one has run just once, in an AQPS race at Le Lion d'Angers in August 2020 for Alain Couetil. However, the style of his success suggests he could prove pretty useful as he powered clear to score by eight lengths in what was unsurprisingly a slowly run race, and he ran pretty straight when clear too. The form has been given some substance as the third has since won twice, including over hurdles at Auteuil, where he and the runner-up pulled 30 lengths clear of 13 others.

LALOR

The oldest and most exposed of the 12 to follow, but interesting all the same as he has moved from Kayley Woollacott to Paul Nicholls. The champion trainer has rekindled many faltering stars from other yards – Tidal Bay being the most obvious – and it wouldn't be a major surprise if he gets a career-best out of the nine-year-old. If he does, he has a horse to go to war with as Lalor is rated just 149. Given how well he goes fresh (he was in the lead four out at Aintree in April) the Paddy Power Gold Cup in November looks the obvious target, and I'll be backing him when the first shows arrive as he'll surely end up favourite if he runs.

LIEUTENANT ROCCO

Well regarded when trained by Colin Tizzard, for whom he won his first two novice hurdles before finding the competition

Lieutenant Rocco: looks well treated on a handicap mark of 147 and can bag a decent prize

too hot behind Monkfish in the 2020 Albert Bartlett, Lieutenant Rocco was then sent to Nick Mitchell, for whom he made steady progress in decent company as a novice chaser with the promise of more to come. He will start this season on a tasty-looking mark of 147, and there's a big prize to be won with him when the ground goes soft.

MY DROGO

Dan Skelton has steadily switched his attention to quality over quantity and My Drogo provided plenty of the former as a novice hurdler last season even if he did sidestep the drubbing the Brits were given at Cheltenham. Having been sent off at 50-1

on his bumper debut at Cheltenham in October, My Drogo switched quickly to hurdles and rattled off a four-timer, starting with a Newbury maiden on good ground in November. Connections chose to swerve Cheltenham in favour of Aintree and were rewarded with another win in the Grade 1 Mersey Novices' Hurdle over 2m4f. There's a healthy argument to say he was actually the best of the British novice hurdlers last season, but his entire career has been about turning him into a top-class chaser, and that's what he will hopefully become over the next few seasons. He certainly has the pedigree, being by Milan out of Nicky Henderson's high-class Grade 2-winning chaser My Petra.

TAMAROC DU MATHAN

Another horse given the kid glove treatment last season was Tamaroc Du Mathan, who ran only four times and was kept away from Cheltenham and Aintree. The Paul Nicholls-trained six-year-old finished his hurdles career for the yard with a rating of just 131, but he made a mockery of that mark on his chase debut in a handicap at Wincanton in November, winning as he liked over that 2m trip. Tamaroc Du Mathan won the Grade 2 Pendil Novices' Chase at Kempton in ready fashion from the useful Ga Law on his first chase effort over further than 2m. He was then sent off at just 13-8 off levels against the high-class Allmankind (11-10) in the Future Champions Novice Chase at Ayr in April,

but was well beaten when unseating two out. That was disappointing for sure, but almost all of Nicholls' runners on Scottish Grand National day ran well below expectations, and it turned out the trainer's horsebox had been held up by two accidents on Friday and what was already a very long trip became an even longer one. He is worth forgiving that effort, and it will be interesting to see what plans Nicholls has for him, although he's likely to be kept away from winter ground.

Tamaroc Du Mathan: best days could be yet to come

BELOW THE RADAR ROBBIE WILDERS

Ten smart performers whose talent might have been underestimated

BEAR GHYLLS

This six-year-old looked destined for the top when landing a bumper by 19 lengths last March and strung together three dominant hurdle victories before losing his unbeaten record in the Ballymore at Cheltenham.

The race was billed as a three-way tussle between Bob Olinger, Gaillard Du Mesnil and Bravemansgame beforehand and Bear Ghylls enhanced his profile by finishing an excellent fourth.

It was his first run on going with 'good' in the description and I suspect he will prefer any ease in the ground. A big season awaits wherever trainer Nicky Martin decides to go.

BENAUD

It is worth noting which high-class horses make the transition from Flat to jumps, and trainer Joseph O'Brien has a potentially exciting recruit to hurdling in Benaud.

The son of Australia finished fourth in the Queen's Vase at Royal Ascot and is rated 102 on the Flat. He is owned by JP McManus and a juvenile hurdling career surely beckons.

He boasts a not-too-dissimilar profile to the ill-fated Sir Erec, who represented the same connections and was classy enough to be sent off a short-priced favourite for the 2019 Triumph Hurdle.

CRACK MOME

Willie Mullins has exercised plenty of patience with the fragile Crack Mome, who has run only twice since he came home 13th in the 2017 Supreme Novices' Hurdle won by Labaik.

He shaped with minor promise on both occasions, particularly when midfield at this year's Punchestown festival in a hot handicap hurdle won by stablemate Koshari following a 731-day absence.

It seems significant top connections are persevering with this low-mileage nine-year-old and granted a clean bill of health he looks well handicapped as he starts the season with a mark of 131.

DEBECE

Tim Vaughan always thought the world of Debece, who claimed third in the 2017 Grade 1 Sefton Novices' Hurdle.

He never scaled those heights again but a first start for Dan Skelton in March prompted a resurgence when he finished second to a subsequent winner.

Debece mostly controlled matters at Sandown, jumping superbly before a mistake at the second-last knocked the wind out of his sails.

The ability remains and he can capture a good staying handicap chase or two this season.

DOLCITA

I rated Dolcita as a Mares' Hurdle dark horse last season but Fergal O'Brien's recent acquisition was a late non-runner.

She shaped well on her sole outing for the stable at Warwick behind impressive winner Molly Ollys Wishes and should be a force in mares' hurdles this term.

The six-year-old was second to Concertista at Cheltenham in 2020 and remains unexposed having run only seven times under rules. There should be more to come.

FASTORSLOW

Fastorslow caught the eye when second to the impressive Lifetime Ambition in the Louis Fitzgerald Hotel Hurdle at this year's Punchestown festival.

Trainer Martin Brassil always targets the meeting with his brightest prospects and this five-year-old could be a Pattern performer.

Running for the first time in 603 days since leaving France, Fastorslow showcased an impressive attitude and had several useful types trailing in his wake.

The smart youngster is open to significant progress, with a record of 1212 in four runs.

LA CAVSA NOSTRA

The Neil Mulholland-trained nine-year-old has not been sighted since he comfortably accounted for Lord Du Mesnil in a novice handicap chase at Sedgefield in 2019.

Factoring in jockey claims he was giving 1lb to the now 153-rated Lord Du Mesnil, who went on to land three consecutive races and eventually run second in the National Hunt Chase.

Despite La Cavsa Nostra's advancing years, he should have more to offer after only three runs in staying handicaps and must be well treated off 128.

MILLINER

I was surprised Milliner remained on the books of the winding-down Gigginstown House Stud operation last season considering his low rating and large absence to overcome.

However, he showed ability in three starts after 762 days off, culminating in a fourth to Mrs Milner in the Pertemps Final at the Cheltenham Festival.

His hurdles mark of 123 looks there for the taking for the all-conquering Henry de Bromhead but Milliner has the scope to make up into a decent chaser this term as well.

O'TOOLE

Splitting Champion Bumper one-two Kilcruit and Sir Gerhard in the Grade 1 Punchestown equivalent was a top-class effort from O'Toole.

Now owned by Simon Munir and Isaac Souede, O'Toole impressed with a 15-length debut success in February and was set a much stiffer task on his next outing but excelled.

His effort was even more meritorious as it was only his second career start and he is a year younger than Kilcruit and Sir Gerhard. It would be a shock were he not among the top novice hurdlers this season.

SAM BROWN

Anthony Honeyball must have been cursing his luck after Sam Brown ran so well behind Imperial Aura in the Colin Parker Memorial Chase at Carlisle last November but failed to make the track again until May.

Good to yielding ground did not suit the heavy-ground lover at Punchestown on that occasion, but his seventh-placed finish behind Brahma Bull was respectable nonetheless.

Sam Brown demonstrated his considerable talent when striking by 15 lengths in a Haydock Grade 2 last January and if this injury-prone nine-year-old gets his conditions and stays healthy, he could make a mockery of his 148 rating.

THIS SEASON'S KEY HORSES

By Dylan Hill

A Plus Tard (Fr)
7 b g Kapgarde - Turboka (Kahyasi)
Henry de Bromhead (Ire)   Cheveley Park Stud

PLACINGS: 12231/2121/3213/212-   RPR **178**c

Starts		1st	2nd	3rd	4th	Win & Pl
16		6	7	3	-	£426,360
	12/20	Leop	3m Gd1 Ch yield			£75,000
	12/19	Leop	2m1f Gd1 Ch soft			£66,441
144	3/19	Chel	2m4f Cls1 Nov List 138-145 Ch Hcap soft			£39,389
	12/18	Naas	2m3f Ch yield..			£7,904
0	4/18	Autl	2m2f List Hdl 4yo Hcap heavy			£39,823
	10/17	Sbri	2m2f Hdl 3yo gd-sft..			£6,974

Brilliant young chaser who took his form to another level when stepped up in trip last season, winning the Savills Chase at Leopardstown on only second run beyond 2m5f and finishing second behind Minella Indo in the Gold Cup; hugely versatile having also proved top class over shorter.

Abacadabras (Fr)
7 b g Davidoff - Cadoubelle Des As (Cadoudal)
Gordon Elliott (Ire)   Gigginstown House Stud

PLACINGS: 104/211212/2152F1-4   RPR **160**+h

Starts		1st	2nd	3rd	4th	Win & Pl
16		6	5	-	2	£347,045
	4/21	Aint	2m4f Cls1 Gd1 Hdl gd-sft			£104,984
	11/20	Punc	2m Gd1 Hdl heavy			£50,000
	12/19	Leop	2m Nov Gd1 Hdl soft			£53,153
	11/19	Navn	2m Nov Gd3 Hdl sft-hvy.................................			£17,275
	10/19	Gowr	2m Mdn Hdl gd-yld.......................................			£7,454
	10/18	Gway	2m¹/₂f NHF 4yo yield......................................			£5,451

Three-time Grade 1 winner, most recently when outclassing a modest field for the grade on first run over 2m4f in the Aintree Hurdle last season; has just come up short in stronger Grade 1 races, not getting close to Honeysuckle in the Irish and Punchestown Champion Hurdles.

Acapella Bourgeois (Fr)
11 ch g Network - Jasmine (Valanjou I)
Willie Mullins (Ire)   Slaneyville Syndicate

PLACINGS: /F2P/013/00261/2510-   RPR **159**+c

Starts		1st	2nd	3rd	4th	Win & Pl
31		9	4	3	2	£201,411
	2/21	Fair	3m1¹/₂f Gd3 Ch sft-hvy			£14,487
	2/20	Fair	3m1f Gd4 Ch heavy			£21,250
	3/19	Clon	2m4f Ch good..			£9,712
	2/17	Navn	3m Nov Gd2 Ch sft-hvy.................................			£21,432
	1/17	Navn	2m4f Ch soft..			£6,833
	3/16	Fair	2m4f Nov Gd2 Hdl yield................................			£19,522
	2/16	Thur	2m4f Nov Gd2 Hdl soft..................................			£19,522
	12/15	Leop	2m4f Mdn Hdl heavy			£6,953
	10/14	Rcpp	1m4f NHF 4-5yo gd-sft			£4,167

Veteran staying chaser who remained as good as ever last season despite advancing years, winning a second successive Bobbyjo Chase at

Fairyhouse; had finished third in the Irish Grand National in 2019 but managed only 13th in the Aintree version last term.

Adagio (Ger)
4 b g Wiener Walzer - Aspidistra (Hernando)
David Pipe   Bryan Drew & Friends / Prof C Tisdall

PLACINGS: 121122-   RPR **146**+h

Starts		1st	2nd	3rd	4th	Win & Pl
6		3	3	-	-	£86,087
	1/21	Chep	2m Cls1 Gd1 Hdl 4yo soft.............................			£28,475
	12/20	Chel	2m1f Cls2 Hdl 3yo soft			£12,512
	11/20	Wwck	2m Cls4 Hdl 3yo good..................................			£3,769

High-class juvenile hurdler last season having been bought out of a French claimer; won a Grade 1 at Chepstow and did best of the British runners in the Triumph Hurdle before filling the same spot at Aintree behind Monmiral (would have been close but for final-flight blunder).

Adrimel (Fr)
6 b/br g Tirwanako - Irise De Gene (Blushing Flame)
Tom Lacey   Lady Bamford & Alice Bamford

PLACINGS: 1/110/111PP-   RPR **143**+h

Starts		1st	2nd	3rd	4th	Win & Pl
8		5	-	-	-	£30,843
	1/21	Wwck	2m5f Cls1 Nov Gd2 Hdl heavy			£12,814
	12/20	Hayd	1m7¹/₂f Cls2 Hdl heavy.................................			£9,583
	11/20	Sand	2m Cls4 Mdn Hdl soft....................................			£3,899
	2/20	Donc	2m¹/₂f Cls5 NHF 4-6yo soft............................			£2,274
	12/19	Uttx	2m Cls5 NHF 4-6yo heavy			£2,274

Has won all five races below the top level, winning three novice hurdles last season to add to two bumper victories, including a Grade 2 at Warwick; pulled up in the Albert Bartlett at Cheltenham as well as at Aintree to take Grade 1 record to 0-3.

Ahoy Senor (Ire)
6 b g Dylan Thomas - Dara Supreme (Darazari)
Lucinda Russell   Mrs C Wymer & PJS Russell

PLACINGS: U/1211-   RPR **153**+h

Starts		1st	2nd	3rd	4th	Win & Pl
3		2	1	-	-	£47,679
	4/21	Aint	3m¹/₂f Cls1 Nov Gd1 Hdl gd-sft......................			£42,328
	3/21	Ayr	2m4¹/₂f Cls4 Mdn Hdl soft..............................			£3,769

Shock 66-1 winner of the Grade 1 Sefton Novices' Hurdle at Aintree last season, proving a strong stayer in beating Bravemansgame by seven lengths; had run just once over hurdles previously, winning a maiden at Ayr; point-to-point winner whose future lies over fences.

Aione (Fr)

8 b g Coastal Path - La Horquela (Acatenango)

Willie Mullins (Ire) | Mrs S Ricci

PLACINGS: 1/12110/ | RPR **143**h

Starts	1st	2nd	3rd	4th	Win & Pl
5	3	1	-	-	£30,107

			Win & Pl
2/20	Naas	2m3f Nov Hdl gd-yld	£10,000
1/20	Gowr	2m4f Mdn Auct Hdl sft-hvy	£10,017
11/19	Punc	2m½f NHF 4-7yo soft	£7,986

Did well to win two novice hurdles two seasons ago given poor hurdling technique and found out when stepped up in trip and class for the Albert Bartlett at Cheltenham, albeit still a reasonable tenth; was already crying out for fences according to his trainer; missed last season through injury.

Ajero (Ire)

6 b g Red Jazz - Eoz (Sadler's Wells)

Kim Bailey | Julie & David R Martin & Dan Hall

PLACINGS: 3/211117- | RPR **142+**h

Starts	1st	2nd	3rd	4th	Win & Pl
7	4	1	1	-	£24,963

				Win & Pl
134	3/21	Hntg	2m Cls3 132-140 Hdl Hcap gd-sft	£6,058
129	2/21	MRas	2m½f Cls3 128-135 Hdl Hcap soft	£8,187
	11/20	Kemp	2m Cls4 Nov Hdl 4-6yo good	£4,419
	10/20	Ludl	2m Cls4 Nov Hdl good	£3,899

Prolific novice hurdler last season, winning four times, albeit kept to lower grades; switched to handicap company for last two wins and scored comfortably at Market Rasen and Huntingdon; distant seventh when stepped up to Grade 1 level at Aintree.

Al Boum Photo (Fr)

9 b g Buck's Boum - Al Gane (Dom Alco)

Willie Mullins (Ire)   Mrs J Donnelly

PLACINGS: 5/1F2F10/11/211/13-2   RPR **175**c

Starts		1st	2nd	3rd	4th	Win & Pl
19		9	3	2	-	£1,006,332
	1/21	Tram	2m5¹/₂f Gd3 Ch soft			£15,804
	3/20	Chel	3m2¹/₂f Cls1 Gd1 Ch gd-sft			£351,688
	1/20	Tram	2m5¹/₂f Gd3 Ch soft			£20,000
	3/19	Chel	3m2¹/₂f Cls1 Gd1 Ch gd-sft			£351,688
	1/19	Tram	2m5¹/₂f List Ch soft			£16,622
	4/18	Fair	2m4f Nov Gd1 Ch sft-hvy			£52,212
	11/17	Navn	2m1f Ch sft-hvy			£8,950
	4/17	Fair	2m4f Nov Gd2 Hdl sft-hvy			£21,432
	1/17	Thur	2m Mdn Hdl 4-5yo yld-sft.....................			£5,256

Dual winner of the Cheltenham Gold Cup, coming out on top in 2019 and 2020 after just a single outing at Tramore both times; followed the same route last season and won again at Tramore before managing only third in the Gold Cup; beaten by Clan Des Obeaux at Punchestown.

Alaphilippe (Ire)

7 b g Morozov - Oscar Bird (Oscar)

Fergal O'Brien   Nic Brereton

PLACINGS: 2F4P1/111215-   RPR **144**+h

Starts		1st	2nd	3rd	4th	Win & Pl
6		4	1	-	-	£26,338
	2/21	Hayd	3m1¹/₂f Cls1 Nov Gd2 Hdl soft.........................			£12,814
	12/20	Sedg	2m4f Cls4 Nov Hdl soft..			£3,769
	11/20	Ayr	2m4¹/₂f Cls4 Mdn Hdl soft...............................			£3,769
	10/20	Ffos	2m Cls5 Mdn NHF 4-6yo heavy.....................			£2,274

Quickly developed into a very useful stayer last season, winning three of first four races over hurdles including a Grade 2 at Haydock by 14 lengths (main rival fell three out); not quite at that level on quicker ground in the Albert Bartlett at Cheltenham but still a creditable fifth.

Al Boum Photo: the dual Gold Cup winner finishes third at Cheltenham last year

RACING POST

Allaho (Fr)

7 b g No Risk At All - Idaho Falls (Turgeon)

Willie Mullins (Ire)   Cheveley Park Stud

PLACINGS: 2/413/2213/6411-2   RPR **178**+c

Starts	1st	2nd	3rd	4th	Win & Pl
13	4	4	2	2	£311,260

3/21	Chel	2m4½f Cls1 Gd1 Ch gd-sft	£150,350
1/21	Thur	2m4f Gd2 Ch sft-hvy	£18,438
1/20	Fair	2m5½f Ch yld-sft	£7,012
2/19	Clon	3m Nov Gd3 Hdl gd-yld	£21,261

Produced a sensational performance when winning last season's Ryanair Chase at Cheltenham by 12 lengths, finally delivering on the biggest stage after two near misses over further; even dropped to 2m at Punchestown but not quite at the same level when second to Chacun Pour Soi.

Allart (Ire)

7 b g Shantou - The Adare Woman (Oscar)

Nicky Henderson   R A Bartlett

PLACINGS: 3/F115/1F-   RPR **155**+c

Starts	1st	2nd	3rd	4th	Win & Pl
7	3	-	1	-	£26,506

12/20	Asct	2m3f Cls1 Nov Gd2 Ch soft	£14,807
2/20	Donc	2m½f Cls4 Nov Hdl soft	£3,769
1/20	Ludl	2m Cls4 Nov Hdl soft	£4,224

Very lightly raced youngster who made a fine winning start over fences last season, beating Fiddlerontheroof in a Grade 2 at Ascot, only to fall next time and miss the rest of the campaign; had finished fifth in the Supreme Novices' Hurdle in 2020.

Allmankind

5 b g Sea The Moon - Wemyss Bay (Sadler's Wells)

Dan Skelton | The Gredley Family

PLACINGS: 1113/311141- | RPR **165**+c

Starts	1st	2nd	3rd	4th	Win & Pl
10	7	-	2	1	£145,138

4/21	Ayr	2m4¹/₂f Cls1 Nov Gd2 Ch good	£14,288
2/21	Wwck	2m Cls1 Nov Gd2 Ch soft	£14,238
12/20	Sand	1m7¹/₂f Cls1 Nov Gd1 Ch soft	£25,929
11/20	Wwck	2m Cls3 Nov Ch good	£7,121
12/19	Chep	2m Cls1 Gd1 Hdl 3yo heavy	£37,018
11/19	Chel	2m¹/₂f Cls1 Gd2 Hdl 3yo soft	£18,224
11/19	Wwck	2m Cls4 Hdl 3yo gd-sft	£4,549

Prolific front-runner who has won Grade 1 novice races over hurdles and fences in the last two seasons; has found things much harder at Cheltenham, with all three defeats under rules coming at that track; won well when stepped up to 2m4f for the first time on final run at Ayr.

Alnadam (Fr)

8 b g Poliglote - Rosadame (Bonbon Rose)

Dan Skelton | Bryan Drew

PLACINGS: 1/81441/21817- | RPR **150**+c

Starts	1st	2nd	3rd	4th	Win & Pl
10	4	1	-	2	£29,693

137	2/21	Sand	2m4f Cls3 123-142 Ch Hcap heavy	£8,317
129	12/20	Sand	2m4f Cls3 Nov 116-135 Ch Hcap soft	£9,747
117	3/20	Hrfd	2m3¹/₂f Cls4 Nov 107-120 Hdl Hcap soft	£3,964
	11/19	Uttx	2m Cls4 Nov Hdl heavy	£3,769

Progressive young chaser who won two 2m4f handicaps at Sandown last season; disappointing favourite at Kempton in between (reportedly unsuited by tight track and quicker ground) and didn't quite stay 3m1f when stepped up in trip for the Ultima at Cheltenham.

Amoola Gold (Ger)

8 b g Mamool - Aughamore Beauty (Dara Monarch)

Dan Skelton | Mr & Mrs Gordon Pink

PLACINGS: /0/25713/3725/11228- | RPR **149**c

Starts	1st	2nd	3rd	4th	Win & Pl
16	3	5	2	-	£43,562

132	10/20	Asct	2m1f Cls1 List 124-150 Ch Hcap soft	£14,238
127	10/20	Weth	1m7f Cls3 125-135 Ch Hcap gd-sft	£7,018
117	11/18	Hrfd	2m Cls3 Nov 116-130 Ch Hcap good	£6,498

Big improver in 2m handicap chases last season, winning at Wetherby and Ascot before also running well off higher marks; neck second to subsequent Grade 1 winner First Flow back at Ascot and also chased home Sky Pirate, though only eighth behind that rival in the Grand Annual.

Andy Dufresne (Ire)

7 b g Doyen - Daytona Lily (Beneficial)

Gordon Elliott (Ire) | John P McManus

PLACINGS: 1/1/1213/113P- | RPR **152**+c

Starts	1st	2nd	3rd	4th	Win & Pl
9	5	1	2	-	£78,853

12/20	Navn	2m1f Nov Gd3 Ch soft	£17,500
10/20	Wxfd	2m Ch soft	£5,500
1/20	Punc	2m¹/₂f Nov Gd2 Hdl soft	£22,250
11/19	Navn	2m4f Mdn Hdl sft-hvy	£7,188
1/19	DRoy	2m NHF 5-7yo yield	£5,550

£330,000 purchase who had a sky-high reputation in younger days but has never quite delivered; won first two starts over fences last season but managed only third behind Monkfish when stepped up in class and was pulled up at Fairyhouse on final run.

Angels Breath (Ire)

7 gr g Shantou - Mystic Masie (Turgeon)

Nicky Henderson | Walters Plant Hire & Ronnie Bartlett

PLACINGS: 1/1273/11/ | RPR **158**c

Starts	1st	2nd	3rd	4th	Win & Pl
6	3	1	1		£65,017

12/19	Asct	2m5f Cls1 Nov Gd2 Ch heavy	£19,933
11/19	Asct	2m3f Cls3 Nov Ch soft	£10,007
12/18	Asct	1m7¹/₂f Cls1 Nov Gd2 Hdl soft	£19,933

Took really well to fences two seasons ago, twice winning easily in small fields at Ascot, but hasn't run since after suffering a tendon injury; fair bit to prove in more competitive races having ultimately disappointed over hurdles after a similarly promising start.

Annie Mc (Ire)

7 b m Mahler - Classic Mari (Classic Cliche)

Jonjo O'Neill | Coral Champions Club

PLACINGS: /2324151/41119/7511- | RPR **153**+c

Starts	1st	2nd	3rd	4th	Win & Pl
15	7	1	1	2	£98,242

2/21	Wwck	2m4f Cls1 List Ch soft	£17,832
12/20	Donc	2m4¹/₂f Cls1 List Ch heavy	£22,667
2/20	Bang	2m4¹/₂f Cls4 Nov Ch soft	£5,718
1/20	Weth	2m3¹/₂f Cls4 Nov Ch soft	£4,606
12/19	Winc	2m3f Cls3 Nov Ch heavy	£9,097
127	3/19	Newb	2m4¹/₂f Cls1 Nov 107-127 Hdl Hcap gd-sft	£24,760
118	1/19	Chep	2m3¹/₂f Cls3 117-129 Hdl Hcap gd-sft	£6,238

Prolific mare who bounced back from a couple of disappointments to win Listed races at Warwick and Doncaster last season; has won all five chases in mares' company yet has finished no better than fifth in three others; missed the Mares' Chase at Cheltenham through injury.

Allmankind: exciting front-runner won four times over fences last season but struggles to find his best form at Cheltenham

RACING POST

Annual Invictus (Ire)

6 b g Mahler - Shantou Rose (Shantou)

Chris Gordon — Thomas Michael Smith

PLACINGS: P/125/21114- **RPR 142h**

Starts	1st	2nd	3rd	4th	Win & Pl
7	3	2	-	1	£23,033

1/21	Plum	2m4¹/₂f Cls3 Nov Hdl 4-7yo soft		£5,913
12/20	Plum	2m Cls4 Nov Hdl soft		£3,769
11/20	Ling	2m Cls4 Nov Hdl heavy		£3,769

Won three novice hurdles last season, most impressively managing to defy a double penalty when stepped up to 2m4f at Plumpton; good fourth on handicap debut in the Betfair Hurdle, rallying strongly to point to return to further.

Any News (Ire)

6 ch g Stowaway - Kisskiss Bang Bang (Zagreb)

Neil Mulholland — Jane Nuala Cartwright

PLACINGS: F/112UP-6 **RPR 144+h**

Starts	1st	2nd	3rd	4th	Win & Pl
6	2	1			£9,254

11/20	Bang	2m¹/₂f Cls4 Mdn Auct Hdl soft		£3,769
10/20	Extr	2m1f Cls5 NHF 4-6yo gd-fm		£2,274

Looked a smart prospect early last season, easily winning a bumper and maiden hurdle before a length second at Cheltenham; lost his way in the spring when pulled up in a Grade 1 at Aintree and fading into sixth in the Swinton at Haydock after travelling well (lost a shoe).

Any Second Now (Ire)

9 b g Oscar - Pretty Neat (Topanoora)

Ted Walsh (Ire) — John P McManus

PLACINGS: /52531F/62U31/99P13- **RPR 163+c**

Starts	1st	2nd	3rd	4th	Win & Pl
25	5	5	5	-	£246,136

143				
3/21	Navn	2m Gd2 Ch heavy		£18,438
2/20	Naas	2m Gd3 Ch heavy		£23,250
3/19	Chel	3m2f Cls2 133-144 Am Ch Hcap gd-sft		£41,510
1/17	Punc	2m Nov Gd2 Hdl soft		£22,440
12/16	Navn	2m Mdn Hdl 4yo yld-sft		£5,426

Has had his last two campaigns geared towards the Grand National and was desperately unlucky when finally getting a chance at Aintree last season, finishing third after being badly hampered; has had limited opportunities in ideal conditions otherwise but has won two 2m Graded chases.

Appreciate It (Ire)

7 b g Jeremy - Sainte Baronne (Saint Des Saints)

Willie Mullins (Ire) — Miss M A Masterson

PLACINGS: 31/3112/1111- **RPR 165+h**

Starts	1st	2nd	3rd	4th	Win & Pl
8	6	1	1		£238,796

3/21	Chel	2m¹/₂f Cls1 Nov Gd1 Hdl soft		£52,799
2/21	Leop	2m Nov Gd1 Hdl sft-hvy		£65,848
12/20	Leop	2m Nov Gd1 Hdl soft		£40,000
11/20	Leop	2m Mdn Hdl heavy		£7,000
2/20	Leop	2m Gd2 NHF 4-7yo yield		£50,000
12/19	Leop	2m4f NHF 4-7yo soft		£6,389

Brilliant winner of last season's Supreme Novices' Hurdle, romping home by 24 lengths to take unbeaten record over hurdles to four and atone for runner-up finish when favourite for the 2020 Champion Bumper; physically imposing type who looks every inch a chaser.

Aramon (Ger)

8 b g Monsun - Aramina (In The Wings)

Willie Mullins (Ire) — Aramon Syndicate

PLACINGS: 12131262/6452/11- **RPR 163h**

Starts	1st	2nd	3rd	4th	Win & Pl
14	5	4	1	1	£296,200

155				
7/20	Gway	2m 131-155 Hdl Hcap yield		£100,000
6/20	Tipp	2m Gd3 Hdl gd-yld		£35,000
12/18	Leop	2m Nov Gd1 Hdl gd-yld		£52,212
11/18	Navn	2m Nov Gd3 Hdl good		£17,688
8/18	Kbgn	2m4f Mdn Hdl good		£6,269

Seemingly much improved when switching to

handicap company in 2020, finishing second in the County Hurdle and winning the Galway Hurdle, but missed the rest of last season through injury; has won just once in eight races at Grade 1 level.

Ashdale Bob (Ire)

6 b g Shantou - Ceol Rua (Bob Back)

Jessica Harrington (Ire)					Diarmuid Horgan
PLACINGS: 435/11F91-2					RPR **147**h

Starts	1st	2nd	3rd	4th	Win & Pl
9	3	1	1	1	£62,161
	4/21	Fair	2m4f Nov Gd2 Hdl yield		£18,438
	12/20	Navn	2m4f Nov Gd2 Hdl sft-hvy		£17,500
	11/20	Navn	2m4f Mdn Hdl soft		£7,500

Developed into a smart novice in second season over hurdles last term; won Grade 2 races at Navan and Fairyhouse before finishing a good second behind Gaillard Du Mesnil in a Grade 1 at Punchestown (raced keenly); likely to go novice chasing and should get 3m.

Ask Me Early: won three times over fences last season and looks open to further improvement

Ask Me Early (Ire)

7 gr g Ask - Cotton Ali (Ala Hounak)

Harry Fry					The Dare Family
PLACINGS: 313/311P1-					RPR **144**+c

Starts	1st	2nd	3rd	4th	Win & Pl
6	3		2	-	£29,218
135	3/21	Uttx	3m Cls2 Nov 119-136 Ch Hcap soft		£14,076
128	1/21	Chep	2m7½f Cls3 Nov 125-144 Ch Hcap soft		£7,018
122	12/20	Chep	2m7½f Cls3 Nov 122-134 Ch Hcap heavy		£7,018

Won three out of four when switched to fences last season, all on soft or heavy ground; diagnosed with a kissing spine after sole disappointment at Sandown and bounced back when winning a good 3m novice handicap chase at Uttoxeter; still very lightly raced.

Aspire Tower (Ire)
5 b g Born To Sea - Red Planet (Pivotal)

Henry de Bromhead (Ire)   Robcour

PLACINGS: 11F2/124-8   RPR **161**h

Starts	1st	2nd	3rd	4th	Win & Pl
8	3	2	-	1	£125,180

10/20	DRoy	2m¹/₂f Gd2 Hdl yld-sft	£30,000
12/19	Leop	2m Gd2 Hdl 3yo soft	£26,577
11/19	Punc	2m¹/₂f Mdn Hdl 3yo soft	£6,922

High-class hurdler who has won all three races over hurdles below Grade 1 but is yet to strike in five attempts at the top level; came closest when second to Sharjah at Leopardstown last season and ran another fine race when fourth in the Champion Hurdle; should stay further.

Asterion Forlonge (Fr)
7 gr g Coastal Path - Belle Du Brizais (Turgeon)

Willie Mullins (Ire)   Mrs J Donnelly

PLACINGS: 1/1114/1FF433-1   RPR **170**+c

Starts	1st	2nd	3rd	4th	Win & Pl
11	5	-	2	2	£168,477

152	4/21	Punc	2m5f Nov 131-152 Ch Hcap yield	£42,143
	11/20	Punc	2m3¹/₂f Ch sft-hvy	£6,250
	2/20	Leop	2m Nov Gd1 Hdl yield	£75,000
	1/20	Naas	2m Mdn Hdl gd-yld	£7,986
	11/19	Thur	2m NHF 5-7yo soft	£5,591

Bounced back in devastating fashion when winning a novice handicap chase at Punchestown by 14 lengths; won a Grade 1 as a novice hurdler but had seemed to lose confidence over fences after a couple of falls; still a work in progress.

Atholl Street (Ire)
6 b g Jeremy - Allthewhile (Old Vic)

Paul Nicholls   Trevor Hemmings

PLACINGS: 6/11P-   RPR **133**+h

Starts	1st	2nd	3rd	4th	Win & Pl
4	2	-	-	-	£7,732

12/20	Tntn	2m¹/₂f Cls4 Nov Hdl gd-sft	£3,769
11/20	Tntn	2m¹/₂f Cls4 Mdn Hdl good	£3,964

Made a big impression in winning novice hurdles at Taunton last season, defying a penalty by 16 lengths in December; sent off 7-4 favourite when stepped up to Grade 2 level at Kempton next time but raced too freely in front and pulled up.

Aye Right (Ire)
8 b g Yeats - Gaybric (Presenting)

Harriet Graham   Geoff & Elspeth Adam

PLACINGS: 612241/12U15/232230-   RPR **160**c

Starts	1st	2nd	3rd	4th	Win & Pl
23	7	8	3	1	£144,543

	1/20	Newc	2m7¹/₂f Cls4 Nov Ch soft	£4,289
136	9/19	Kels	2m5f Cls2 124-136 Hdl Hcap good	£11,696
130	4/19	Ayr	3m¹/₂f Cls3 Nov 111-135 Hdl Hcap good	£10,007
122	1/19	Ayr	2m5¹/₂f Cls3 120-136 Hdl Hcap soft	£9,357
	10/18	Kels	2m5f Cls4 Nov Hdl good	£4,549
	9/18	Kels	2m5f Cls4 Nov Hdl gd-fm	£4,224
	11/17	Carl	2m1f Cls5 NHF 4-6yo soft	£2,274

Beating at the door in top staying handicaps

Bachasson (Fr)
10 gr g Voix Du Nord - Belledonne I (Shafoun)

Willie Mullins (Ire)   Edward O'Connell

PLACINGS: F21/11F/14/361/1111-   RPR **165**+c

Starts	1st	2nd	3rd	4th	Win & Pl
25	15	2	1	1	£195,673

3/21	Gowr	2m4f Gd2 Ch sft-hvy	£18,438
1/21	Naas	1m7¹/₂f Gd3 Hdl heavy	£14,487
12/20	Punc	2m3¹/₂f Hdl heavy	£8,500
11/20	Clon	2m4f Gd2 Ch heavy	£25,000
3/20	Clon	2m4f Ch soft	£9,004
12/18	Punc	2m4f Hdl good	£10,903
1/18	Tram	2m5f List Ch heavy	£16,327
11/17	Thur	2m4f List Ch sft-hvy	£14,981
2/17	Gowr	2m4f Ch heavy	£7,371
10/15	Tipp	2m Nov Gd3 Hdl good	£15,116
9/15	Gway	2m2f Nov Hdl good	£9,093
7/15	Gway	2m Nov Hdl 4yo good	£10,078
7/15	Slig	2m Mdn Hdl 4yo good	£5,616
9/14	Stra	1m4f NHF 3yo v soft	£5,000
7/14	Vitt	1m4f NHF 3yo gd-sft	£4,583

Won all four races last season, mixing hurdles and fences, though has been kept in much calmer waters in recent years after falling in the 2018 Gold Cup (twice long odds-on last term and never bigger than 9-4); best over fences and has won his last six completed chases.

Balko Des Flos (Fr)
10 ch g Balko - Royale Marie (Garde Royale)

Henry de Bromhead (Ire)   Racehorseclub

PLACINGS: 214/43973/44/4764U2-   RPR **160**c

Starts	1st	2nd	3rd	4th	Win & Pl
32	6	4	6	7	£616,860

	3/18	Chel	2m5f Cls1 Gd1 Ch soft	£200,263
146	8/17	Gway	2m6¹/₂f 137-160 Ch Hcap good	£126,068
	1/17	Fair	2m5¹/₂f Ch soft	£5,879
	1/16	Punc	2m4f Mdn Hdl sft-hvy	£6,088
	5/15	Slig	2m2f NHF 4yo yield	£5,349
	1/15	Leop	2m NHF 4yo soft	£4,279

Looked in decline for much of last season but then ran a remarkable race to finish second in the Grand National at Aintree at 100-1, albeit well beaten by Minella Times; had won the Ryanair in his heyday in 2018 but future surely lies in long-distance handicaps now.

Ballyadam (Ire)
6 b g Fame And Glory - Grass Tips (Bob Back)

Henry de Bromhead (Ire)   Cheveley Park Stud

PLACINGS: 131/114224-   RPR **147**h

Starts	1st	2nd	3rd	4th	Win & Pl
8	3	2	1	2	£93,611

11/20	Fair	2m Nov Gd1 Hdl soft	£35,000
10/20	DRoy	2m¹/₂f Mdn Hdl soft	£5,000
3/20	Dpat	2m1¹/₂f NHF 4-7yo yield	£5,000

High-class novice hurdler last term, winning the Royal Bond and punching his weight in Grade 1 company all season; pushed Appreciate It close

www.cavalor.com
Consumer line 7/7
+44 (0)1352 746100

BRONCHIX PULMO

> FOR PULMONARY SUPPORT AND ELASTICITY

Richard Hughes; *"I have used Bronchix Pulmo syrup and Bronchix Pulmo syringes on two individual horses who have unfortunately been categorised as "bleeders". The product is simple and easy to use and we have had great success with it. We now would not do without it."*

at Leopardstown and might have done the same in the Supreme but for a late blunder; well below par over 2m4f at Aintree.

Ballyandy

10 b g Kayf Tara - Megalex (Karinga Bay)

Nigel Twiston-Davies — Options O Syndicate

PLACINGS: P4133/642318/223339-					RPR **158**h
Starts	1st	2nd	3rd	4th	Win & Pl
32	8	6	8	5	£358,397
1/20	Hayd	1m7½f Cls1 Gd2 Hdl heavy			£42,713
142 1/19	Uttx	2m4f Cls2 116-142 Hdl Hcap soft			£9,384
9/17	Prth	2m4f Cls3 Nov Ch heavy			£7,507
135 2/17	Newb	2m½f Cls1 Gd3 126-146 Hdl Hcap soft			£88,273
3/16	Chel	2m½f Cls1 Gd1 NHF 4-6yo good			£39,865
2/16	Newb	2m½f Cls1 List NHF 4-6yo heavy			£11,390
11/15	Chel	2m½f Cls1 List NHF 4-6yo gd-sft			£11,390
10/15	Worc	2m Cls6 NHF 3-5yo gd-sft			£1,560

Standing dish in good 2m hurdles in the last two seasons and earned a deserved win in the 2020 Champion Hurdle Trial at Haydock; ran his best races in handicap company last season, finishing second in the Welsh Champion Hurdle and the Greatwood.

Barbados Buck's (Ire)

6 b g Getaway - Buck's Blue (Epervier Bleu)

Paul Nicholls — The Stewart Family

PLACINGS: 275/21110-					RPR **142+**h
Starts	1st	2nd	3rd	4th	Win & Pl
7	3	1			£14,644
1/21	Kemp	3m½f Cls3 Nov Hdl soft			£5,913
12/20	Sthl	3m½f Cls4 Nov Hdl gd-sft			£3,769
11/20	Sthl	3m½f Cls4 Nov Hdl gd-sft			£3,769

Won three novice hurdles last season, all just beyond 3m, doing well to defy a double penalty at Kempton; shortest-priced British-trained runner for the Albert Bartlett at Cheltenham at 8-1 but failed to land a blow in 11th; likely to go novice chasing.

Bareback Jack (Ire)

5 b g Getaway - Dubh Go Leir (Definite Article)

Donald McCain — T G Leslie

PLACINGS: 1/1114-					RPR **137+**h
Starts	1st	2nd	3rd	4th	Win & Pl
4	3	-	-	1	£22,795
2/21	Muss	1m7½f Cls2 Nov Hdl soft			£12,996
1/21	Catt	1m7½f Cls4 Nov Hdl soft			£3,769
11/20	Muss	1m7½f Cls4 Nov Hdl good			£3,899

Won first three novice hurdles last season, including a competitive Scottish Supreme at Musselburgh (upsides Third Time Lucki at the last when left in charge); disappointed when up in grade behind My Drogo at Kelso; likely to go novice chasing.

Beacon Edge (Ire)

7 b g Doyen - Laurel Gift (Presenting)

Noel Meade (Ire) — Gigginstown House Stud

PLACINGS: 14/3122/113314-F					RPR **162**h
Starts	1st	2nd	3rd	4th	Win & Pl
13	5	2	3	2	£92,866
2/21	Navn	2m5f Gd2 Hdl heavy			£18,438
10/20	Gway	2m4½f Gd3 Hdl soft			£13,750
10/20	Dpat	2m3f Hdl yield			£5,750
10/19	Punc	2m Mdn Hdl yield			£6,922
10/18	Ayr	2m Cls5 NHF 4-6yo good			£2,274

Developed into a very smart stayer last season, with three wins including the Boyne Hurdle at Navan before a fine fourth in the Stayers' Hurdle at Cheltenham; beaten when falling two out at Punchestown on final run; could go novice chasing.

Bear Ghylls (Ire)

6 br g Arcadio - Inch Princess (Oscar)

Nicky Martin   Bradley Partnership

| PLACINGS: 1/1114- | | | | | RPR **150**h |

Starts	1st	2nd	3rd	4th	Win & Pl
5	4	-	-	1	£21,148

130	1/21	Extr	2m2¹/₂f Cls3 113-132 Hdl Hcap soft	£5,913
	11/20	Ffos	2m Cls4 Nov Hdl soft	£3,899
	10/20	Ling	2m3¹/₂f Cls4 Mdn Hdl soft	£3,769
	3/20	Wwck	2m Cls5 NHF 4-6yo soft	£2,599

Smart youngster who won his first four races under rules, culminating in a comfortable win on handicap debut at Exeter last season despite jumping poorly; finished a good fourth in a red-hot Ballymore at Cheltenham, coping well with quicker ground; likely to go novice chasing.

Beauport (Ire)

5 b g Califet - Byerley Beauty (Brian Boru)

Nigel Twiston-Davies   Bryan & Philippa Burrough

| PLACINGS: 43131- | | | | | RPR **135+**h |

Starts	1st	2nd	3rd	4th	Win & Pl
5	2	-	2	1	£33,367

122	3/21	Sand	2m4f Cls1 Nov Gd3 117-132 Hdl 4-7yo Hcap soft	£28,230
	1/21	Font	2m5¹/₂f Cls4 Nov Hdl soft	£3,769

Easy winner of a gruelling EBF Final at Sandown, showing tremendous reserves of stamina in a notably tough test (first three in the market all pulled up); was a 28-1 shot that day after managing only third down in trip at Fontwell; likely to need further.

Belargus (Fr)

6 b g Authorized - Belga Wood (Woodman)

Nick Gifford   John P McManus

| PLACINGS: 561/974437/2F21F1- | | | | | RPR **142+**c |

Starts	1st	2nd	3rd	4th	Win & Pl
15	3	2	1	2	£33,535

130	4/21	Sand	2m4f Cls2 Nov 126-142 Ch Hcap good	£13,008
121	2/21	Sand	1m7¹/₂f Cls3 121-130 Ch Hcap heavy	£7,018
	1/19	Asct	1m7¹/₂f Cls3 Hdl 4yo gd-sft	£6,758

Slow learner over fences but flourished towards the end of second campaign as a novice last season; finally got off the mark by nine lengths at Sandown and put a fall behind him to win there again in a good novice handicap on final day of the season.

Passing the stands at Sandown in the Grade 3 hurdle won in good style by Beauport

Belfast Banter (Ire)

6 b g Jeremy - Sumtin Nice (Simply Great)

Peter Fahey (Ire)   Direct Bloodstock

PLACINGS: 12F54/222531256211-0   RPR **149+h**

Starts		1st	2nd	3rd	4th	Win & Pl
19		4	6	2	1	£119,155
129	4/21	Aint	2m¹/₂f Cls1 Nov Gd1 Hdl gd-sft.....................£42,239
	3/21	Chel	2m1f Cls1 Gd3 129-155 Hdl Hcap gd-sft........£42,203
	10/20	Gway	2m¹/₂f Mdn Auct Hdl soft.................................£10,000
	7/19	NAbb	2m1f Cls5 NHF 4-6yo gd-fm.............................£2,274

One of last season's most remarkable success stories, winning at Cheltenham and Aintree having earlier needed ten attempts to get off the mark over hurdles; won the County Hurdle off bottom weight before stepping up to Grade 1 company successfully at Aintree.

Bennys King (Ire)

10 b g Beneficial - Hellofafaithful (Oscar)

Dan Skelton   Mezzone Family

PLACINGS: 2104/P/11/6152/5123-   RPR **162c**

Starts		1st	2nd	3rd	4th	Win & Pl
19		5	6	1	1	£107,505
147	12/20	Asct	2m3f Cls2 124-150 Ch Hcap heavy...............£15,640
134	11/19	Newb	2m6¹/₂f Cls2 124-145 Ch Hcap gd-sft...........£25,024
126	12/18	MRas	2m5¹/₂f Cls3 Nov 106-126 Ch Hcap soft..........£7,798
120	12/18	Chep	2m3¹/₂f Cls4 97-120 Ch Hcap heavy................£4,938
122	12/16	Uttx	2m4f Cls3 103-129 Hdl Hcap soft...................£9,097

Progressive chaser over the last two seasons and landed one of his biggest wins in a handicap at Ascot last term; matched that level in two subsequent runs, though found a higher mark just beyond him in another handicap and looked short of Grade 1 level when third in the Ascot Chase.

Benson

6 b g Beat Hollow - Karla June (Unfuwain)

Dr Richard Newland   Pump & Plant Services

PLACINGS: 5/814U7/1114-   RPR **140+**h

Starts	1st	2nd	3rd	4th	Win & Pl
10	4	-	-	2	£39,248
127	12/20	Sand	2m Cls1 List 123-147 Hdl Hcap heavy		£22,508
	11/20	Hrfd	2m Cls4 Nov Hdl gd-sft		£3,769
	10/20	Hrfd	2m Cls4 Mdn Hdl gd-fm		£3,769
	11/19	MRas	2m¹/₂f Cls5 NHF 4-6yo soft		£2,274

Prolific as a second-season novice hurdler last season, twice winning at Hereford before a successful handicap debut in a Listed race at Sandown; eyecatching fourth in another big 2m handicap at Ascot on final run having got behind early (sent off favourite).

Billaway (Ire)

9 b g Well Chosen - Taipans Girl (Taipan)

Willie Mullins (Ire)   J Turner

PLACINGS: 12/26312/212/21125-2   RPR **147+**c

Starts	1st	2nd	3rd	4th	Win & Pl
15	4	8	1	-	£55,203
	1/21	Naas	3m1f Hunt Ch heavy		£7,112
	12/20	DRoy	2m5¹/₂f Hunt Ch soft		£4,500
	1/20	Naas	3m Hunt Ch soft		£7,513
	3/19	Dpat	2m7¹/₂f Mdn Hunt Ch gd-yld		£5,550

High-class hunter chaser who has been desperately unlucky not to win at one of the big spring festivals; finished second at Cheltenham last season for the second successive year when beaten a short head by Porlock Bay before missing out by a nose to Bob And Co at Punchestown.

Black Op (Ire)

10 br g Sandmason - Afar Story (Desert Story)

Tom George   R S Brookhouse

PLACINGS: 221/33304/122/4967-F   RPR **157**c

Starts	1st	2nd	3rd	4th	Win & Pl
20	4	4	3	3	£154,228
	10/19	Strf	2m5f Cls4 Ch soft		£5,458
	4/18	Aint	2m4f Cls1 Nov Gd1 Hdl soft		£56,141
	1/18	Donc	2m5f Cls5 Mdn Hdl soft		£3,119
	2/17	Donc	2m1¹/₂f Cls6 NHF 4-6yo good		£1,949

Smart novice chaser two seasons ago, finishing second behind Champ and Slate House in Graded races, but struggled last season; faced some stiff tasks but also disappointed twice in handicaps when ninth in the Ladbrokes Trophy and falling (weakening at the time) at Punchestown.

Bennys King: smart handicap chaser heads to victory at Ascot last December

Black Tears

7 b m Jeremy - Our Girl Salley (Carroll House)

Gordon Elliott (Ire)   Mrs Caren Walsh & John Lightfoot

PLACINGS: 22145/63P23122/3311-   RPR **155+**h

Starts	1st	2nd	3rd	4th	Win & Pl
21	5	8	4	1	£205,043
	3/21	Chel	2m4f Cls1 Gd1 Hdl soft		£50,643
	3/21	Punc	2m4f Gd3 Hdl soft		£14,487
133	2/20	Leop	2m2f 111-140 Hdl Hcap yield		£50,000
	2/19	Fair	2m Mdn Hdl good		£6,382
	3/18	Cork	2m NHF 4-7yo sft-hvy		£5,451

Tough mare whose two best performances have come at the Cheltenham Festival, beating Concertista in last season's Mares' Hurdle to improve on Coral Cup second in 2020; had been 0-10 in Graded/Listed company until winning at 2-5 at Punchestown in early March.

Blue Lord (Fr)

6 b g Blue Bresil - Lorette (Cachet Noir)

Willie Mullins (Ire)   Simon Munir & Isaac Souede

PLACINGS: 123F-3   RPR **155+**h

Starts	1st	2nd	3rd	4th	Win & Pl
5	1	1	2	-	£37,651
	11/20	Punc	2m1¹/₂f Mdn Hdl soft		£6,000

Very highly tried last season, with all four runs in Grade 1 company after a winning Irish debut; finished placed three times and was running even better, albeit held in second, when falling at the last behind Appreciate It in the Supreme; needs to learn to settle.

Bob And Co (Fr)

10 b g Dom Alco - Outre Mer (Sleeping Car)

Paul Nicholls   David Maxwell Racing

PLACINGS: 1565345P3/P11/1U1-12   RPR **155+**c

Starts	1st	2nd	3rd	4th	Win & Pl
32	10	2	4	3	£227,035
	4/21	Punc	3m¹/₂f Hunt Ch yield		£13,170
	4/21	Hexm	3m Cls6 Am Hunt Ch good		£1,797
	2/21	Font	2m6f Cls3 Am Hunt Ch soft		£7,018
	2/20	Font	3m2f Cls6 Am Hunt Ch soft		£1,280
	2/20	Bang	2m4¹/₂f Cls6 Am Hunt Ch soft		£1,419
	5/18	Roya	2m4¹/₂f Hdl heavy		£6,372
	5/18	Pina	2m2¹/₂f Ch gd-sft		£7,221
	9/16	Autl	2m5¹/₂f Ch 5-6yo v soft		£19,412
	10/15	Autl	2m5¹/₂f Ch 4yo soft		£24,186
	6/15	Autl	2m1¹/₂f Ch 4yo v soft		£20,465

Leading hunter chaser who has won five of his last six completed races; unseated rider three out at the Cheltenham Festival (in contention at the time) but bounced back to win at Hexham and followed up in thrilling fashion at Punchestown; disappointing second at Stratford in May.

Bob Olinger (Ire)

6 b g Sholokhov - Zenaide (Zaffaran)

Henry de Bromhead (Ire)   Robcour

PLACINGS: 11/2111-					RPR **163+**h
Starts	1st	2nd	3rd	4th	Win & Pl
5	4	1	-	-	£108,150

3/21	Chel	2m5f Cls1 Nov Gd1 Hdl gd-sft	£52,753
1/21	Naas	2m4f Nov Gd1 Hdl heavy	£42,143
12/20	Navn	2m4f Mdn Hdl sft-hvy	£6,000
3/20	Gowr	2m2f NHF 4-7yo sft-hvy	£5,000

Brilliant novice hurdler last season; stepped up in trip after a creditable second behind Ferny Hollow and won his last three races, including a comprehensive defeat of Grade 1 winners Gaillard Du Mesnil and Bravemansgame in the Ballymore at Cheltenham; goes novice chasing.

Bravemansgame (Fr)

6 b g Brave Mansonnien - Genifique (Nickname)

Paul Nicholls   John Dance & Bryan Drew

PLACINGS: 1/36/211132-					RPR **154+**h
Starts	1st	2nd	3rd	4th	Win & Pl
8	3	2	2	-	£64,407

12/20	Newb	2m4¹/₂f Cls1 Nov Gd1 Hdl soft	£23,848
11/20	Newb	2m4¹/₂f Cls3 Nov Hdl good	£6,498
11/20	Extr	2m1f Cls3 Nov Hdl good	£5,913

Among last season's leading British novice hurdlers, completing a hat-trick when winning the Challow Hurdle by ten lengths; solid third in the Ballymore at Cheltenham but slightly disappointing when second at Aintree (stepped up to 3m); likely to go novice chasing.

Brewin'upastorm (Ire)

8 b g Milan - Daraheen Diamond (Husyan)

Olly Murphy

Mrs Barbara Hester

PLACINGS: /14/14F42/11U/65115-

RPR **158+**h

Starts	1st	2nd	3rd	4th	Win & Pl
15	6	1	-	3	£100,003

	2/21	Font	2m3f Cls1 Gd2 Hdl gd-sft	£28,609
148	1/21	Tntn	2m3f Cls2 122-148 Hdl Hcap soft	£9,495
	11/19	Tntn	2m2f Cls4 Nov Ch good	£6,590
	10/19	Carl	2m Cls3 Ch gd-sft	£7,473
	12/18	Hntg	2m Cls4 Nov Hdl gd-sft	£5,523
	1/18	Hrfd	2m Cls5 Am NHF 4-6yo soft	£2,599

Badly lost his way over fences last season (said to have taken a mental toll on him) but bounced back when reverting to hurdles, winning twice including a Grade 2 at Fontwell over McFabulous; jumped poorly again in the Aintree Hurdle and did remarkably well to run on into fifth.

Bob Olinger: impressive winner of the Ballymore Novices' Hurdle

Brinkley (Fr)

6 gr g Martaline - Royale Majesty (Nikos)

David Pipe — Brocade Racing

PLACINGS: 731/P110- — RPR **149+h**

Starts	1st	2nd	3rd	4th	Win & Pl
7	3	-	1	-	£20,172

140	2/21	Extr	2m7f Cls2 133-146 Hdl Hcap heavy	£9,384
130	1/21	Winc	2m5½f Cls3 115-130 Hdl Hcap heavy	£5,913
	2/20	Newb	2m4½f Cls4 Nov Hdl soft	£3,769

Won handicap hurdles at Wincanton and Exeter last season, most notably a Pertemps qualifier; gained both those wins on heavy ground and seemed unsuited by quicker conditions when well beaten at Cheltenham; likely to go novice chasing.

Bristol De Mai (Fr)

10 gr g Saddler Maker - La Bole Night (April Night)

Nigel Twiston-Davies — Simon Munir & Isaac Souede

PLACINGS: /11632/1F34/229/12P- — RPR **175c**

Starts	1st	2nd	3rd	4th	Win & Pl
36	11	11	5	2	£809,151

	11/20	Hayd	3m1½f Cls1 Gd1 Ch heavy	£90,032
	11/18	Hayd	3m1½f Cls1 Gd1 Ch good	£112,540
	11/17	Hayd	3m1½f Cls1 Gd1 Ch heavy	£113,072
	11/17	Weth	3m Cls1 Gd2 Ch soft	£57,218
154	1/17	Hayd	3m Cls1 Gd2 142-162 Ch Hcap soft	£28,475
	2/16	Sand	2m4f Cls1 Nov Gd1 Ch gd-sft	£25,628
	1/16	Hayd	2m4f Cls1 Nov Gd2 Ch heavy	£18,438
	12/15	Leic	2m4f Cls3 Nov Ch soft	£6,330
	11/15	Wwck	2m Cls3 Nov Ch 4-5yo gd-sft	£9,384
	12/14	Chep	2m Cls1 Gd1 Hdl 3yo heavy	£19,933
	9/14	Autl	2m2f Hdl 3yo v soft	£19,200

Haydock specialist who won the Betfair Chase for a third time last season with an excellent win over Clan Des Obeaux; yet to win a big race elsewhere and form tailed off last season (pulled up in the Grand National after a comprehensive defeat by Native River at Sandown).

Burning Victory (Fr)

5 br m Nathaniel - M'Oubliez Pas (El Corredor)

Willie Mullins (Ire) — Mrs Audrey Turley

PLACINGS: 11/77 — RPR **142h**

Starts	1st	2nd	3rd	4th	Win & Pl
4	2	-	-	-	£89,755

	3/20	Chel	2m1f Cls1 Gd1 Hdl 4yo soft	£73,506
	2/20	Fair	2m Gd3 Hdl 4yo heavy	£16,250

Won the Triumph Hurdle in 2020 on just her second run over hurdles, picking up the pieces after Goshen's dramatic exit; missed nearly all of last season through injury, finishing seventh when finally back at Punchestown, but has since won twice on the Flat in France.

Burrows Saint (Fr)

8 b g Saint Des Saints - La Bombonera (Mansonnien)

Willie Mullins (Ire) — Mrs S Ricci

PLACINGS: /1203/4111/531/2624- — RPR **148c**

Starts	1st	2nd	3rd	4th	Win & Pl
21	5	6	2	3	£424,571

	12/19	Punc	2m3½f Hdl gd-yld	£10,649
144	4/19	Fair	3m5f 135-157 Ch Hcap gd-yld	£243,243
	3/19	Limk	3m½f Nov Gd3 Ch good	£22,590
	3/19	Gowr	2m4f Ch soft	£8,047
	11/17	Punc	2m4f Mdn Hdl 4yo sft-hvy	£7,108

Brilliant winner of the Irish Grand National as a novice in 2019 on just his fourth run over fences; has run in just four chases since when laid out for the last two Grand Nationals, finally getting his chance last season only to not quite see out the trip in fourth.

Buveur D'Air (Fr)

10 b g Crillon - History (Alesso)

Nicky Henderson — John P McManus

PLACINGS: 11/1111/121F2/12/24- — RPR **156+h**

Starts	1st	2nd	3rd	4th	Win & Pl
26	17	5	1	2	£1,230,068

	5/19	Punc	2m Gd1 Hdl gd-yld	£159,459
	2/19	Sand	2m Cls1 List Hdl soft	£17,286
	12/18	Newc	2m Cls1 Gd1 Hdl soft	£62,629
	3/18	Chel	2m½f Cls1 Gd1 Hdl heavy	£266,384
	2/18	Sand	2m Cls1 List Hdl soft	£17,085
	12/17	Kemp	2m Cls1 Gd1 Hdl soft	£68,340
	12/17	Newc	2m Cls1 Gd1 Hdl soft	£61,897
	4/17	Aint	2m4f Cls1 Gd1 Hdl good	£112,260
	3/17	Chel	2m½f Cls1 Gd1 Hdl gd-sft	£227,800
	2/17	Sand	2m Cls1 List Hdl heavy	£14,238
	12/16	Wwck	2m Cls4 Nov Ch soft	£5,198
	12/16	Hayd	1m7½f Cls2 Nov Ch soft	£11,574
	4/16	Aint	2m½f Cls1 Nov Gd1 Hdl soft	£42,203
	1/16	Hntg	2m Cls4 Nov Hdl gd-sft	£3,249
	11/15	Newb	2m½f Cls3 Mdn Hdl soft	£6,498
	10/14	Nant	1m4f NHF 3yo gd-sft	£6,250
	8/14	Sjdm	1m5f NHF 3yo soft	£4,167

Dual Champion Hurdle winner and eight-time Grade I winner, although aura of invincibility had gone even before a serious injury in the Fighting Fifth two seasons ago; well below his best in just two runs last term, but far from disgraced when fourth in the Aintree Hurdle.

Buzz (Fr)

7 gr g Motivator - Tiysha (Araafa)

Nicky Henderson — Thurloe For Royal Marsden Cancer Charity

PLACINGS: 114/31252- — RPR **157h**

Starts	1st	2nd	3rd	4th	Win & Pl
8	3	2	1	1	£89,649

137	11/20	Asct	1m7½f Cls2 112-138 Hdl Hcap soft	£11,261
	2/20	Donc	2m½f Cls4 Nov Hdl good	£3,769
	1/20	Tntn	2m½f Cls4 Mdn Hdl soft	£5,133

Developed into a high-class hurdler last season;

Buzz: smart prospect looks highly likely to enjoy a successful campaign

ran away with a competitive handicap hurdle at Ascot and continued to run well in similar races under big weights; handled step up in trip and grade when second behind Abacadabras in the Aintree Hurdle.

Cadzand (Ire)

6 b g Stowaway - Queens Mark (Roselier)

Dan Skelton   Chelsea Thoroughbreds

PLACINGS: 1/32/21101-   RPR **138+**h

Starts	1st	2nd	3rd	4th	Win & Pl
7	3	2	1	-	£19,536
	3/21	Sthl	2m4¹/₂f Cls4 Nov Hdl gd-sft		£3,769
129	12/20	Kemp	2m Cls3 114-141 Hdl Hcap soft		£9,747
	11/20	Wwck	2m Cls4 Nov Hdl gd-sft		£3,769

Won three times over hurdles last season, most impressively at Kempton on handicap debut; disappointed when favourite to follow up in the Betfair Hurdle but bounced back to win under a double penalty at Southwell; likely to go novice chasing.

Calico (Ger)

5 b g Soldier Hollow - Casanga (Rainbow Quest)

Dan Skelton   John J Reilly

PLACINGS: 1214-   RPR **137**h

Starts	1st	2nd	3rd	4th	Win & Pl
4	2	1	-	1	£14,607
	3/21	Wwck	2m Cls4 Nov Hdl soft		£3,769
	1/21	Ludl	2m Cls4 Nov Hdl heavy		£3,899

Smart German Flat horse who quickly took to hurdles last season, chasing home Cape Gentleman in a Grade 2 at Kempton on just his second run and winning twice on softer ground either side of that; solid fourth in the Scottish Champion Hurdle on handicap debut.

Call Me Lord (Fr)

8 b/br g Slickly - Sosa (Cape Cross)

Nicky Henderson   Simon Munir & Isaac Souede

PLACINGS: 321/73/2120/4274453-   **RPR 155+h**

Starts		1st	2nd	3rd	4th	Win & Pl
22		6	4	4	3	£272,663
	12/19	Chel	2m1f Cls1 Gd2 Hdl soft			£78,778
143	4/18	Sand	2m5¹/₂f Cls1 Gd2 Hdl gd-sft			£31,323
135	1/18	Sand	2m Cls2 117-143 Hdl Hcap heavy			£15,640
	4/17	Sand	2m Cls2 109-135 Hdl 4yo Hcap good			£31,280
	3/17	Comp	2m2f Hdl 4yo heavy			£19,692
	12/16	Cagn	2m¹/₂f Hdl 3yo soft			£11,294

Dual Grade 2 winner who was campaigned mainly at that level last season but couldn't quite match his best form; did better after wind surgery in the spring, finishing fifth in a 3m Grade 1 at Aintree (didn't quite stay) and an unlucky third at Sandown (every chance when mistake last).

Calva D'Auge (Fr)

6 b g Air Chief Marshal - Hill Ou Elle (Tiger Hill)

Paul Nicholls   Owners Group

PLACINGS: 026P22/124115/6111-   **RPR 144+h**

Starts		1st	2nd	3rd	4th	Win & Pl
16		6	4	-	1	£62,033
140	4/21	Tntn	3m Cls3 114-140 Hdl Hcap gd-fm			£4,956
136	12/20	Newb	2m4¹/₂f Cls2 128-136 Hdl Hcap soft			£9,471
132	11/20	Tntn	2m3f Cls3 115-132 Hdl Hcap good			£6,173
	2/20	Plum	2m Cls4 Nov Hdl heavy			£4,094
	1/20	Winc	1m7¹/₂f Cls3 Nov Hdl soft			£7,798
	11/19	Plum	2m Cls4 Mdn Hdl heavy			£4,094

Progressive in handicap hurdles last season, winning three times, including when stepped up to 3m for the first time on final run at Taunton; benefited from having sights lowered since novice days when well beaten on both runs at Graded level.

Canelo (Ire)

8 ch g Mahler - Nobody's Darling (Supreme Leader)

Alan King   John P McManus

PLACINGS: 225141/3601/012143F-   **RPR 152c**

Starts		1st	2nd	3rd	4th	Win & Pl
17		5	3	2	2	£69,637
142	12/20	Weth	3m Cls1 Gd3 135-148 Ch Hcap soft			£17,085
130	11/20	Aint	2m4f Cls3 Nov 122-136 Ch Hcap gd-sft			£7,018
125	3/20	Hntg	2m4f Cls3 115-131 Ch Hcap heavy			£16,245
	4/18	Font	2m5¹/₂f Cls4 Nov Hdl good			£4,094
	2/18	Donc	2m3¹/₂f Cls4 Nov Hdl 4-7yo gd-sft			£4,094

Progressive for much of the last two seasons and was winning for the third time in five races when

landing the Rowland Meyrick at Wetherby last Christmas; just found out by higher mark when third and fourth in other handicaps before falling in the Grand National.

Cape Gentleman (Ire)

5 ch g Champs Elysees - Hawaiian Heat (Galileo)

Emmet Mullins (Ire)   Mrs Margaret O'Rourke

PLACINGS: 1P1-93   **RPR 144h**

Starts		1st	2nd	3rd	4th	Win & Pl
5		2	-	1	-	£38,903
	2/21	Kemp	2m Cls1 Nov Gd2 Hdl good			£12,814
	12/20	Punc	2m4f Mdn Hdl 4yo heavy			£6,000

Very useful dual-purpose performer who won twice when sent hurdling last season, most notably in a Grade 2 novice at Kempton; slightly disappointing on handicap debut at Punchestown but did much better when third in the Galway Hurdle (sent off favourite).

Capodanno (Fr)

5 ch g Manduro - Day Gets Up (Muhtathir)

Willie Mullins (Ire)   John P McManus

PLACINGS: 2/3134-1   **RPR 153+h**

Starts		1st	2nd	3rd	4th	Win & Pl
6		2	1	2	1	£45,819
132	4/21	Punc	3m 125-140 Hdl Hcap yield			£26,339
	1/21	Clon	2m Mdn Hdl heavy			£5,268

Stunning 12-length winner of a 25-runner handicap hurdle over 3m at Punchestown in April, showing massive improvement on yielding ground after running on heavy in novice races for much of the winter; likely to go novice chasing.

Captain Guinness (Ire)

6 b g Arakan - Presenting D'Azy (Presenting)

Henry de Bromhead (Ire)   Declan Landy

PLACINGS: 12B/P12F3-U   **RPR 157+c**

Starts		1st	2nd	3rd	4th	Win & Pl
9		2	2	1	-	£38,635
	12/20	Punc	2m Ch heavy			£6,250
	12/19	Navn	2m Mdn Hdl soft			£7,986

Unlucky to repeatedly bump into brilliant pair Energumene and Shishkin, facing one of those rivals in last four runs but producing some good accounts, including when third (best of those ridden prominently) in the Arkle; had also fallen when running well in the Irish Arkle.

Carefully Selected (Ire)

9 b g Well Chosen - Knockamullen Girl (Alderbrook)

Willie Mullins (Ire)　　　　　　　　Miss M A Masterson

PLACINGS: 21/1123/1/3111U/　　　　　　　RPR **154**c

Starts	1st	2nd	3rd	4th	Win & Pl
10	6	1	2	-	£104,189

1/20	Naas	3m Nov Gd3 Ch soft	£22,500
1/20	Punc	2m4f Nov Gd3 Ch soft	£21,250
11/19	Fair	2m5f Ch soft	£7,720
3/19	Limk	2m6f Mdn Hdl heavy	£7,214
2/18	Naas	2m NHF 4-7yo soft	£7,087
12/17	Leop	2m4f NHF 4-7yo soft	£6,318

Top-class bumper performer who showed his big engine over fences two seasons ago; won first three chases but couldn't get away with continued jumping errors when odds-on for the National Hunt Chase (held in third when unseated at the last); missed last season through injury.

Caribean Boy (right): heading to victory in the Berkshire Novices' Chase at Newbury last season

Caribean Boy (Fr)

7 gr g Myboycharlie - Caribena (Linamix)

Nicky Henderson　　　　　　Simon Munir & Isaac Souede

PLACINGS: F7515692/31/1347P-　　　　　RPR **156**c

Starts	1st	2nd	3rd	4th	Win & Pl
15	3	1	2	1	£74,608

	11/20	Newb	2m4f Cls1 Nov Gd2 Ch good	£17,085
138	2/20	Hayd	2m4f Cls3 Nov 127-138 Ch Hcap heavy	£9,747
	10/17	Autl	2m1½f Hdl 3yo v soft	£19,692

Couldn't build on impressive reappearance win at Newbury last season but shaped with enough promise in first two handicaps, notably when a staying-on seventh in the Plate at Cheltenham, to go off favourite for the Topham (pulled up); could do better at 3m.

Cash Back (Fr)

9 b g Linda's Lad - Holding (Useful)

Willie Mullins (Ire)　　　　　　　　Watch This Space Syndicate

PLACINGS: 2677/22/12/5112F/FF-　　　　　　RPR **148**c

Starts	1st	2nd	3rd	4th	Win & Pl
16	3	5	-	-	£81,965

1/20	Naas	2m Nov Ch yield	£11,162
11/19	Navn	2m1f Ch soft	£9,051
3/19	Thur	2m Mdn Hdl gd-yld	£6,105

Talented chaser but has fallen three times in a row after crashing out of both races last season; had won twice as a novice in 2019-20 and pushed Notebook in a Grade 1 before falling in the Arkle; running well behind Chacun Pour Soi when falling at the last on latest run.

Castlebawn West (Ire)

8 b g Westerner - Cooksgrove Lady (Anshan)

Willie Mullins (Ire)　Mrs R Boyd, Mrs M J Armstrong & Exors Of Late J B

PLACINGS: 41/21P4/6514U/31-　　　　　　RPR **166**c

Starts	1st	2nd	3rd	4th	Win & Pl
13	4	1	1	3	£106,242

148	12/20	Leop	3m 136-148 Ch Hcap yield	£69,915
1/20	Fair	2m5f Ch yield	£7,012
12/18	Leop	2m4f Mdn Hdl gd-yld	£8,177
3/18	Clon	2m NHF 5-7yo heavy	£5,451

Lightly raced chaser who put up a superb front-running performance to win last season's Paddy

RACING POST

Power Chase at Leopardstown, building on a promising third on his handicap debut first time out; has great scope according to his trainer and could be a Grand National type.

Castlegrace Paddy (Ire)

10 b g Flemensfirth - Thunder Road (Mtoto)
Pat Fahy (Ire) — Clipper Logistics Group

PLACINGS: 5/14F5/3451/145222-5 — RPR **159**c

Starts	1st	2nd	3rd	4th	Win & Pl
23	6	4	1	5	£188,707
	11/20	Navn	2m Gd2 Ch sft-hvy	£17,500
	3/20	Navn	2m Gd2 Ch heavy	£21,250
	12/18	Cork	2m¹/₂f Gd2 Ch soft	£31,327
	3/18	Thur	2m2f Nov List Ch soft	£16,327
	12/17	Fair	2m Ch heavy	£7,897
	3/17	Gowr	2m Mdn Hdl sft-hvy	£6,844

Hugely consistent chaser who has finished first or second in his last five races below Grade 1 level, claiming the notable scalp of A Plus Tard in last season's Fortria Chase at Navan; no better than third in eight runs in Grade 1 races.

Cepage (Fr)

9 b g Saddler Maker - Sience Fiction (Dom Alco)
Venetia Williams — The Bellamy Partnership

PLACINGS: /23414/2/24617/P144- — RPR **161**+c

Starts	1st	2nd	3rd	4th	Win & Pl
27	6	4	4	8	£191,509
154	1/21	Chep	2m3¹/₂f Cls2 128-154 Ch Hcap heavy	£12,996
154	1/20	Chel	2m4¹/₂f Cls1 Gd3 128-154 Ch Hcap soft	£39,423
136	3/18	Kemp	2m4¹/₂f Cls2 127-139 Ch Hcap soft	£25,024
119	12/16	Newb	2m¹/₂f Cls4 99-119 Ch Hcap gd-sft	£4,549
	5/16	Lign	2m5¹/₂f Ch 4yo v soft	£4,588
	4/16	Pari	2m3f Hdl 4yo v soft	£7,412

Cheltenham specialist who has run well in many big handicap chases at the track, although only win last season came in calmer waters at Chepstow; proved stamina for 3m with two more good efforts subsequently, including a solid fourth in the Ultima back at Cheltenham.

Chacun Pour Soi: star 2m chaser who ended last season on a high with victory at the Punchestown festival

132

Chacun Pour Soi (Fr)

9 b g Policy Maker - Kruscyna (Ultimately Lucky)

Willie Mullins (Ire)   Mrs S Ricci

PLACINGS: 1253/1/121/1113-1   RPR **179**c

Starts	1st	2nd	3rd	4th	Win & Pl
13	8	2	2	-	£505,504

4/21	Punc	2m Gd1 Ch yield	£131,696
2/21	Leop	2m1¹/₂f Gd1 Ch soft	£65,848
12/20	Leop	2m1f Gd1 Ch yield	£50,000
12/20	Cork	2m¹/₂f Gd2 Ch sft-hvy	£35,000
2/20	Leop	2m1f Gd1 Ch yield	£75,000
5/19	Punc	2m Nov Gd1 Ch yield	£61,126
3/19	Naas	2m Ch yld-sft	£8,047
8/15	Diep	2m1f Hdl 3yo v soft	£8,558

Very fragile since joining Willie Mullins but finally withstood a busy campaign last season and proved himself the leading 2m chaser despite an odds-on defeat in the Champion Chase; faded up the hill in third that day but bounced back with a thrilling defeat of Allaho at Punchestown.

Champ (Ire)

9 b g King's Theatre - China Sky (Definite Article)

Nicky Henderson   John P McManus

PLACINGS: 12/2/111121/11F1/2P-   RPR **170+**c

Starts	1st	2nd	3rd	4th	Win & Pl
15	9	4	-	-	£286,108

	3/20	Chel	3m¹/₂f Cls1 Nov Gd1 Ch soft	£98,764
	11/19	Newb	2m4f Cls1 Nov Gd2 Ch gd-sft	£22,887
	11/19	Newb	2m6¹/₂f Cls3 Ch gd-sft	£7,018
	4/19	Aint	3m¹/₂f Cls1 Nov Gd1 Hdl soft	£56,130
	12/18	Newb	2m4¹/₂f Cls1 Nov Gd1 Hdl gd-sft	£25,628
139	12/18	Newb	2m4¹/₂f Cls2 120-145 Hdl Hcap soft	£25,992
	5/18	Wwck	2m5f Cls4 Nov Hdl gd-sft	£4,549
	5/18	Prth	2m4f Cls4 Mdn Hdl good	£4,224
	1/17	Sthl	1m7¹/₂f Cls6 Mdn NHF 4-6yo soft	£2,053

Ran just twice during a frustrating campaign last season, finishing a fine second in his Gold Cup prep run over an inadequate trip only for his jumping to fall apart when pulled up at Cheltenham (has since had back surgery); had beaten Minella Indo and Allaho when winning at the festival 12 months earlier.

Champ Kiely (Ire)

5 b g Ocovango - Cregg So (Moscow Society)

Willie Mullins (Ire)   Miss M A Masterson

PLACINGS: U-1					RPR **121+**b
Starts	1st	2nd	3rd	4th	Win & Pl
1	1	-	-	-	£5,267
	5/21	Limk	2m NHF yld-sft		.....£5,268

Made a winning bumper debut at Limerick in May, knuckling down well to score by half a length having raced keenly; big horse who looks a likely improver in good staying novice hurdles.

Champagne Gold (Ire)

6 b g Presenting - Kon Tiky (Perrault)

Henry de Bromhead (Ire)   Barry Maloney

PLACINGS: P/42/21320-0					RPR **144**h
Starts	1st	2nd	3rd	4th	Win & Pl
6	1	2	1	-	£29,912
	10/20	Wxfd	2m¹/₂f Mdn Hdl sft-hvy		.....£5,000

Useful novice hurdler last season and produced best run when worn down close home in a valuable contest at Leopardstown on handicap debut; disappointed in similar contests at Cheltenham and Punchestown (had been just 6-1 for the County Hurdle).

Chantry House (Ire)

7 br g Yeats - The Last Bank (Phardante)

Nicky Henderson   John P McManus

PLACINGS: U11/113/13111-					RPR **167+**c
Starts	1st	2nd	3rd	4th	Win & Pl
9	7	-	2	-	£167,518
	4/21	Aint	3m1f Cls1 Nov Gd1 Ch gd-sft		.....£44,690
	3/21	Chel	2m4f Cls1 Nov Gd1 Ch gd-sft		.....£73,918
	2/21	Weth	2m5¹/₂f Cls4 Nov Ch soft		.....£4,289
	11/20	Asct	2m3f Cls3 Nov Ch soft		.....£10,463
	2/20	Newb	2m¹/₂f Cls3 Nov Hdl good		.....£6,758
	12/19	Chel	2m1f Cls3 Nov Hdl 4-6yo gd-sft		.....£9,384
	3/19	Wwck	2m Cls5 NHF 4-6yo soft		.....£2,599

High-class novice chaser last season who landed a Grade 1 double at Cheltenham and Aintree; benefited from high-profile falls both times, though, with red-hot favourite Envoi Allen falling early in the Marsh and Espoir De Romay falling in front two out when stepped up to 3m1f at Aintree.

Chantry House: won four out of five last season, including a big-race double at Cheltenham and Aintree

Chatham Street Lad (Ire)

9 br g Beneficial - Hearts Delight (Broken Hearted)

Michael Winters (Ire) Vivian Healy

PLACINGS: 69U471123/5/1511341- RPR **163**+c

Starts	1st	2nd	3rd	4th	Win & Pl
23	7	2	2	3	£149,649

	3/21	Limk	3m¹/₂f Nov Gd3 Ch heavy.............................£14,487
141	12/20	Chel	2m4¹/₂f Cls1 Gd3 138-157 Ch Hcap soft £59,798
128	11/20	Cork	2m¹/₂f 117-138 Ch Hcap heavy £10,500
118	10/20	Baln	2m1f 90-118 Ch Hcap soft................................£5,500
127	1/19	Cork	2m4f 112-140 Hdl Hcap soft...........................£13,851
117	12/18	Cork	2m 95-123 Hdl Hcap sft-hvy £8,722
	1/18	Cork	2m Nov Hdl heavy..£9,267

Failed when first sent chasing in 2018 but came on in leaps and bounds last season, winning four races including the Caspian Caviar Gold Cup at Cheltenham by 15 lengths; only fourth in Grade 1 novice company in the Marsh but did better when stepped up to 3m to win at Limerick.

Cheddleton

6 br g Shirocco - Over Sixty (Overbury)

Jennie Candlish P & Mrs G A Clarke

PLACINGS: 1/2113/4113- RPR **152**+c

Starts	1st	2nd	3rd	4th	Win & Pl
9	5	1	2	1	£36,468

	12/20	Hayd	2m¹/₂f Cls3 Nov Ch heavy £6,882
	11/20	Carl	2m Cls3 Ch soft..£7,018
	1/20	Kels	2m Cls4 Nov Ch heavy £4,224
	12/19	Bang	2m Cls4 Nov Hdl heavy....................................£4,094
	3/19	Hayd	1m7¹/₂f Cls4 NHF 4-6yo soft £3,899

Looked potentially smart in comfortably winning novice chases at Carlisle and Haydock last season but tailed off behind Allmankind at Warwick when stepped up in class; had also come up short at Grade 2 level as a novice hurdler after winning two softer races.

Chris's Dream (Ire)

9 b g Mahler - Janebailey (Silver Patriarch)

Henry de Bromhead (Ire) Robcour

PLACINGS: 2119/1215/P110/25PU- RPR **163**+c

Starts	1st	2nd	3rd	4th	Win & Pl
19	6	3	-	-	£175,562

	2/20	Gowr	2m4f Gd2 Ch heavy £30,000
146	11/19	Navn	3m 121-149 Ch Hcap soft £53,153
	2/19	Navn	3m Nov Gd2 Ch yield.....................................£23,919
	12/18	Navn	2m4f Ch yield..£7,904
	2/18	Clon	3m Nov Gd3 Hdl heavy £20,409
	12/17	Limk	2m3f Mdn Hdl soft...£5,791

Big improver two seasons ago and ran well in the Gold Cup until looking a non-stayer; proved himself at 3m when a neck second in Down Royal's Champion Chase behind The Storyteller last season but disappointed subsequently, including when pulled up in the Ryanair.

Cilaos Emery (Fr)

9 b g Califet - Queissa (Saint Preuil)

Willie Mullins (Ire) Luke McMahon

PLACINGS: 51/42/1/11F14/218-42 RPR **167**+c

Starts	1st	2nd	3rd	4th	Win & Pl
18	8	4	-	3	£253,046

	2/21	Naas	2m Gd3 Ch soft..£14,487
	2/20	Gowr	2m Gd3 Hdl heavy...£30,000
	12/19	Cork	2m Gd3 Ch soft..£45,180
	11/19	Naas	2m Gd3 Ch sft-hvy £17,275
	1/19	Gowr	2m Ch soft..£8,047
	4/17	Punc	2m¹/₂f Nov Gd1 Hdl gd-yld............................£50,427
	12/16	Navn	2m Mdn Hdl sft-hvy £6,331
	4/16	Punc	2m NHF 4yo gd-yld...£5,426

Talented two-miler who has won five of his last seven races below Grade 1 level, most impressively when an easy winner of a Grade 3 chase at Naas last season; failed to build on that subsequently and has done better over hurdles at the top level.

Clan Des Obeaux (Fr)

9 b g Kapgarde - Nausicaa Des Obeaux (April Night)

Paul Nicholls Mr & Mrs P K Barber, G Mason & Sir A Ferguson

PLACINGS: 123/41152/218/2321-1 RPR **178**+c

Starts	1st	2nd	3rd	4th	Win & Pl
27	10	8	2	3	£830,835

	4/21	Punc	3m¹/₂f Gd1 Ch yield.......................................£131,696
	4/21	Aint	3m1f Cls1 Gd1 Ch gd-sft................................£84,963
	12/19	Kemp	3m Cls1 Gd1 Ch soft....................................£144,050
	2/19	Asct	3m Cls1 Gd2 Ch gd-sft...................................£28,475
	12/18	Kemp	3m Cls1 Gd1 Ch gd-sft.................................£142,375
	11/17	Hayd	2m5¹/₂f Cls2 Ch heavy £32,490
	3/17	Extr	2m3f Cls3 Nov Ch gd-sft..................................£7,148
	11/16	Newb	2m4f Cls1 Nov Gd2 Ch gd-sft.........................£19,933
	12/15	Newb	2m¹/₂f Cls4 Hdl 3yo soft £3,249
	4/15	Lrsy	1m4f NHF 3yo gd-sft...£3,876

Four-time Grade 1 winner comprising two King Georges and a brilliant spring double last season; had been only third chasing a King George hat-trick but benefited from missing Cheltenham (0-6 at that track and no better than fifth in two Gold Cups) to win at Aintree and Punchestown.

Classic Getaway (Ire)

5 br g Getaway - Classic Magic (Classic Cliche)

Willie Mullins (Ire) Cheveley Park Stud

PLACINGS: 1-1 RPR **125**+b

Starts	1st	2nd	3rd	4th	Win & Pl
1	1	-	-	-	£5,267

	5/21	Tipp	2m4f NHF 4-7yo heavy....................................£5,268

Bought for £570,000 after winning sole point-to-point last season and made an impressive winning start in May, landing a Tipperary bumper by 15 lengths; big jumping type likely to be sent over hurdles sooner rather than later.

Clondaw Castle (Ire)

9 b g Oscar - Lohort Castle (Presenting)

Tom George   J French, D McDermott, S Nelson & T Syder

PLACINGS: 7/521144/291/213212-   RPR **167**+c

Starts	1st	2nd	3rd	4th	Win & Pl
21	8	5	2	2	£211,404

154	2/21	Kemp	3m Cls1 Gd3 132-158 Ch Hcap good................£42,713
151	11/20	Newb	2m4f Cls2 129-151 Ch Hcap good.................£18,768
143	2/20	Wwck	2m4f Cls2 130-148 Ch Hcap gd-sft...............£31,280
134	2/19	Hntg	2m¹/₂f Cls3 Nov 119-134 Ch Hcap good.............£9,653
	1/19	Leic	2m Cls3 Nov Ch gd-fm...............................£8,058
	1/18	Kels	2m Cls4 Nov Hdl soft...............................£4,159
	11/17	Hntg	2m Cls4 Mdn Hdl gd-sft.............................£3,249
	3/17	Strf	2m¹/₂f Cls4 Mdn NHF 4-6yo soft.....................£3,249

Produced a big career-best when stepped up to 3m for the first time to win a valuable handicap chase at Kempton in February; couldn't quite build on that when a distant second behind Clan Des Obeaux in the Bowl at Aintree, taking record at Grade 1 and Grade 2 level to 0-7.

Cloth Cap (Ire)

9 b g Beneficial - Cloth Fair (Old Vic)

Jonjo O'Neill   Trevor Hemmings

PLACINGS: 716F/3113/4328/311P-   RPR **165**+c

Starts	1st	2nd	3rd	4th	Win & Pl
20	5	4	4	3	£198,098

	3/21	Kels	2m7¹/₂f Cls1 List Ch gd-sft.......................£25,628
136	11/20	Newb	3m2f Cls1 Gd3 136-162 Ch Hcap good........£113,900
125	11/18	Catt	3m1f Cls3 122-135 Ch Hcap good.................£10,007
118	11/18	Strf	2m6¹/₂f Cls4 104-122 Ch Hcap good...............£5,588
111	12/17	Hntg	2m4¹/₂f Cls4 86-112 Hdl Hcap gd-sft..............£5,198

Massive improver last term, relishing quicker ground having struggled on soft the previous season; easily won the Ladbrokes Trophy and a Listed chase at Kelso; 9lb well in and favourite for the Grand National but pulled up after weakening quickly (made a respiratory noise).

Coeur Sublime (Ire)

6 b g Elusive Pimpernel - Love Knot (Lomitas)

Gearoid O'Loughlin (Ire)   C Jones

PLACINGS: 12F423/130/47-   RPR **152**h

Starts	1st	2nd	3rd	4th	Win & Pl
11	2	2	2	2	£86,459

11/19	DRoy	2m¹/₂f Gd2 Hdl yld-sft..............................£26,577
11/18	DRoy	2m¹/₂f Hdl 3yo gd-yld..............................£8,177

Looked a seriously promising youngster when sent off just 12-1 for the Champion Hurdle in 2020 but has beaten just three rivals in three races since then; at least shaped encouragingly when fourth of five in last season's Morgiana Hurdle, travelling well before blowing up.

Coko Beach (Fr)

6 gr g Cokoriko - Solana Beach (Take Risks)

Gordon Elliott (Ire)   Gigginstown House Stud

PLACINGS: 1932/512F09/2423117-   RPR **153**c

Starts	1st	2nd	3rd	4th	Win & Pl
17	4	2	1	1	£127,069

	2/21	Navn	3m Nov Gd2 Ch heavy...............................£18,438
138	1/21	Gowr	3m1f 135-156 Ch Hcap heavy.....................£52,679
	10/19	Punc	2m2¹/₂f Hdl gd-yld................................£10,649
	10/18	Nant	2m1¹/₂f Hdl 3yo v soft.............................£6,796

Excellent winner of last season's Thyestes Chase, taking a big step forward on handicap chase debut when stepped up to 3m for the first time over fences; backed that up with a fine Grade 2 win at Navan and ran well for a long way when seventh in the Irish Grand National.

Commander Of Fleet (Ire)

7 b g Fame And Glory - Coonagh Cross (Saddlers' Hall)

Gordon Elliott (Ire)   Gigginstown House Stud

PLACINGS: 11/1412/P/001-   RPR **143**h

Starts	1st	2nd	3rd	4th	Win & Pl
9	4	1	-	1	£162,950

	3/21	Thur	3m Hdl yield.......................................£6,058
	2/19	Leop	2m6f Nov Gd1 Hdl gd-yld..........................£66,441
	11/18	Punc	2m4¹/₂f Mdn Hdl 4yo good............................£7,359
	4/18	Punc	2m¹/₂f NHF 4-5yo yld-sft.........................£52,212

Top-class novice hurdler three seasons ago, winning a Grade 1 at Leopardstown and beating all bar Minella Indo in the Albert Bartlett; struggled on first two runs after long layoff last season, including on chase debut, but got back to winning ways over hurdles at Thurles.

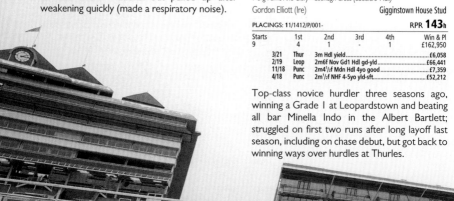

Concertista (Fr)

7 ch m Nathaniel - Zagzig (Selkirk)

Willie Mullins (Ire)   Simon Munir & Isaac Souede

PLACINGS: 2/4331/112-3				RPR **156+**h
Starts	1st	2nd	3rd	4th
9	3	2	3	1
				Win & Pl
				£165,209
12/20	Leop	2m4f Gd3 Hdl soft		£17,500
11/20	Fair	2m3¹/₂f Gd2 Hdl soft		£40,000
3/20	Chel	2m1f Cls1 Nov Gd2 Hdl soft		£50,643

Beaten a head at 10-11 in last season's Mares' Hurdle at Cheltenham, suffering a second narrow festival defeat to go with a runaway win in 2020; had looked last season's top mare with two good wins before that but yet to land a Grade 1 after another odds-on defeat at Punchestown.

Conflated (Ire)

7 b g Yeats - Saucy Present (Presenting)

Gordon Elliott (Ire)   Gigginstown House Stud

PLACINGS: /U241/F31344/321314-				RPR **152+**c
Starts	1st	2nd	3rd	4th
17	4	2	4	4
				Win & Pl
				£60,534
3/21	Naas	2m4¹/₂f Nov Gd3 Ch sft-hvy		£14,487
12/20	Navn	2m4f Ch soft		£6,250
11/19	Fair	2m Mdn Hdl soft		£6,922
3/19	Clon	2m NHF 5-7yo good		£5,550

Useful novice chaser last season, winning twice including a soft Grade 3 at Naas (sent off just 4-9 to beat three rivals); no better than third in five runs at a higher level; should stay 3m, though beaten a long way on only run over that trip last season.

Coole Cody (Ire)

10 b g Dubai Destination - Run For Cover (Lafontaine I)

Evan Williams   Wayne Clifford

PLACINGS: P6200/834P/12216344-				RPR **148**c
Starts	1st	2nd	3rd	4th
28	6	6	2	4
				Win & Pl
				£148,407
137	11/20	Chel	2m4f Cls1 Gd3 134-158 Ch Hcap soft	£74,035
	8/20	NAbb	2m5f Cls3 Nov Ch good	£6,303
136	11/17	Chel	2m5f Cls3 111-137 Hdl Hcap soft	£12,512
	9/17	NAbb	2m5¹/₂f Cls4 Nov Hdl gd-sft	£3,899
	9/17	NAbb	2m2¹/₂f Cls4 Nov Hdl gd-sft	£6,498
	3/17	Winc	2m4f Cls5 Mdn Hdl heavy	£2,599

Had run over fences just twice prior to last season but made rapid progress in that sphere and won the Paddy Power Gold Cup at Cheltenham; mixed form subsequently but finished a good fourth back over course and distance in the Plate; has also run well over 3m and beyond.

Copperhead

7 ch g Sulamani - How's Business (Josr Algarhoud)

Colin Tizzard   Mrs G C Pritchard

PLACINGS: 79/03811/5111F/PP50-				RPR **137**h
Starts	1st	2nd	3rd	4th
17	5	-	1	-
				Win & Pl
				£61,947
	2/20	Asct	3m Cls1 Nov Gd2 Ch soft	£24,027
134	12/19	Newb	3m2f Cls3 118-135 Ch Hcap soft	£11,631
125	12/19	Winc	3m1f Cls3 101-127 Ch Hcap good	£16,245
116	2/19	Sand	2m4f Cls4 Nov 107-116 Hdl Hcap soft	£4,549
104	1/19	Extr	2m2¹/₂f Cls4 100-119 Hdl Hcap gd-sft	£4,094

Desperately out of sorts last season but had developed into a very useful staying chaser before that, completing a hat-trick in the Reynoldstown

Cloth Cap: created a fine impression when landing last season's Ladbrokes Trophy

at Ascot in 2020; pulled up in the Ladbrokes Trophy on only run over fences last term and no better than fifth (of six) in three runs over hurdles.

Copperless

6 b g Kayf Tara - Presenting Copper (Presenting)

Olly Murphy   Aiden Murphy & Alan Peterson

PLACINGS: 211F-1   RPR **139+**h

Starts	1st	2nd	3rd	4th	Win & Pl
5	1				£65,594

126	5/21	Hayd	1m7¹/₂f Cls1 Gd3 122-144 Hdl Hcap soft	£56,950
117	3/21	Tntn	2m¹/₂f Cls4 104-117 Hdl Hcap good	£3,769
	10/20	MRas	2m¹/₂f Cls4 Mdn Hdl good	£3,769

Lightly raced hurdler who flourished in the spring having been quickly switched to handicaps; ran away with the Swinton at Haydock in May having fallen two out when going well in a similar race at Aintree; raised 14lb but could have more to offer in top handicaps.

Craigneiche (Ire)

7 br g Flemensfirth - Itsalark (Definite Article)

Nicky Henderson   Robert Kirkland

PLACINGS: 131/12-   RPR **143+**h

Starts	1st	2nd	3rd	4th	Win & Pl
5	3	1	1	-	£41,559

127	1/21	Asct	2m3¹/₂f Cls1 Gd3 127-147 Hdl Hcap soft	£19,933
	1/20	Donc	2m5f Cls5 Mdn Hdl soft	£2,794
	6/19	MRas	2m¹/₂f Cls5 NHF 4-6yo good	£2,274

Did brilliantly for one so inexperienced in top handicaps last season, winning first time out at Ascot and finishing second in the Coral Cup at Cheltenham; had missed more than a year after getting off the mark over hurdles in January 2020 and has still run just four times over hurdles.

Cyrname (Fr)

9 b g Nickname - Narquille (Passing Sale)

Paul Nicholls   Mrs Johnny De La Hey

PLACINGS: 121214/3711/12F/1PP-   RPR **173+**c

Starts	1st	2nd	3rd	4th	Win & Pl
22	8	4	2	1	£360,603

	10/20	Weth	3m Cls1 Gd2 Ch soft	£39,865
	11/19	Asct	2m5f Cls1 Gd2 Ch soft	£39,865
	2/19	Asct	2m5f Cls1 Gd1 Ch gd-sft	£85,425
150	1/19	Asct	2m5f Cls2 135-152 Ch Hcap gd-sft	£46,920
	2/18	Kemp	2m4¹/₂f Cls1 Nov Gd2 Ch good	£18,224
	12/17	Kemp	2m Cls1 Nov Gd2 Ch soft	£23,491
130	11/17	Hntg	2m¹/₂f Cls3 Nov 123-131 Ch Hcap good	£7,798
	1/16	Pau	2m1¹/₂f Cls1 4yo v soft	£11,294

Highest-rated chaser in Britain and Ireland for two of the last three seasons on Racing Post Ratings after three terrific wins over 2m5f at Ascot; inconsistent subsequently, proving

himself going left-handed and over 3m when winning last season's Charlie Hall Chase only to flop twice more.

Daly Tiger (Fr)

8 b g Tiger Groom - Reine Tresor (Saint Cyrien)

Noel Meade (Ire)   Gigginstown House Stud

PLACINGS: 123/15/1P3539/19125-   RPR **161+**c

Starts	1st	2nd	3rd	4th	Win & Pl
16	5	2	3		£111,451

147	1/21	Fair	2m1f 134-156 Ch Hcap heavy	£39,509
137	11/20	Punc	2m3¹/₂f 126-150 Ch Hcap sft-hvy	£37,500
	10/19	Tipp	2m1f Ch yield	£6,389
	11/18	Punc	2m Mdn Hdl good	£7,087
	11/17	Thur	2m NHF 4yo yield	£5,265

Big improver last season, winning valuable handicaps at Punchestown and Fairyhouse; raised a total of 20lb for those two victories and struggled when forced into Graded races, finishing a distant second behind Cilaos Emery at Naas and last of five at Navan.

Dame De Compagnie (Fr)

8 b m Lucarno - Programmee (Kahyasi)

Nicky Henderson   John P McManus

PLACINGS: 1/322/1521/511/1U9-7   RPR **147+**c

Starts	1st	2nd	3rd	4th	Win & Pl
15	6	3	1	-	£123,036

	1/21	Ayr	2m¹/₂f Cls4 Nov Ch heavy	£4,289
140	3/20	Chel	2m5f Cls1 Gd3 138-154 Hdl Hcap soft	£56,270
132	12/19	Chel	2m4¹/₂f Cls2 111-137 Hdl Hcap soft	£18,768
	4/18	Chel	2m4¹/₂f Cls1 Nov List Hdl good	£14,238
	11/17	Uttx	2m Cls4 Mdn Hdl good	£3,249
	4/16	Lrsy	1m4f NHF 3yo	£3,676

Won the Coral Cup at Cheltenham in 2020, capping an impressive comeback season after a long layoff; won on chase debut last season but unseated rider in the Scilly Isles (nudged along at the time but still in touch) and disappointed back over hurdles at Cheltenham.

Dark Raven (Ire)

4 br g Malinas - Mary Wilkie (Oscar)

Willie Mullins (Ire)   Simon Munir & Isaac Souede

PLACINGS: 11-   RPR **133+**b

Starts	1st	2nd	3rd	4th	Win & Pl
2	2	-	-	-	£57,946

	4/21	Fair	2m NHF 4-5yo yield	£52,679
	3/21	Leop	2m NHF 4yo yield	£5,268

Won both bumpers at Leopardstown and Fairyhouse by wide margins last season, hacking up by 11 lengths at the big Easter festival in a valuable sales race; looks to be a smart novice hurdler in the making.

RoR
Retraining of Racehorses

Racing to a new career at ror.org.uk

Source a Horse

ourceahorse.ror.org.uk

A new website for selling or loaning a horse directly out of a trainer's yard and for all former racehorses.

Owner/Trainer Helpline

A dedicated helpline to assist in the placement of horses coming out of training.

Rehoming Direct

RoR has compiled a checklist to safeguard your horse's future when moved directly into the sport horse market.

Retrainers

RoR has a list of retrainers recommended by rainers who can start he retraining process nd assess each horse.

Visit
ror.org.uk
for rehoming options and advice

Equine Charities

Retrain former racehorses for a donation, as well as care for vulnerable horses with the help of RoR funding.

oR is British horseracing's official charity or the welfare of horses retired from racing.

T: 01488 648998

Darver Star (Ire)

9 b g Kalanisi - Maggies Oscar (Oscar)

Gavin Cromwell (Ire)   SSP Number Twentytwo Syndicate

PLACINGS: 316/1111323/13277-66					RPR **155**c
Starts	1st	2nd	3rd	4th	Win & Pl
21	6	2	4	1	£192,473
	10/20	Punc	2m1f Ch yield...		£6,250
	10/19	Limk	2m5f Nov List Hdl heavy.......................................		£18,072
	9/19	List	2m4f Nov Hdl yield..		£11,959
133	8/19	Klny	2m1f 109-137 Hdl Hcap yld-sft..........................		£26,577
	8/19	Dpat	2m3f Hdl gd-yld...		£10,649
106	4/19	Wxfd	2m4f 105-123 Hdl Hcap yield..............................		£9,157

Finished third in the 2020 Champion Hurdle but couldn't live up to expectations over fences last season; finished second behind Franco De Port in a Grade 1 over Christmas but was well beaten the next twice and did little better when reverting to hurdles at Punchestown.

Dashel Drasher

8 b g Passing Glance - So Long (Nomadic Way)

Jeremy Scott   Mrs B Tully & R Lock

PLACINGS: 06/3341111/2U1/3111-					RPR **171**+c
Starts	1st	2nd	3rd	4th	Win & Pl
17	9	1	3	1	£172,977
152	2/21	Asct	2m5f Cls1 Gd1 Ch soft..		£59,620
	1/21	Asct	2m5f Cls2 132-154 Ch Hcap soft........................		£32,844
	12/20	Asct	2m5f Cls2 Ch heavy...		£18,768
	12/19	Hayd	2m5¹/₂f Cls2 Nov Ch soft.....................................		£12,996
	4/19	Chel	2m4¹/₂f Cls2 Nov Hdl good..................................		£12,380
	3/19	Newb	2m4¹/₂f Cls3 Nov Hdl gd-sft................................		£6,238
	2/19	Asct	2m3¹/₂f Cls3 Nov Hdl gd-sft................................		£15,857
	1/19	Chep	2m3¹/₂f Cls4 Nov Hdl gd-sft................................		£4,094
	2/18	Winc	1m7¹/₂f Cls5 NHF 4-6yo heavy.............................		£2,274

Developed into a high-class chaser last season, winning his last three races including the Grade 1 Ascot Chase (weak race for the grade with favourite Cyrname disappointing); missed

Cheltenham owing to quick ground, though had been prolific on good/good to soft over hurdles.

De Rasher Counter

9 b g Yeats - Dedrunknmunky (Rashar)

Emma Lavelle   Makin' Bacon Partnership

PLACINGS: 21F72/3P7121/614P/2-					RPR **143**h
Starts	1st	2nd	3rd	4th	Win & Pl
19	5	4	2	1	£203,662
149	11/19	Newb	3m2f Cls1 Gd3 135-160 Ch Hcap gd-sft........		£142,375
140	3/19	Uttx	3m Cls2 Nov 118-140 Ch Hcap heavy..............		£25,024
133	12/18	Newb	2m6¹/₂f Cls3 Nov 129-148 Ch Hcap gd-sft........		£7,343
124	1/18	Font	2m3f Cls3 105-127 Ch Hcap heavy..................		£6,238
	3/17	Clon	2m NHF 5-7yo sft-hvy.......................................		£5,265

Won what looked a really strong Ladbrokes Trophy two seasons ago, capping a hugely progressive 12 months; missed most of last season through injury having disappointed in two subsequent runs (fourth in the Cotswold Chase and pulled up in a gruelling Midlands National).

Decimation (Ire)

6 b g Milan - Babies Present (Presenting)

Henry de Bromhead (Ire)   Gigginstown House Stud

PLACINGS: 22212-3					RPR **142**h
Starts	1st	2nd	3rd	4th	Win & Pl
6	1	4	1	-	£17,897
	2/21	DRoy	2m¹/₂f Mdn Hdl heavy..		£5,268

Unlucky not to win more than once in novice hurdles last season, finishing second four times in addition to a ten-length victory at Down Royal; produced best run when beaten a neck by Ashdale Bob in a Grade 2 at Fairyhouse but disappointed when favourite next time at Punchestown.

Defi Bleu (Fr)

8 b g Saddler Maker - Glycine Bleue (Le Nain Jaune)

Gordon Elliott (Ire)   **Gigginstown House Stud**

PLACINGS: /18/213203/P/3F4712-   RPR **149**c

Starts	1st	2nd	3rd	4th	Win & Pl
15	3	3	3	1	£45,463

3/21	Wxfd	3m1f Ch heavy	£5,795
11/18	Navn	2m4f Mdn Hdl good	£7,087
12/17	Navn	2m NHF 4-7yo good	£5,528

Useful hurdler (third in the Martin Pipe at Cheltenham and placed twice in Graded novices) who gradually reached a similar level over fences last season after more than a year out; got off the mark at the fifth attempt and finished second behind Chatham Street Lad in a 3m Grade 3 at Limerick.

Defi Du Seuil (Fr)

8 b g Voix Du Nord - Quarvine Du Seuil (Lavirco)

Philip Hobbs   **John P McManus**

PLACINGS: 1/47/51211/21114/P5-   RPR **153**c

Starts	1st	2nd	3rd	4th	Win & Pl
23	14	3	-	2	£618,912

1/20	Asct	2m1f Cls1 Gd1 Ch heavy	£85,425
12/19	Sand	1m7¹/₂f Cls1 Gd1 Ch soft	£84,405
11/19	Chel	2m Cls1 Gd2 Ch soft	£42,203
3/19	Chel	2m4f Cls1 Nov Gd1 Ch gd-sft	£88,209
2/19	Sand	2m4f Cls1 Nov Gd1 Ch soft	£31,691
12/18	Extr	2m3f Cls2 Nov Ch soft	£16,245
4/17	Aint	2m1f Cls1 Gd1 Hdl 4yo good	£56,181
3/17	Chel	2m1f Cls1 Gd1 Hdl 4yo good	£71,188
1/17	Chel	2m1f Cls1 Gd2 Hdl 4yo soft	£17,085
12/16	Chep	2m Cls1 Gd1 Hdl 3yo soft	£28,475
12/16	Chel	2m1f Cls2 Hdl 3yo gd-sft	£12,512
11/16	Chel	2m¹/₂f Cls1 Gd2 Hdl 3yo gd-sft	£17,165
10/16	Ffos	2m Cls5 Mdn Hdl 3yo good	£2,599
4/16	Pari	1m4f NHF 3yo v soft	£5,882

Seven-time Grade 1 winner who mopped up several top races at around 2m in Britain two seasons ago, including the Tingle Creek and Clarence House; fourth at 2-5 in the Champion Chase that year, though, and showed little sparkle in just two runs last season.

Dashel Drasher: high-class performer over fences last season

Delta Work (Fr)

8 br g Network - Robbe (Video Rock)

Gordon Elliott (Ire) — Gigginstown House Stud

PLACINGS: 4312/1113/14115/5U3- **RPR 163c**

Starts		1st	2nd	3rd	4th	Win & Pl
21		8	3	5	2	£531,183
	2/20	Leop	3m Gd1 Ch yield			£118,856
	12/19	Leop	3m Gd1 Ch yield			£93,018
	4/19	Punc	3m¹/₂f Nov Gd1 Ch yld-sft			£53,153
	12/18	Leop	3m Nov Gd1 Ch good			£52,212
	12/18	Fair	2m4f Nov Gd1 Ch good			£46,991
	11/18	DRoy	2m3¹/₂f Ch good			£8,177
139	3/18	Chel	3m Cls1 Gd3 135-155 Hdl Hcap soft			£56,950
	5/17	Punc	2m¹/₂f Mdn Hdl good			£6,844

Prolific Grade 1 winner since going chasing and added the Savills Chase and Irish Gold Cup two seasons ago to three top-level victories as a novice; below his best last season and missed the spring after fracturing a hind leg when third defending his Irish Gold Cup crown.

Demachine (Ire)

7 b g Flemensfirth - Dancingonthemoon (Milan)

Kerry Lee — West Coast Haulage

PLACINGS: 7332/1132- **RPR 148+c**

Starts		1st	2nd	3rd	4th	Win & Pl
8		2	2	3	-	£27,513
132	11/20	Asct	3m Cls3 Nov 118-134 Ch Hcap soft			£9,747
122	10/20	Uttx	2m6¹/₂f Cls3 Nov 121-135 Ch Hcap gd-sft			£7,018

Took really well to fences last season, winning novice handicaps at Uttoxeter and Ascot on first two runs; had wind surgery after finishing only third at Newbury and got back on track with a career-best second in the Reynoldstown at Ascot when just outstayed by Remastered.

Dickie Diver (Ire)

8 b g Gold Well - Merry Excuse (Flemensfirth)

Nicky Henderson — John P McManus

PLACINGS: 1/214/24- **RPR 144c**

Starts		1st	2nd	3rd	4th	Win & Pl
5		1	2	-	2	£22,979
	2/19	Chep	2m3¹/₂f Cls4 Mdn Hdl gd-sft			£3,574

Very useful novice hurdler three seasons ago (won twice and finished fourth in the Albert Bartlett) but has run just twice since then; good second on chase debut at Newbury on back of

Demachine: young, talented and unexposed over fences

monster layoff last season before finishing fourth behind Monkfish at Cheltenham.

Dingo Dollar (Ire)
9 ch g Golden Lariat - Social Society (Moscow Society)

Sandy Thomson   M Warren J Holmes R Kidner & J Wright

PLACINGS: 112/4362P/355U/0P12-   RPR **154**+c

Starts		1st	2nd	3rd	4th	Win & Pl
23		5	4	2	2	£126,443
137	3/21	Newc	2m7½f Cls3 Ch Hcap gd-sft 120-142			£7,018
	2/18	Donc	3m Cls4 Nov Ch gd-sft			£4,494
130	12/17	Newb	2m7½f Cls3 Nov Ch Hcap soft 125-137			£6,498
	4/17	Font	3m1½f Cls4 Nov Hdl good			£3,249
	1/17	Bang	2m7f Cls4 Mdn Hdl gd-sft			£3,249

Rejuvenated after a switch in yard last season, winning easily at Newcastle and just getting worn down late in the Scottish Grand National; had run well in similar top handicaps in 2018-19 before becoming disappointing; back up to a career-high mark.

Diol Ker (Fr)
7 b g Martaline - Stiren Bleue (Pistolet Bleu)

Noel Meade (Ire)   Gigginstown House Stud

PLACINGS: 2F1/532/1/F34129-6   RPR **156**+h

Starts		1st	2nd	3rd	4th	Win & Pl
11		2	2	2	1	£26,154
	12/20	Limk	2m4f Hdl heavy			£6,750
	11/19	Fair	2m4f Mdn Hdl heavy			£5,857

Seen as a fine chasing prospect but struggled in three runs when switched to fences last season; did better back over hurdles, winning at Limerick and unlucky to be narrowly beaten by Sams Profile in the Galmoy Hurdle, though only ninth in Grade 1 company at Aintree.

Discorama (Fr)
8 b g Saddler Maker - Quentala (Lone Bid)

Paul Nolan (Ire)   Thomas Friel & Andrew Gemmell

PLACINGS: 3725/15F2/22833/257-   RPR **154**+c

Starts		1st	2nd	3rd	4th	Win & Pl
19		2	7	3	-	£117,010
	11/18	Naas	2m3f Ch yield			£7,904
	12/17	Fair	2m2f Mdn Hdl soft			£7,108

Has won only once each over hurdles and fences but has been placed three times at the Cheltenham Festival, most recently when a fine third in the Ultima in 2020; lightly raced last season, finishing a close second at Galway first time out and seventh in the Grand National.

Do Your Job (Ire)
7 b g Fame And Glory - Full Of Birds (Epervier Bleu)

Michael Scudamore   Mark Dunphy

PLACINGS: 152/112422-   RPR **146**h

Starts		1st	2nd	3rd	4th	Win & Pl
8		2	4	-	1	£39,321
	10/20	Ayr	2m Cls4 Nov Hdl 4-6yo soft			£3,769
	10/20	Ffos	2m Cls4 Nov Hdl 4-6yo heavy			£3,769

Very useful novice hurdler last season and briefly

threatened a Grade 1 victory when second to Belfast Banter at Aintree; form had tailed off slightly after two early-season wins but bounced back in the spring after wind surgery; likely to go novice chasing.

Does He Know
6 b g Alkaased - Diavoleria (Slip Anchor)

Kim Bailey   Yes He Does Syndicate

PLACINGS: 1/22/111085-   RPR **144**h

Starts		1st	2nd	3rd	4th	Win & Pl
8		3	2	-	-	£36,283
	11/20	Chel	2m5f Cls1 Nov Gd2 Hdl gd-sft			£14,807
	10/20	Chel	2m5f Cls2 Nov Hdl good			£10,047
	10/20	Ludl	2m5f Cls4 Nov Hdl gd-fm			£3,899

Won three novice hurdles last season, twice at Cheltenham including a 2m5f Grade 2 in November; struggled subsequently but unsuited by softer ground on handicap debut at Exeter and far from disgraced in fifth when stepped up in class for the Ballymore.

Dolos (Fr)
8 b g Kapgarde - Redowa (Trempolino)

Paul Nicholls   Mrs Johnny De La Hey

PLACINGS: 2/22315/12714/44267-   RPR **164**c

Starts		1st	2nd	3rd	4th	Win & Pl
31		6	9	6	3	£194,106
157	2/20	Sand	1m7½f Cls2 Ch Hcap soft 140-157			£19,577
154	5/19	Kemp	2m2f Cls2 Ch Hcap good 128-154			£14,389
149	2/19	Kemp	2m2f Cls2 Ch Hcap soft 132-154			£18,768
	11/17	Asct	2m3f Cls3 Ch gd-sft			£9,986
	4/17	Chep	2m Cls4 Nov Hdl good			£3,899
	10/16	Chep	2m Cls4 Nov Hdl 3yo good			£3,899

Has done well in small-field 2m handicap chases and very nearly defied a mark of 158 at Sandown in February (was going for a third straight win in that race); otherwise struggled last season and failed to beat a single rival in the Game Spirit Chase and Celebration Chase.

Domaine De L'Isle (Fr)
8 b g Network - Gratiene De L'Isle (Altayan)

Sean Curran   12 Oaks Racing & Ian Hutchins

PLACINGS: P5P4/361115/4P84911-   RPR **149**+c

Starts		1st	2nd	3rd	4th	Win & Pl
22		7	2	2	3	£129,907
144	4/21	Chel	3m2f Cls2 Ch Hcap good 124-150			£9,626
137	3/21	Kemp	2m4½f Cls3 Ch Hcap good 127-141			£15,335
140	1/20	Asct	2m5f Cls2 Ch Hcap heavy 127-153			£46,920
130	12/19	Newc	2m7½f Cls3 Ch Hcap soft 122-132			£16,505
120	12/19	Chep	2m3½f Cls4 Ch Hcap soft 98-120			£4,289
	6/18	Clun	2m2f Ch good			£5,097
	5/18	Pmnl	2m4f Ch 5-6yo good			£5,522

Streaky chaser who has proved prolific when in form, winning his final two races last season and three in a row during the previous campaign; mark dropped 9lb in between winning sequences and ended back on career-high rating after latest win when stepped up in trip at Cheltenham.

Dreal Deal (Ire)

6 b g Arvico - Fleur Rose (Flemensfirth)

Ronan McNally (Ire)   Ronan M P McNally

PLACINGS: 3/20000880/11117-   RPR **140+**h

Starts	1st	2nd	3rd	4th	Win & Pl
12	4	-	-	-	£34,968

	1/21	Punc	2m Nov Gd2 Hdl heavy £18,438
111	11/20	Cork	2m 85-113 Hdl Hcap sft-hvy £5,500
106	10/20	Punc	2m4¹/₂f 97-117 Hdl Hcap yld-sft £5,500
84	9/20	Navn	2m6f 80-101 Hdl Hcap good..................£5,000

Astonishing improver last season, completing a six-timer (including twice on the Flat) with a Grade 2 novice hurdle win at Punchestown having failed to finish better than eighth in previous 11 runs under rules; well below best on only subsequent run at Aintree.

Dreams Of Home (Ire)

5 b g Jet Away - Knocktartan (King's Ride)

Donald McCain   Colin Taylor & Miss Kay Wilding

PLACINGS: 1111   RPR **133+**h

Starts	1st	2nd	3rd	4th	Win & Pl
3	3	-	-	-	£11,306

3/21	Newc	2m Cls4 Nov Hdl gd-sft................£3,769
2/21	Carl	2m1f Cls4 Nov Hdl heavy..............£3,769
1/21	Weth	2m Cls4 Mdn Hdl heavy................£3,769

Won all three novice hurdles last season, albeit when kept to ordinary company; easily defied a double penalty by nine lengths at Newcastle, proving versatility on good to soft ground after winning twice on heavy; likely to appreciate going beyond 2m.

Duffle Coat (Ire)

4 gr g Alhebayeb - Humilis (Sadler's Wells)

Gordon Elliott (Ire)   R Stokes

PLACINGS: 1111-   RPR **138**h

Starts	1st	2nd	3rd	4th	Win & Pl
4	4	-	-	-	£36,099

11/20	Chel	2m¹/₂f Cls1 Gd2 Hdl 3yo gd-sft.........£14,807
10/20	Weth	2m Cls1 List Hdl 3yo gd-sft..............£8,543
10/20	Gowr	2m Hdl 3yo good............................£6,750
9/20	Punc	2m¹/₂f Mdn Hdl 3yo yield...................£6,000

Missed the second half of last season but had been disputing Triumph Hurdle favouritism up to that point after winning all four starts; showed stamina is his forte when beating subsequent Grade 1 winner Adagio at Cheltenham, powering home after getting detached early.

Dusart (Ire)

6 b g Flemensfirth - Dusty Too (Terimon)

Nicky Henderson   R A Bartlett

PLACINGS: 13-   RPR **146+**h

Starts	1st	2nd	3rd	4th	Win & Pl
2	1	-	1	-	£11,762

11/20	Newb	2m1¹/₂f Cls4 Nov Hdl good £3,769

Missed much of last season but showed big promise in just two runs in novice hurdles;

claimed a good scalp in Soaring Glory on hurdling debut and was sent off joint-favourite for a Grade 1 at Aintree despite subsequent layoff, finishing third behind Belfast Banter; likely to go novice chasing.

Dysart Dynamo (Ire)

5 b g Westerner - Dysart Dancer (Accordion)

Willie Mullins (Ire)   Ms Eleanor Manning

PLACINGS: 1-1   RPR **135+**b

Starts	1st	2nd	3rd	4th	Win & Pl
2	2	-	-	-	£11,062

4/21	Punc	2m NHF 4-7yo yield..........................£5,795
3/21	Clon	2m2¹/₂f NHF 5-7yo soft £5,268

Easy winner of both bumpers at Clonmel and Punchestown last spring; did particularly well to win on second start having taken a fierce hold off a slow gallop, still finding enough to draw clear in the closing stages; nice prospect for novice hurdles.

Early Doors (Fr)

8 b g Soldier Of Fortune - Ymlaen (Desert Prince)

Joseph O'Brien (Ire)   John P McManus

PLACINGS: /112930/521/2262/01-   RPR **153**h

Starts	1st	2nd	3rd	4th	Win & Pl
17	5	5	2	-	£228,213

139	7/20	Gway	2m6¹/₂f 135-158 Ch Hcap gd-yld..................£100,000
145	12/19	Chel	2m4¹/₂f Cls2 126-145 Cond Hdl Hcap gd-sft....£43,330
	11/17	Naas	2m Gd3 Hdl 4yo sft-hvy......................£17,083
	10/17	Wxfd	2m Mdn Hdl 4yo soft...........................£6,055
	2/17	Punc	2m¹/₂f NHF 4yo heavy..........................£5,265

Finally got things right over fences when winning the Galway Plate in 2020 after a disappointing novice campaign; missed the rest of last season through injury but capable of more handicap success on hurdles form having produced a high-class performance to win the Martin Pipe at Cheltenham in 2019.

Easy Game (Fr)

7 b g Barastraight - Rule Of The Game (Lavirco)

Willie Mullins (Ire)   Nicholas Peacock

PLACINGS: 3/7212F/01127U1-5P21   RPR **165+**c

Starts	1st	2nd	3rd	4th	Win & Pl
25	9	5	2	1	£243,306

9/21	List	2m4f Ch gd-yld..............................£11,063
4/21	Fair	2m4f Gd2 Ch yield...........................£42,143
10/20	Gowr	2m4f Gd2 Ch good...........................£17,500
8/20	Tram	2m5¹/₂f Ch good................................£6,250
12/19	Leop	2m5f Ch yield...................................£9,318
12/18	Navn	2m4f Nov Gd2 Hdl yield.....................£22,190
11/18	Navn	2m4f Nov Gd3 Hdl good.....................£22,190
7/18	Gway	2m¹/₂f Nov Hdl 4yo good....................£10,903
7/18	Klny	2m4¹/₂f Mdn Hdl good.........................£6,269

Has had a fine summer, finishing second in the Galway Plate and winning at Listowel; had also won two Grade 2 chases last season, both over 2m4f, but was twice tailed off in stronger company at Leopardstown and Punchestown to go 0-6 at the top level.

Easysland (Fr)

7 b/br g Gentlewave - Island Du Frene (Useful)

David Cottin (Fr)   John P McManus

| PLACINGS: 7/651FF011/11111/42- | | | | | RPR 153c |

Starts		1st	2nd	3rd	4th	Win & Pl
19		9	1	1	1	£182,778
	3/20	Chel	3m6f Cls2 Ch soft			£40,235
	2/20	Pau	3m7¹/₂f List Ch v soft			£30,508
139	12/19	Chel	3m6f Cls2 122-148 Ch Hcap gd-sft........			£21,896
	11/19	Comp	3m3f List Ch heavy			£20,757
	10/19	Comp	2m7¹/₂f Ch heavy			£9,081
	2/19	Pau	2m4¹/₂f Ch 5-6yo heavy......................			£11,243
	1/19	Pau	2m4¹/₂f Ch 5-6yo v soft			£12,108
	11/18	Drtl	2m5f Ch 4-5yo soft			£6,372
	2/18	Pau	2m1¹/₂f Hdl 4yo heavy........................			£13,593

Wide-margin winner of the Cross Country Chase at the Cheltenham Festival in 2020 but well beaten in two runs over the same course last season, including a distant second behind Tiger Roll in March; connections expressed dissatisfaction with lofty handicap mark.

Echoes In Rain (Fr)

5 b m Authorized - Amarantine (King's Best)

Willie Mullins (Ire)   Barnane Stud

| PLACINGS: 5/1411-1 | | | | | RPR 146+h |

Starts		1st	2nd	3rd	4th	Win & Pl
6		4	-	-	1	£97,704
	4/21	Punc	2m1¹/₂f Nov Gd1 Hdl yield			£52,679
	4/21	Fair	2m Nov Gd2 Hdl yield......................			£18,438
	2/21	Naas	1m7¹/₂f Nov Gd2 Hdl soft..................			£18,438
	12/20	Naas	2m Mdn Hdl 4yo heavy			£6,000

Won four out of five novice hurdles last season; signed off with a Grade 1 win against geldings at Punchestown having earlier beaten Belfast Banter at Naas and won a Grade 2 at Fairyhouse by 15 lengths; potential Champion Hurdle horse if continuing to settle better.

Editeur Du Gite (Fr)

7 b g Saddex - Malaga De St Sulpice (Saint Cyrien)

Gary Moore   The Preston Family, Friends & T Jacobs

| PLACINGS: 2/1/P6/252P11- | | | | | RPR 144+c |

Starts		1st	2nd	3rd	4th	Win & Pl
10		3	3	-	-	£77,706
132	4/21	Aint	2m Cls1 Gd3 123-149 Ch Hcap gd-sft........			£42,203
125	3/21	Newb	2m1¹/₂f Cls3 115-129 Ch Hcap good.........			£7,018
	5/18	Comp	2m2f Hdl 4yo heavy..........................			£19,115

Work in progress for some time but penny dropped last spring when winning handicap chases at Newbury and Aintree, relishing return to quicker ground; beat subsequent

Punchestown winner Sully D'Oc AA in latest victory with more in hand than bare margin.

Edwardstone

7 b g Kayf Tara - Nothingtaloose (Luso)

Alan King   Robert Abrey & Ian Thurtle

| PLACINGS: 222/1126/5U1353- | | | | | RPR 152h |

Starts		1st	2nd	3rd	4th	Win & Pl
13		3	4	2		£57,125
141	1/21	MRas	2m1¹/₂f Cls2 123-141 Hdl Hcap heavy..............			£9,384
	12/19	Aint	2m1f Cls3 Nov Hdl gd-sft...................			£7,798
	11/19	Winc	1m7¹/₂f Cls3 Nov Hdl 4-6yo good			£6,238

Won at Market Rasen last season and ran well in several top handicap hurdles, coming closest when third in the Betfair Hurdle and a three-length fifth in the County; had novice chase campaign aborted after unseating rider at Doncaster but likely to have a crack at fences again.

Eklat De Rire (Fr)

7 b g Saddex - Rochdale (Video Rock)

Henry de Bromhead (Ire)   P Davies

| PLACINGS: 121/11U- | | | | | RPR 158+c |

Starts		1st	2nd	3rd	4th	Win & Pl
5		3	1			£29,990
	1/21	Naas	3m1f Nov Gd3 Ch heavy.....................			£14,487
	12/20	Punc	3m1¹/₂f Ch heavy			£6,250
	3/20	Thur	2m7f Mdn Hdl sft-hvy.......................			£7,000

Won first two races over fences last season, jumping outstandingly well for an inexperienced horse, but unseated his rider around halfway when facing his acid test in the Brown Advisory Chase at Cheltenham; gained both wins on heavy ground and trainer concerned about good.

El Barra (Fr)

7 br g Racinger - Oasaka (Robin Des Champs)

Willie Mullins (Ire)   Mrs S Ricci

| PLACINGS: 2/10421-1 | | | | | RPR 138+h |

Starts		1st	2nd	3rd	4th	Win & Pl
6		3	1	-	1	£23,928
	4/21	Punc	2m Nov Hdl yield............................			£10,536
	4/21	Fair	2m Mdn Hdl yield			£6,321
	11/20	Thur	2m NHF 5-7yo soft			£4,500

Steady improver in novice hurdles last season, getting off the mark at the fourth attempt at Fairyhouse before following up in a stronger contest at Punchestown by a head; likely to go novice chasing.

Eldorado Allen (Fr)

7 gr g Khalkevi - Hesmeralda (Royal Charter)

Colin Tizzard   J P Romans & Terry Warner

PLACINGS: 23/1U/230/114225-					RPR **158**c
Starts	1st	2nd	3rd	4th	Win & Pl
13	3	4	2	1	£85,618
	11/20	Chel	2m Cls1 Nov Gd2 Ch gd-sft		£17,387
	10/20	NAbb	2m¹/₂f Cls3 Nov Ch gd-sft		£8,058
	11/18	Sand	2m Cls4 Mdn Hdl heavy		£6,498

Won a Grade 2 novice chase at Cheltenham last season but seemed slightly fortunate (main rival fell two out) and couldn't win again; flattered to finish second in the Arkle when ridden to pick up the pieces and well held in fourth and fifth in two other runs at Grade 1 level.

Elegant Escape (Ire)

9 b g Dubai Destination - Graineuaile (Orchestra)

Colin Tizzard   J P Romans

PLACINGS: 212133/121668/236P0/					RPR **167**c
Starts	1st	2nd	3rd	4th	Win & Pl
151	6	6	3	1	£347,277
	12/18	Chep	3m5¹/₂f Cls1 Gd3 133-155 Ch Hcap soft		£85,425
	11/18	Sand	3m Cls1 List Ch soft		£17,085
	2/18	Extr	3m Cls2 Ch heavy		£12,512
	12/17	Newb	2m7¹/₂f Cls1 Nov Gd2 Ch gd-sft		£23,048
	11/16	Asct	2m5¹/₂f Cls2 Nov Hdl gd-sft		£12,512
	10/16	Chep	2m3¹/₂f Cls4 Mdn Hdl gd-sft		£3,899

Strong stayer who won the 2018 Welsh Grand National and ran well under a big weight again when third in the 2019 Ladbrokes Trophy; not quite as effective in conditions races and twice well beaten in the Cheltenham Gold Cup; missed last season through injury.

Elimay (Fr)

7 gr m Montmartre - Hyde (Poliglote)

Willie Mullins (Ire)   John P McManus

PLACINGS: 13222/26/1111/22121-					RPR **159**c
Starts	1st	2nd	3rd	4th	Win & Pl
17	7	7	1	1	£240,082
	4/21	Fair	2m5f List Ch yield		£11,853
	2/21	Naas	2m List Ch soft		£11,853
	1/20	Thur	2m4¹/₂f Nov Gd2 Ch yield		£28,750
	12/19	Cork	2m¹/₂f Nov Gd3 Ch yield		£21,261
	5/19	Klny	2m1f List Hdl good		£16,622
	5/19	Punc	2m4f Hdl yield		£13,851
	5/17	Autl	2m1¹/₂f Hdl 3yo v soft		£19,692

High-class mare who has won four of her six races over fences, beaten only by Allaho at Thurles and subsequent Punchestown giant-killer Colreevy in a thriller in the inaugural Mares' Chase at Cheltenham; effective over 2m-2m5f and trainer feels she should stay 3m.

Elixir D'Ainay (Fr)

7 ch g Muhtathir - Perle Du Bocage (Agent Bleu)

Willie Mullins (Ire)   John P McManus

PLACINGS: 6/1/2/125F/					RPR **151**h
Starts	1st	2nd	3rd	4th	Win & Pl
7	2	2	-	-	£41,988
	11/19	Naas	2m3f Mdn Hdl sft-hvy		£7,188
	11/17	Pari	1m4f NHF 3yo soft		£14,530

Running a big race in the 2020 Supreme Novices'

Hurdle at Cheltenham when badly hampered and falling two out but hasn't run since; had been highly tried earlier that season, finishing second behind Envoi Allen in a 2m4f Grade 1 but failing to stay further in another Grade 1 at Leopardstown.

Elixir De Nutz (Fr)
7 gr g Al Namix - Nutz (Turgeon)

Colin Tizzard				Terry Warner
PLACINGS: 16/F2111/77/2-				RPR **126**c

Starts	1st	2nd	3rd	4th	Win & Pl
10	4	2	-	-	£68,796

1/19	Sand	2m Cls1 Nov Gd1 Hdl soft...................£28,475
12/18	Chel	2m1f Cls3 Nov Hdl 4-6yo good.............£9,285
11/18	Chel	2m1½f Cls1 Nov Gd2 Hdl good..........£18,006
10/17	Agtn	1m6f NHF 3yo gd-sft.............................£6,838

Top-class novice hurdler three seasons ago, winning the Tolworth Hurdle, but has had nothing go right since then, running just three times; beaten 15 lengths into second when favourite on chase debut last December and didn't run again.

Elle Est Belle
5 b m Fame And Glory - Katalina (Hernando)

Dan Skelton				Mrs Suzanne Lawrence
PLACINGS: 1132-				RPR **123**b

Starts	1st	2nd	3rd	4th	Win & Pl
4	2	1	1	-	£23,978

| 11/20 | Chel | 2m1½f Cls1 List NHF 4-6yo soft ....£7,049 |
| 10/20 | Aint | 2m1f Cls4 NHF 4-6yo soft ....£3,754 |

Best of the British-trained runners in last season's Champion Bumper when finishing third behind Sir Gerhard; did well in mares' bumpers either side of that, dead-heating in a Listed race at Cheltenham and finishing second behind a subsequent Flat winner in a Grade 2 at Aintree.

Embittered (Ire)
7 b g Fame And Glory - Kilbarry Classic (Classic Cliche)

Joseph O'Brien (Ire)				Gigginstown House Stud
PLACINGS: 13/415363/2244F-0201				RPR **149**c

Starts	1st	2nd	3rd	4th	Win & Pl
17	3	3	3	3	£68,987

8/21	Klny	2m1f Ch good....................................£5,795
11/19	Naas	2m Mdn Hdl sft-hvy £7,986
12/18	Punc	2m NHF 4yo good..............................£5,724

Scored over fences at Killarney in August but before that hadn't won since landing a maiden hurdle in 2019; finished third in the County

Hurdle in 2020, however, and was favourite when falling in the Grand Annual back at Cheltenham last season after twice finishing fourth in Grade 1 novice chases.

Emitom (Ire)
7 b g Gold Well - Avenging Angel (Heron Island)

Warren Greatrex				The Spero Partnership
PLACINGS: 1/11112/614/236P-				RPR **140+**c

Starts	1st	2nd	3rd	4th	Win & Pl
13	6	2	1	1	£85,399

2/20	Hayd	3m1½f Cls1 Gd2 Hdl heavy £22,887
3/19	Newb	2m4½f Cls4 Nov Hdl gd-sft £4,549
1/19	Ling	2m Cls4 Nov Hdl gd-sft.......................£4,159
11/18	Ffos	2m4f Cls4 Mdn Hdl soft......................£4,159
11/18	Asct	1m7½f Cls4 NHF 4-6yo good................£4,549
4/18	Wwck	2m Cls5 NHF 4-6yo gd-sft £2,599

Developed into a high-class staying hurdler two seasons ago, finishing fourth in the Stayers' Hurdle at Cheltenham after winning the Rendlesham; had high hopes when sent chasing last season but was beaten twice and fared even worse back over hurdles after a break.

Empire Steel (Ire)
7 gr g Aizavoski - Talk Of Rain (Turgeon)

Sandy Thomson				Alan Wight
PLACINGS: 4/3313/121P-				RPR **152+**c

Starts	1st	2nd	3rd	4th	Win & Pl
6	3	1	1	-	£19,518

2/21	Kels	2m7½f Cls3 Nov Ch soft.......................£7,742
120 10/20	Ayr	2m4½f Cls4 Nov 104-120 Ch Hcap soft...........£4,289
12/19	Carl	2m1f Cls4 Mdn Hdl soft.......................£4,874

Won two of first three races over fences last season, including a wide-margin win over Grade 1 winner Protektorat at Kelso; hard to assess that run (second well below par) and pulled up when stepped up to Grade 1 level at Aintree; still lightly raced after just six runs under rules.

Energumene (Fr)
7 br g Denham Red - Olinight (April Night)

Willie Mullins (Ire)				Tony Bloom
PLACINGS: 1/311/111-1				RPR **171+**c

Starts	1st	2nd	3rd	4th	Win & Pl
7	6	-	1	-	£157,029

4/21	Punc	2m Nov Gd1 Ch yield...........................£60,580
2/21	Leop	2m1½f Nov Gd1 Ch soft......................£65,848
1/21	Naas	2m Nov Ch heavy................................£10,272
11/20	Gowr	2m4f Ch heavy...................................£7,750
3/20	Gowr	2m Nov Mdn Hdl sft-hvy.....................£6,750
1/20	Thur	2m NHF 4-7yo yield............................£5,008

Brilliant novice chaser last season, easily

Eldorado Allen: heading to victory in a Grade 2 novice chase at Cheltenham

winning all four races to maintain unbeaten record over obstacles; missed eagerly awaited Arkle showdown with Shishkin when lame but bounced back spectacularly at Punchestown when beating Grade 1 winner Janidil by 16 lengths.

Enrilo (Fr)

7 bl g Buck's Boum - Rock Treasure (Video Rock)
Paul Nicholls — Martin Broughton & Friends

PLACINGS: 141/1513/21P11d- — RPR **151+c**

Starts	1st	2nd	3rd	4th	Win & Pl
12	6	1	2	1	£67,693

138	2/21	Newb	2m7¹/₂f Cls3 Nov 128-141 Ch Hcap gd-sft	£7,018
	11/20	Extr	3m Cls2 Nov Ch good	£12,021
	12/19	Sand	2m4f Cls1 Nov Gd2 Hdl good	£17,085
	10/19	Winc	2m4f Cls4 Nov Hdl good	£5,198
	2/19	Kemp	2m Cls5 NHF 4-6yo good	£3,119
	10/18	Worc	2m Cls5 NHF 4-6yo good	£2,274

Had a good first campaign over fences last season, winning twice and improving again on first run beyond 3m when first past the post in the bet365 Gold Cup; suffered double whammy of being demoted to third and raised 4lb but open to further improvement.

Entoucas (Fr)

7 b g Network - Mousse Des Bois (Chef De Clan)
Joseph O'Brien (Ire) — John P McManus

PLACINGS: 1/226/32213/222442-3 — RPR **151+c**

Starts	1st	2nd	3rd	4th	Win & Pl
16	2	8	3	2	£67,334

	2/20	Naas	2m Mdn Hdl gd-yld	£6,750
	10/17	Nant	1m4f NHF 3yo soft	£7,692

Still a maiden over fences but made the frame in five big 2m handicap chases last season, coming closest when a short-head second in the Grand Annual at Cheltenham; sent off favourite on final run at Punchestown despite rising mark but managed only third.

Envoi Allen (Fr)

7 b g Muhtathir - Reaction (Saint Des Saints)
Henry de Bromhead (Ire) — Cheveley Park Stud

PLACINGS: 1/1111/1111/111F-P — RPR **165+c**

Starts	1st	2nd	3rd	4th	Win & Pl
13	11	-	-	-	£342,066

	1/21	Punc	2m4f Nov Gd3 Ch heavy	£18,438
	11/20	Fair	2m4f Nov Gd1 Ch soft	£35,000
	10/20	DRoy	2m3¹/₂f Ch yield	£5,500
	3/20	Chel	2m5f Nov Gd1 Hdl soft	£70,338
	1/20	Naas	2m4f Nov Gd1 Hdl gd-yld	£47,838
	12/19	Fair	2m Nov Gd1 Hdl yld-sft	£47,838
	11/19	DRoy	2m¹/₂f Mdn Hdl soft	£7,986
	3/19	Chel	2m²/₂f Cls1 Gd1 NHF 4-6yo soft	£42,203
	2/19	Leop	2m Gd2 NHF 4-7yo gd-yld	£46,509
	12/18	Navn	2m List NHF 4-7yo yield	£14,967
	12/18	Fair	2m NHF 4yo good	£5,451

Hugely exciting dual Cheltenham Festival winner who had won his first 11 races under rules, including three over fences, before things went wrong last spring; fell when odds-on to win the Marsh Novices' Chase and was pulled up at Punchestown with a fractured hind leg.

Epatante (Fr)

7 b m No Risk At All - Kadjara (Silver Rainbow)
Nicky Henderson — John P McManus

PLACINGS: 211/119/111/123-3 — RPR **158+h**

Starts	1st	2nd	3rd	4th	Win & Pl
13	8	2	2	-	£531,707

	11/20	Newc	2m Cls1 Gd1 Hdl good	£45,814
	3/20	Chel	2m¹/₂f Cls1 Gd1 Hdl soft	£264,610
	12/19	Kemp	2m Cls1 Gd1 Hdl soft	£74,035
	11/19	Newb	2m¹/₂f Cls1 List 122-141 Hdl Hcap gd-sft	£28,475
137	2/19	Extr	2m1f Cls4 Nov Hdl gd-sft	£4,549
	11/18	Kemp	2m Cls4 Nov Hdl good	£4,094
	11/17	StCl	1m4¹/₂f Gd1 NHF 3yo heavy	£21,368
	9/17	Le L	1m4f NHF 3yo v soft	£7,692

Won the Champion Hurdle in 2020 during a brilliant unbeaten campaign but didn't hit those heights last season despite another Grade 1 win in the Fighting Fifth; beaten at 1-5 in the Christmas Hurdle and managed only third behind Honeysuckle at Cheltenham and Punchestown.

Eric Bloodaxe (Ire)

6 bl g Saint Des Saints - Diorissima (Sholokhov)
Joseph O'Brien (Ire) — Gigginstown House Stud

PLACINGS: 117/4 — RPR **124b**

Starts	1st	2nd	3rd	4th	Win & Pl
4	2	-	-	1	£15,284

	12/19	Leop	2m NHF 4-7yo yield	£6,389
	12/19	Fair	2m NHF 4yo yld-sft	£5,324

Impressive winner of bumpers at Fairyhouse and Leopardstown in December 2019, beating subsequent Cheltenham hero Ferny Hollow; lame when well beaten at Leopardstown and missed more than a year before finishing fourth behind Kilcruit at Punchestown in April.

Escaria Ten (Fr)

7 b g Maresca Sorrento - Spartes Eria (Ballingarry)
Gordon Elliott (Ire) — McNeill Family

PLACINGS: 1/23110/5123P- — RPR **155c**

Starts	1st	2nd	3rd	4th	Win & Pl
10	3	2	2	-	£36,439

	12/20	Thur	3m1f Ch soft	£7,000
	1/20	Ayr	3m¹/₂f Cls4 Nov Hdl heavy	£4,289
	1/20	Cork	3m Mdn Hdl soft	£7,188

Smart novice chaser last season; did well at around 3m, hacking up at Thurles and pushing Eklat De Rire at Naas, before improved as expected over further when a close third in the National Hunt Chase at Cheltenham; pulled up in the Irish Grand National.

Artist & Sculptor

ady to mount, Leopardstown" oil on board

Espanito Bello (Fr)

7 gr g Turgeon - Flower Flight (Ungaro)

Barry Connell (Ire)   Barry Connell

PLACINGS: 1/1P/02/74120-   RPR **157+**c

Starts	1st	2nd	3rd	4th	Win & Pl
10	3	2	-	1	£30,684
	12/20 Naas	2m3f Ch heavy			£6,250
	3/19 Naas	2m3f Mdn Hdl yield			£8,324
	1/18 Naas	2m NHF 4yo sft-hvy			£5,724

Very useful novice chaser last season; thrashed subsequent Thyestes winner Coko Beach at Naas and might well have beaten that rival again in a 3m Grade 2 at Navan but for a mistake at the last; disappointing in the Irish Grand National on final run.

Espoir De Romay (Fr)

7 b g Kap Rock - Miss Du Seuil (Lavirco)

Kim Bailey   The Midgelets

PLACINGS: 3/1310/121F-   RPR **167+**c

Starts	1st	2nd	3rd	4th	Win & Pl
9	4	1	2	-	£31,703
140	3/21 Leic	2m4f Cls3 130-140 Ch Hcap heavy			£7,018
	11/20 Hntg	2m4f Cls3 Nov Ch good			£7,310
132	1/20 Winc	2m4f Cls3 112-132 Cond Am Hdl Hcap soft			£7,148
	11/19 Wwck	2m3f Cls4 Nov Hdl gd-sft			£4,549

Very smart novice chaser last season and might well have beaten Chantry House in a Grade 1 at Aintree but for falling two out; had won two out of three completed races over fences, beaten only by Royale Pagaille; still very lightly raced and open to further improvement.

Esprit Du Large (Fr)

7 b g No Risk At All - Tuffslolyloly (Double Bed)

Evan Williams   Mr & Mrs William Rucker

PLACINGS: 71410/211F/F3FP-   RPR **154+**c

Starts	1st	2nd	3rd	4th	Win & Pl
13	4	1	1	1	£54,528
	12/19 Sand	1m7¹/₂f Cls1 Nov Gd1 Ch soft			£31,095
	11/19 Extr	2m3f Cls3 Ch soft			£7,798
	3/19 Hrfd	2m3¹/₂f Cls4 Nov Hdl gd-sft			£4,094
	12/18 Uttx	2m Cls4 Mdn Hdl soft			£4,094

Won a Grade 1 novice chase two seasons

ago but has failed to get round in four out of five races since then; might well have won at Chepstow last season had stamina held up over 2m3f but took a tired fall when headed at the last; pulled up when reverting to hurdles.

Faivoir (Fr)

6 b g Coastal Path - Qape Noir (Subotica)

Dan Skelton   Mrs Suzanne Lawrence

PLACINGS: 1211/21411311-   RPR **146**h

Starts	1st	2nd	3rd	4th	Win & Pl
11	7	2	1	1	£51,619
	4/21 Chel	2m4¹/₂f Cls2 Nov Hdl good			£7,805
	3/21 Newb	2m4¹/₂f Cls3 Nov Hdl gd-sft			£5,913
	1/21 Hayd	1m7¹/₂f Cls1 Nov Gd2 Hdl heavy			£12,814
	12/20 Ludl	2m Cls4 Nov Hdl soft			£3,899
	10/20 Chel	2m¹/₂f Cls3 Mdn Hdl good			£7,221
	3/20 Hntg	2m Cls5 NHF 4-6yo gd-sft			£2,274
	2/20 Bang	2m¹/₂f Cls5 NHF 4-6yo soft			£2,274

Five-time winner in novice hurdles last season, progressing all the time; kept away from big spring festivals but did impress when winning at Cheltenham in April, coping with step up to 2m4f under a penalty for previous Grade 2 win at Haydock; could go novice chasing.

Fakiera (Fr)

6 b/br g Cokoriko - Stella D'Engilbert (Network)

Gordon Elliott (Ire)   Tim O'Driscoll

PLACINGS: 4/4222/11240-   RPR **145+**h

Starts	1st	2nd	3rd	4th	Win & Pl
10	2	4	-	3	£39,337
	11/20 Navn	2m4f Nov Gd3 Hdl soft			£13,750
	11/20 Fair	2m Mdn Hdl soft			£5,000

Won two novice hurdles last season but just came up short in top company; appeared to be crying out for 3m when second and fourth on next two runs and duly sent off just 4-1 for the Albert Bartlett at Cheltenham but shaped like a non-stayer when fading into tenth.

Fakir D'Oudairies (Fr)

6 b g Kapgarde - Niagaria Du Bois (Grand Tresor)

Joseph O'Brien (Ire) — John P McManus

PLACINGS: 4B1142/21122/2P221-3 — RPR **167+c**

Starts	1st	2nd	3rd	4th	Win & Pl
20	5	8	1	3	£412,487

4/21	Aint	2m4f Cls1 Gd1 Ch gd-sft	£104,963
12/19	Fair	2m4f Nov Gd1 Ch soft	£47,838
11/19	Navn	2m1f Ch sft-hvy	£9,051
1/19	Chel	2m1f Cls1 Gd2 Hdl 4yo gd-sft	£18,006
1/19	Cork	2m Mdn Hdl 4-5yo soft	£7,492

Impressive winner of last season's Melling Chase at Aintree, maintaining fine record at around 2m4f (won a Grade 1 novice and second in the Ryanair on two previous attempts); has also done well over shorter but disappointing in two runs over 3m, including a distant third at Punchestown.

Fanion D'Estruval (Fr)

6 b g Enrique - Urfe D'Estruval (Martaline)

Venetia Williams — David Wilson

PLACINGS: 17/11115/2F445- — RPR **160c**

Starts	1st	2nd	3rd	4th	Win & Pl
12	5	1		2	£93,075

137	11/19	Newb	2m¹/₂f Cls3 Nov 124-142 Ch Hcap soft	£12,449
	7/19	Autl	2m1¹/₂f Ch 4yo v soft	£22,486
	6/19	Toul	2m1¹/₂f Ch 4yo gd-sft	£9,081
	5/19	Comp	2m2f Hdl 4yo v soft	£19,459
	4/19	Angl	2m3f Hdl 4-5yo gd-sft	£5,622

Four-time winner in France who made a big impression when easily winning a novice handicap chase on British debut in

November 2019; has since come up just short in stronger company, finishing no better than fourth in five runs in Graded races over 2m-2m4f.

Farclas (Fr)

7 gr g Jukebox Jury - Floriana (Seattle Dancer)

Gordon Elliott (Ire) — Gigginstown House Stud

PLACINGS: 215/6F55P/111/53425- — RPR **155+c**

Starts	1st	2nd	3rd	4th	Win & Pl
17	4	3	1	1	£193,168

6/19	Rosc	2m Nov Ch good	£8,324
5/19	Punc	2m Nov Ch good	£11,099
5/19	DRoy	2m3¹/₂f Ch good	£6,659
3/18	Chel	2m1f Cls1 Gd1 Hdl 4yo soft	£71,188

Former Triumph Hurdle winner who became a hardy handicap chaser last season after more than a year off; made the first five in five big-field chases, coming closest when second in the Plate at Cheltenham before coping with a much longer trip when fifth in the Grand National.

Faivoir: prolific over hurdles and not hard to see him doing well over fences this season

Farinet (Fr)

6 gr g Lord Du Sud - Mendy Tennise (Kadalko)

Venetia Williams   M Hammond, E Coombs & T Henriques

PLACINGS: 514/3P4/3231-   RPR **139**+c

Starts	1st	2nd	3rd	4th	Win & Pl
10	2	1	3	2	£68,200

125	3/21	Sand	2m4f Cls1 Nov List 125-145 Ch Hcap soft £22,744
	10/18	Autl	2m2f Hdl 3yo v soft £19,115

French recruit who made a quick impression in just two runs in Britain towards the end of last season, getting off the mark at the second attempt in a Listed novice handicap chase at Sandown in good style; should stay further and totally unexposed.

Farouk D'Alene (Fr)

6 b g Racinger - Mascotte D'Alene (Ragmar)

Gordon Elliott (Ire)   Gigginstown House Stud

PLACINGS: 1/11/141-   RPR **146**h

Starts	1st	2nd	3rd	4th	Win & Pl
5	4	-	-	1	£36,756

	12/20	Limk	2m7f Nov Gd2 Hdl heavy £17,500
	10/20	DRoy	2m6f Mdn Hdl yld-sft £6,500
	2/20	Naas	2m NHF 4-7yo sft-hvy £6,500
	12/19	DRoy	2m1f NHF 4-7yo sft-hvy £5,324

Beaten only once in five races under rules (also won only point) and put that sole defeat behind him when edging out subsequent Albert Bartlett winner Vanillier at Limerick last Christmas; missed the rest of last season after a setback; looks a fine chasing type.

Felix Desjy (Fr)

8 ch g Maresca Sorrento - Lamadoun (Smadoun)

Gordon Elliott (Ire) — Gigginstown House Stud

PLACINGS: 65/1752151/2/F1138F- — RPR **157**+c

Starts	1st	2nd	3rd	4th	Win & Pl
18	7	2	1	-	£159,539

11/20	Punc	2m Nov Gd2 Ch sft-hvy	£17,500
10/20	Klny	2m1f Ch good	£5,500
4/19	Aint	2m¹/₂f Cls1 Nov Gd1 Hdl soft	£56,130
1/19	Punc	2m Nov Gd2 Hdl good	£23,653
10/18	Gway	2m¹/₂f Mdn Auct Hdl yield	£10,903
11/17	DRoy	2m NHF 4-7yo soft	£7,897
10/17	Punc	2m NHF 4-7yo soft	£5,265

Returned from more than a year out last season and soon matched smart hurdles form when sent chasing, winning a Grade 2 at Punchestown; beaten favourite when third in a Grade 1 at Leopardstown and regressed further in two subsequent runs, jumping poorly.

Ferny Hollow (Ire)

6 b/br g Westerner - Mirazur (Good Thyne)

Willie Mullins (Ire) — Cheveley Park Stud

PLACINGS: 1/2211/1- — RPR **147**+h

Starts	1st	2nd	3rd	4th	Win & Pl
5	3	2	-	-	£57,988

11/20	Gowr	2m Mdn Hdl heavy	£7,000
3/20	Chel	2m1¹/₂f Cls1 Gd1 NHF 4-6yo soft	£42,203
2/20	Fair	2m NHF 5-7yo heavy	£5,000

Hugely exciting prospect who ran out a brilliant winner of the Champion Bumper at Cheltenham in 2020, beating Appreciate It; claimed the scalp of another subsequent festival winner, Bob Olinger, on hurdles debut last season only to miss the rest of the campaign through injury.

Fiddlerontheroof (Ire)

7 b g Stowaway - Inquisitive Look (Montjeu)

Colin Tizzard — Taylor, Burley & O'Dwyer

PLACINGS: /5321/22110/2122223- — RPR **158**c

Starts	1st	2nd	3rd	4th	Win & Pl
15	4	8	2	-	£118,275

11/20	Extr	2m3f Cls3 Ch gd-sft	£7,018
1/20	Sand	2m Cls1 Nov Gd1 Hdl soft	£28,475
12/19	Sand	2m Cls3 Nov Hdl heavy	£6,256
3/19	Navn	2m NHF 5-7yo soft	£5,827

Won the Tolworth two seasons ago but looked short of Grade 1 quality over fences last season, winning just once in seven races despite going off 9-4 or shorter five times; still ran well when a clear second behind Monkfish in the Brown Advisory at Cheltenham, looking a strong stayer.

Fidelio Vallis (Fr)

6 b g Saint Des Saints - Quora Vallis (Mansonnien)

Paul Nicholls — J Hales

PLACINGS: 2/7F11/24211-11 — RPR **153**+c

Starts	1st	2nd	3rd	4th	Win & Pl
12	6	3	-	1	£55,880

143	5/21	Wwck	2m Cls2 127-145 Ch Hcap gd-sft	£11,707
137	5/21	Kemp	2m2f Cls2 120-137 Ch Hcap good	£11,774
	4/21	Sthl	2m Cls4 Nov Ch good	£3,594
	3/21	Font	2m2f Cls4 Ch gd-fm	£3,594
	3/20	Kemp	2m Cls4 Nov Hdl gd-sft	£4,159
	2/20	Winc	1m7¹/₂f Cls4 Nov Hdl soft	£4,224

Dual hurdles winner who soon stepped up to another level over fences last spring, winning four in a row including good handicaps at Kempton and Warwick; did well to defy top weight when completing four-timer given probably best suited by return to further than 2m on a right-handed track.

Fifty Ball (Fr)

6 b g Cokoriko - Voix De Montot (Voix Du Nord)

Gary Moore — Steven Packham

PLACINGS: 4474/511/321120- — RPR **139**h

Starts	1st	2nd	3rd	4th	Win & Pl
13	4	2	1	3	£56,686

120	12/20	Sand	2m Cls4 Nov 112-120 Hdl Hcap heavy	£5,198
113	10/20	Asct	2m Cls4 Nov 101-119 Cond Hdl Hcap gd-sft	£5,198
	10/19	Sabl	1m5¹/₂f Hdl 4yo soft	£9,009
	9/19	Lrsy	1m4f NHF 4yo good	£4,279

Progressed rapidly during first season in Britain last term having won two French bumpers; easily won two novice handicap hurdles before running a huge race when second in the Betfair Hurdle; disappointed in the County Hurdle on final run.

Financier

8 ch g Dubawi - Desired (Rainbow Quest)

Kerry Lee — Will Roseff

PLACINGS: 1305/P13/27F1- — RPR **153**+c

Starts	1st	2nd	3rd	4th	Win & Pl
10	2	1	2	-	£16,778

136	3/21	Hrfd	2m Cls3 134-140 Ch Hcap soft	£6,756
	2/20	Ludl	2m Cls4 Ch soft	£6,238

Impressive ten-length winner of a good handicap chase at Hereford on final run last season, belatedly building on narrow defeat at Chepstow first time out; progress had been blighted by jumping errors on two runs in between; raised 9lb for latest win.

Ferny Hollow: 2020 Champion Bumper winner made a promising start over hurdles last season before injury ruled him out for the rest of the season

Finest Evermore (Ire)

5 b m Yeats - St Helans Bay (Heron Island)

Willie Mullins (Ire)   J Turner

PLACINGS: 2/1113-   RPR **135**+h

Starts	1st	2nd	3rd	4th	Win & Pl
5	3	1	1	-	£20,383
9/20	List	2m4f Nov Hdl soft................................£8,500
8/20	Tipp	2m4f Mdn Hdl 4yo soft..........................£5,000
7/20	Cork	2m NHF 4-5yo yld-sft............................£4,500

Promising mare who won on first three runs for Willie Mullins early last season, twice by wide margins when sent hurdling; disappointing third when odds-on to follow up in a Listed race at Punchestown and missed the rest of the season through injury.

First Flow (Ire)

9 b g Primary - Clonroche Wells (Pierre)

Kim Bailey   A N Solomons

PLACINGS: 1P/5/22132111/1116-6   RPR **169**+c

Starts		1st	2nd	3rd	4th	Win & Pl
20		10	3	1	2	£166,373
	1/21	Asct	2m1f Cls1 Gd1 Ch soft.............................£59,513
154	12/20	Weth	1m7f Cls2 133-154 Ch Hcap heavy.................£12,021
148	11/20	Asct	2m1f Cls2 138-159 Ch Hcap soft..................£15,640
	3/20	Carl	2m Cls3 Nov Ch heavy..............................£9,747
	2/20	Donc	2m¹/₂f Cls4 Nov Ch heavy..........................£4,289
141	2/20	Leic	2m Cls3 Nov 125-141 Ch Hcap heavy..............£6,498
	12/19	Hrfd	2m Cls3 Nov Ch soft...............................£8,769
	1/18	Hayd	1m7¹/₂f Cls1 Nov Gd2 Hdl heavy..................£17,085
	12/17	Newb	2m1¹/₂f Cls4 Hdl heavy.............................£4,549
	11/17	Ling	2m Cls4 Nov Hdl soft..............................£5,198

Progressive chaser who graduated to the top level last season, making it six wins in a row when beating Politologue in the Clarence House Chase at Ascot; disappointed twice in the spring on quicker ground, albeit not beaten far in the Champion Chase; has gained all ten wins on soft or heavy.

First Flow (left): classy chaser who has an impressive record on testing ground

Five O'Clock (Fr)

6 b g Cokoriko - Rodika (Kapgarde)

Willie Mullins (Ire)   Mrs S Ricci

PLACINGS: 0/32/2117/   RPR **143**h

Starts	1st	2nd	3rd	4th	Win & Pl
7	2	2	1	-	£47,940
	2/20 Thur	2m5f Nov Gd3 Hdl soft			£25,000
	1/20 Limk	2m Mdn Hdl sft-hvy			£5,509

French recruit who won two novice hurdles two seasons ago, most impressively when stepped up to 2m5f to win a Grade 3 at Thurles by six lengths; had a troubled passage when seventh in the Martin Pipe at Cheltenham; missed last season through injury; likely to go novice chasing.

Flash Collonges (Fr)

6 b g Saddler Maker - Prouesse Collonges (Apple Tree)

Paul Nicholls   The Gi Gi Syndicate

PLACINGS: 1F211-   RPR **147**+h

Starts	1st	2nd	3rd	4th	Win & Pl
5	3	1	-	-	£23,300
133	3/21 Kels	2m5f Cls2 115-138 Hdl Hcap gd-sft			£12,512
	1/21 Winc	2m5½f Cls4 Nov Hdl gd-sft			£3,769
	11/20 Extr	2m5½f Cls3 Nov Hdl good			£5,913

Looked a smart novice hurdler in winning three out of four completed starts last season, albeit in modest company; put narrow odds-on defeat behind him with wide-margin wins at Wincanton and Kelso, latterly off 133 on handicap debut; likely to go novice chasing.

Flooring Porter (Ire)

6 b g Yeats - Lillymile (Revoque)

Gavin Cromwell (Ire)   Flooring Porter Syndicate

PLACINGS: 780714162/132111-P   RPR **168**+h

Starts	1st	2nd	3rd	4th	Win & Pl
16	6	2	1	1	£262,258
	3/21 Chel	3m Cls1 Gd1 Hdl gd-sft			£135,048
	12/20 Leop	3m Gd1 Hdl soft			£50,000
136	12/20 Navn	3m½f 128-154 Hdl Hcap soft			£45,000
122	7/20 Gowr	3m½f 107-122 Hdl Hcap good			£7,250
105	10/19 Cork	3m 80-107 Hdl Hcap yield			£6,655
	8/19 Bell	2m½f Mdn Hdl good			£6,123

Astonishing improver last season when seemingly transformed by front-running tactics, going from winning a Navan handicap at 22-1 off 136 to running away with the Stayers' Hurdle just two runs later; pulled up at Punchestown on final run; had long been earmarked for chasing.

Franco De Port (Fr)

6 br g Coastal Path - Ruth (Agent Bleu)

Willie Mullins (Ire) — Bruton Street V

PLACINGS: 1/172P/11252-F — RPR **159c**

Starts	1st	2nd	3rd	4th	Win & Pl
11	4	3	-	-	£116,954

			Win & Pl
12/20	Leop	2m1f Nov Gd1 Ch yield	£40,000
11/20	Thur	2m2f Ch soft	£5,500
11/19	Gowr	2m Nov Hdl 4yo heavy	£8,253
3/19	Autl	2m1½f Hdl 4yo heavy	£19,459

Surprised even his trainer when winning a Grade 1 novice chase at Leopardstown last Christmas; largely outclassed in four subsequent runs at the top level, though still ran well when second behind Energumene in the Irish Arkle and Janidil in the Underwriting Exchange Gold Cup.

Freewheelin Dylan (Ire)

9 b g Curtain Time - Gaye Future (Beat All)

Dermot McLoughlin (Ire) — Miss S Mangan

PLACINGS: 75/7F12310/1F5981-46 — RPR **149c**

Starts	1st	2nd	3rd	4th	Win & Pl
28	6	3	3	2	£283,138

			Win & Pl
137	4/21	Fair	3m5f 135-153 Ch Hcap yield	£192,857
135	7/20	Kbgn	3m1f 127-140 Ch Hcap gd-yld	£37,500
130	11/19	Punc	2m6½f 111-132 Ch Hcap soft	£13,820
121	9/19	Kbgn	3m1f 103-133 Ch Hcap gd-yld	£10,649
111	8/18	Kbgn	3m1f 93-118 Ch Hcap good	£6,814
	6/17	List	3m Hunt Ch heavy	£5,791

Caused one of the biggest upsets of modern times when winning last season's Irish Grand National at 150-1, leading virtually throughout on first run for six months; largely known as a summer jumper given preference for good ground but now has Aintree as his aim.

French Dynamite (Fr)

6 b g Kentucky Dynamite - Matnie (Laveron)

Mouse Morris (Ire) — Robcour

PLACINGS: 11514/2512-4 — RPR **158+h**

Starts	1st	2nd	3rd	4th	Win & Pl
9	3	2	-	2	£51,869

			Win & Pl
3/21	Leop	2m2½f Hdl yield	£8,955
2/20	Thur	2m4½f Nov Hdl gd-yld	£9,000
11/19	Thur	2m Mdn Hdl 4yo soft	£5,857

Ran consistently well in good staying hurdles last season, though had to drop markedly in class to gain sole win at 1-7; finished second in two Grade 2 races and no better than fourth in two runs at Grade 1 level, most recently at Punchestown; should make a fine chaser.

Frero Banbou (Fr)

6 b g Apsis - Lady Banbou (Useful)

Venetia Williams — P Davies

PLACINGS: 24711/73314- — RPR **144+c**

Starts	1st	2nd	3rd	4th	Win & Pl
10	3	1	2	2	£60,779

			Win & Pl
124	3/21	Sand	1m7½f Cls3 113-126 Ch Hcap gd-sft	£7,018
	4/19	Autl	2m1½f Ch 4yo v soft	£21,622
	3/19	Le L	2m1f Ch 4yo v soft	£8,649

Dual French chase winner who found his feet

Frodon (right): tough and admirable chaser who goes particularly well at Cheltenham

last spring on first season in Britain, running away with a handicap chase at Sandown by nine lengths; raised 13lb for that and only fourth in the Red Rum Chase at Aintree; still quite lightly raced.

Friend Or Foe (Fr)

6 b g Walk In The Park - Mandchou (Mansonnien)

Paul Nicholls   Gordon & Su Hall

PLACINGS: 44101/242124-1   RPR **148+**c

Starts	1st	2nd	3rd	4th	Win & Pl
12	4	3	-	4	£32,826

	5/21	Uttx	2m Cls4 Ch good	£4,008
128	12/20	Winc	1m7½f Cls3 102-132 Hdl Hcap soft	£5,913
	4/19	Chep	2m Cls4 Nov Hdl good	£4,094
	12/18	Tntn	2m¹/₂f Cls4 Hdl 3yo gd-sft	£5,133

Grand chasing type who made a winning start over fences at Uttoxeter in May before being put away; had been progressive over hurdles last season despite winning only once, finishing second three times off rising marks before a below-par fourth in the Kingwell Hurdle.

Frodon (Fr)

9 b g Nickname - Miss Country (Country Reel)

Paul Nicholls   P J Vogt

PLACINGS: 50/12111/3314/14151-   RPR **171**c

Starts	1st	2nd	3rd	4th	Win & Pl
40	17	3	7	3	£970,788

	4/21	Sand	2m6½f Cls1 Gd2 Ch good	£23,919
	12/20	Kemp	3m Cls1 Gd1 Ch gd-sft	£116,178
164	10/20	Chel	3m1f Cls2 138-164 Ch Hcap good	£30,140
	1/20	Kemp	2m4½f Cls1 Gd2 Ch gd-sft	£34,170
	3/19	Chel	2m4½f Cls1 Gd1 Ch gd-sft	£196,945
	1/19	Chel	3m1½f Cls1 Gd2 Ch gd-sft	£56,536
164	12/18	Chel	2m4½f Cls3 138-164 Ch Hcap good	£74,035
158	10/18	Aint	2m4f Cls1 Gd2 138-158 Ch Hcap good	£45,016
154	1/18	Chel	2m5f Cls1 Gd3 131-154 Ch Hcap heavy	£42,713
	2/17	Kemp	2m4½f Cls1 Nov Gd2 Ch good	£18,793
	2/17	Muss	2m4f Cls3 Nov Ch good	£7,798
149	12/16	Chel	2m5f Cls1 Gd3 132-158 Ch Hcap soft	£56,950
	11/16	Winc	2m4f Cls1 Nov Gd2 Ch good	£28,486
	9/16	Font	2m5f Cls4 Nov Ch good	£5,198
	9/16	NAbb	2m¹/₂f Cls3 Nov Ch good	£7,187
	2/16	Hayd	1m7¹/₂f Cls2 Hdl 4yo heavy	£9,747
	4/15	Autl	1m7f Hdl 3yo heavy	£20,465

Prolific chaser who has won eight times across the last three seasons, all in tough races, most notably last year's King George at Kempton; has a remarkable record at Cheltenham, including a victory in the 2019 Ryanair Chase, but just found wanting when only fifth in the Gold Cup.

Full Back (Fr)

6 b g Sinndar - Quatre Bleue (Cyborg)

Gary Moore   Ashley Head

PLACINGS: 2514/311P2-   RPR **145**c

Starts	1st	2nd	3rd	4th	Win & Pl
8	3	1	1	1	£20,881

	1/21	Extr	3m Cls3 Ch soft	£7,018
	12/20	Plum	3m1¹/₂f Cls4 Ch soft	£7,533
	1/20	Font	2m3f Cls4 Mdn Hdl soft	£3,769

Good winner of 3m novice chases at Plumpton

and Exeter last season on soft ground; flopped when up in class for the Reynoldstown at Ascot, jumping poorly, but did better when just beaten at Fontwell under a double penalty on ground perhaps quicker than ideal (finished lame).

Funambule Sivola (Fr)

6 b g Noroit - Little Memories (Montjeu)

Venetia Williams   My Racing Manager Friends

PLACINGS: 22/0F55/1512112-   RPR **158+**c

Starts	1st	2nd	3rd	4th	Win & Pl
13	4	4			£66,011

141	3/21	Asct	2m1f Cls2 Nov 129-141 Ch Hcap good	£16,243
133	2/21	Chep	2m Cls2 126-145 Ch Hcap good	£11,930
124	12/20	Newb	2m¹/₂f Cls3 113-125 Ch Hcap soft	£7,018
112	11/20	Weth	1m7f Cls4 Nov 112-120 Ch Hcap gd-sft	£4,289

Made the most of an extremely lenient opening mark last season, winning four times in handicaps having been switched to fences; only horse to give Shishkin a race when second in a Grade 1 at Aintree but made to pay by the handicapper, going up another 7lb.

Fury Road (Ire)

7 b g Stowaway - Molly Duffy (Oscar)

Gordon Elliott (Ire)   Gigginstown House Stud

PLACINGS: 4151/311143/142P-P   RPR **159**h

Starts	1st	2nd	3rd	4th	Win & Pl
13	5	1	2	2	£135,867

	11/20	Punc	2m5¹/₂f Gd2 Hdl heavy	£30,000
	12/19	Limk	2m7f Nov Gd2 Hdl heavy	£39,865
	11/19	Navn	2m4f Nov Gd3 Hdl soft	£22,590
	11/19	DRoy	2m6f Mdn Hdl yld-sft	£7,986
	2/19	Fair	2m NHF 5-7yo gd-yld	£5,550

Won well first time out last season (second win at Grade 2 level, with a neck third in the Albert Bartlett in between) but disappointed subsequently; twice a beaten favourite in stronger races and was pulled up at the Cheltenham and Punchestown festivals; likely to go novice chasing.

Fusil Raffles (Fr)

6 b g Saint Des Saints - Tali Des Obeaux (Panoramic I)

Nicky Henderson   Simon Munir & Isaac Souede

PLACINGS: 121/11P0/11P12P-   RPR **161**c

Starts	1st	2nd	3rd	4th	Win & Pl
13	7	2	-	-	£172,514

	12/20	Chel	2m4¹/₂f Cls2 Nov Ch soft	£12,820
	10/20	Chel	2m Cls2 Nov Ch good	£12,512
	9/20	Uttx	2m Cls4 Nov Ch good	£4,289
	11/19	Winc	1m7¹/₂f Cls1 Gd2 Hdl gd-sft	£34,572
	5/19	Punc	2m Gd1 Hdl 4yo gd-yld	£53,153
	2/19	Kemp	2m Cls1 Gd2 Hdl 4yo good	£17,085
	7/18	Seno	2m2f Hdl 3yo soft	£5,947

High-class hurdler who took really well to fences last season, winning three times (twice at Cheltenham) and finishing second behind Chantry House in the Marsh; prone to throw in the odd bad run, though had an excuse when pulled up at Aintree (broke blood vessels).

Gaillard Du Mesnil (Fr)

5 gr g Saint Des Saints - Athena Du Mesnil (Al Namix)

Willie Mullins (Ire)   Mrs J Donnelly

PLACINGS: 621222/2112-1   RPR **155+**h

Starts	1st	2nd	3rd	4th	Win & Pl
11	4	6	-	-	£171,603
	4/21 Punc	2m4f Nov Gd1 Hdl yield			£52,679
	2/21 Leop	2m6f Nov Gd1 Hdl sft-hvy			£65,848
	12/20 Leop	2m4f Mdn Hdl 4yo soft			£6,000
	8/19 Sjdm	1m5f NHF 3yo gd-sft			£4,279

Won two Grade I novice hurdles last season, making the most of Bob Olinger's late defection at Punchestown after an honourable second behind that rival in the Ballymore at Cheltenham; likely to go novice chasing.

Gallyhill (Ire)

6 b g Getaway - Tanit (Xaar)

Nicky Henderson   Claudio Michael Grech

PLACINGS: 1/12P-   RPR **138+**h

Starts	1st	2nd	3rd	4th	Win & Pl
3	1	1	-	-	£7,043
	1/21 Newb	2m¹/₂f Cls4 Nov Hdl heavy			£3,769

Bought for £450,000 after winning sole point-to-point and made winning start over hurdles last season; pulled up when stepped up to Grade I level at Aintree (reported to have had breathing issues).

Galopin Des Champs (Fr)

5 bl g Timos - Manon Des Champs (Marchand De Sable)

Willie Mullins (Ire)   Mrs Audrey Turley

PLACINGS: 12P61-1   RPR **161+**h

Starts	1st	2nd	3rd	4th	Win & Pl
142	3	1	-	-	£104,940
	4/21 Punc	3m Nov Gd1 Hdl yield			£52,679
	3/21 Chel	2m4¹/₂f Cls2 132-143 Cond Hdl Hcap gd-sft			£32,498
	5/20 Autl	2m2f Hdl 4yo v soft			£16,475

Massive improver last spring, proving a handicap blot in the Martin Pipe at Cheltenham and then running away with a strong Grade I at Punchestown by 12 lengths when stepped up to 3m; could be a Stayers' Hurdle candidate but trainer is tempted to go chasing.

Galvin (Ire)

7 b g Gold Well - Burren Moonshine (Moonax)

Gordon Elliott (Ire)   R A Bartlett

PLACINGS: 1111162/F422/11111-   RPR **159+**c

Starts	1st	2nd	3rd	4th	Win & Pl
16	10	3	-	1	£145,017
	3/21 Chel	3m6f Cls1 Nov Gd2 Ch gd-sft			£52,753
	10/20 Chel	3m¹/₂f Cls2 Nov Ch good			£12,558
	10/20 Tipp	2m4f Nov Gd3 Ch good			£13,750
	8/20 Klny	2m5f Nov Ch yield			£6,250
	7/20 Klny	2m5f Ch yield			£6,250
	2/19 Ayr	2m Cls4 Nov Hdl soft			£4,094
	1/19 Navn	2m Nov Hdl yield			£8,879
	8/18 Prth	2m Cls4 Mdn Hdl good			£4,549
	7/18 Limk	2m NHF 4-7yo gd-yld			£5,996
	7/18 Rosc	2m NHF 4-7yo soft			£5,451

Flourished as a second-season novice chaser last season, winning all five races; ran up a sequence through the summer before returning to land the National Hunt Chase at Cheltenham; felt to be best after a break.

Ganapathi (Fr)

5 br g Samum - Une Dame D'Avril (Meshaheer)

Willie Mullins (Ire)   Mrs J Donnelly

PLACINGS: 1/1250-F   RPR **146+**h

Starts	1st	2nd	3rd	4th	Win & Pl
6	2	1	-	-	£19,349
	11/20 Cork	2m Mdn Hdl 4yo heavy			£6,000
	11/19 Pnml	1m4f NHF 3yo heavy			£5,180

Very useful novice hurdler last season, finishing second in a Grade 2 at Punchestown and running a big race in a 2m4f Grade I back there until falling at the last; had failed to stay 2m6f at Leopardstown and disappointed when 6-1 for the County Hurdle at Cheltenham in between.

Gars De Sceaux (Fr)

5 gr g Saddler Maker - Replique (April Night)

Gordon Elliott (Ire)   John P McManus

PLACINGS: 1/211-   RPR **148+**h

Starts	1st	2nd	3rd	4th	Win & Pl
3	2	1	-	-	£18,262
	3/21 Navn	2m7f Nov Hdl sft-hvy			£10,009
	1/21 Navn	2m4f Mdn Hdl heavy			£6,321

Won two out of three novice hurdles last season, most impressively at Navan when destroying a useful field (all previous hurdle winners) by nine lengths; relished step up to 2m7f that day and looks a fine staying chaser in the making.

Gauloise (Fr)

5 ch m Samum - Sans Histoire (Blushing Flame)

Willie Mullins (Ire)   Kenneth Alexander

PLACINGS: 1/11302-1   RPR **144+**h

Starts	1st	2nd	3rd	4th	Win & Pl
7	4	1	1	-	£61,207
	4/21 Punc	2m Nov List Hdl yield			£15,804
	12/20 Thur	2m Nov List Hdl soft			£15,000
	11/20 Thur	2m Mdn Hdl soft			£6,500
	4/19 Lign	1m4f NHF 3yo soft			£4,730

Very useful mare who won two Listed novice hurdles last season, hacking up at Punchestown by ten lengths on final run; had been placed twice at a higher level, including when a half-length second behind Skyace in a Grade I at Fairyhouse, but disappointed at Cheltenham.

Gentleman De Mee (Fr)

5 b g Saint Des Saints - Koeur De Mee (Video Rock)

Willie Mullins (Ire)   John P McManus

PLACINGS: 22/10-7   RPR **136**h

Starts	1st	2nd	3rd	4th	Win & Pl
5	1	2	-	-	£18,645
	2/21 Naas	1m7¹/₂f Mdn Hdl soft			£6,321

Sent off favourite for last season's Martin Pipe

IN THE
PADD🔗CK

DISCOVER THE THRILL OF SHARED OWNERSHIP

Compare over 100 syndicates and racing clubs across Britain to help find the right horse to suit your budget

Scan the QR code and start searching today!

Hurdle at Cheltenham on just his second run outside France but managed only tenth; highly promising seventh in another competitive handicap at Punchestown, fading late after a sweeping move to the front (had also got loose beforehand).

Gentlemansgame

5 gr g Gentlewave - Grainne Ni Maille (Terimon)

Mouse Morris (Ire)   Robcour

PLACINGS: 1123-2				RPR **147**h
Starts	1st	2nd	3rd	4th	Win & Pl
4	1	2	1	-	£47,303
1/21	Cork	2m Mdn Hdl 4-5yo sft-hvy		£6,321

Very useful novice hurdler last season, twice finishing second in Grade 1 races behind Gaillard Du Mesnil and Galopin Des Champs; disappointing third at odds-on at Fairyhouse in between when too keen over shorter 2m4f trip; likely to go novice chasing.

Getabird (Ire)

9 b g Getaway - Fern Bird (Revoque)

Willie Mullins (Ire)   Mrs S Ricci

PLACINGS: 01/11/11017P/12/P1/				RPR **156**c
Starts	1st	2nd	3rd	4th	Win & Pl
12	7	1	-	-	£102,183
11/19	Gowr	2m4f Ch heavy		£10,649
12/18	Punc	2m Ch yield		£7,632
4/18	Fair	2m Nov Gd2 Hdl heavy		£26,106
1/18	Punc	2m Nov Gd2 Hdl sft-hvy		£23,235
12/17	Punc	2m4f Mdn Hdl heavy		£6,844
1/17	Gowr	2m NHF 5-7yo soft		£6,833
12/16	Fair	2m NHF 4yo gd-yld		£4,070

Long held in high regard (sent off just 7-4 for the Supreme Novices' Hurdle in 2018) but has run just twice since the end of that year and not at all since a winning reappearance in November 2019; still totally unexposed over fences; best going right-handed.

Getaway Trump (Ire)

8 b g Getaway - Acinorev (Cape Cross)

Paul Nicholls   Owners Group

PLACINGS: 24411/33P/3141321F-5				RPR **153**c
Starts	1st	2nd	3rd	4th	Win & Pl
22	7	2	4	5	£136,784
140	3/21	Donc	2m¹/₂f Cls2 126-140 Ch Hcap good	£12,558
	11/20	Fknm	2m5f Cls3 Nov Ch good	£8,837
	10/20	Wwck	2m Cls4 Ch good	£4,289
147	4/19	Sand	2m Cls2 Nov 122-147 Hdl Hcap good	£61,900
	4/19	Ayr	2m Cls3 Nov Hdl good	£9,942
	12/18	Extr	2m1f Cls4 Nov Hdl 4-6yo heavy	£4,874
	11/18	Plum	2m4¹/₂f Cls4 Nov Hdl good	£4,094

Notably strong traveller who continues to promise more than he delivers despite winning three times last season; largely kept to small fields over fences but had shown best form over hurdles in big fields, notably winning a valuable novice handicap at Sandown.

Good Risk At All (Fr)

5 ch g No Risk At All - Sissi Land (Grey Risk)

Sam Thomas   Walters Plant Hire

PLACINGS: 211-				RPR **135+**b
Starts	1st	2nd	3rd	4th	Win & Pl
3	2	1	-	-	£22,339
2/21	Newb	2m¹/₂f Cls1 List NHF 4-6yo gd-sft	£11,390
11/20	Chel	2m¹/₂f Cls1 List NHF 4-6yo soft	£10,251

Last season's top British-trained bumper horse on Racing Post Ratings on the strength of a fine win in a Listed race at Newbury; defied a penalty that day having also won in the same grade at Cheltenham earlier in the season; good prospect for novice hurdles.

Goshen (Fr)

5 b g Authorized - Hyde (Poliglote)

Gary Moore   Steven Packham

PLACINGS: 111U/018-5				RPR **167+**h
Starts	1st	2nd	3rd	4th	Win & Pl
8	4	-	-	-	£50,863
2/21	Winc	1m7¹/₂f Cls1 Gd2 Hdl heavy	£21,628
1/20	Asct	1m7¹/₂f Cls3 Hdl 4yo heavy	£7,018
12/19	Sand	2m Cls2 Hdl 3yo soft	£12,512
11/19	Font	2m¹/₂f Cls4 Hdl 3yo soft	£4,094

Talented but enigmatic hurdler still most famous for throwing away the 2020 Triumph Hurdle at the last; put some disappointments behind him with a runaway win in last season's Kingwell Hurdle but hung uncontrollably in the Champion Hurdle before managing only fifth at Punchestown.

Grand Paradis (Fr)

5 gr g Martaline - Outre Mer (Sleeping Car)

Gordon Elliott (Ire)   Andrew Brown & Gemma Brown

PLACINGS: 1411-				RPR **150+**h
Starts	1st	2nd	3rd	4th	Win & Pl
4	3	-	-	1	£25,808
2/21	Thur	2m5f Nov Gd3 Hdl heavy	£14,487
2/21	Fair	2m Mdn Hdl heavy	£6,321
11/20	Fair	2m NHF 4yo soft	£4,500

Won three out of four races, following a debut bumper win with two wide-margin victories over hurdles, including a 2m5f Grade 3 at Thurles; gained both hurdles wins on heavy ground and was withdrawn due to quicker ground at Fairyhouse in the spring; looks a future chaser.

Grand Roi (Fr)

5 b g Spanish Moon - Ultra D'Anjou (Nononito)

Gordon Elliott (Ire)   Noel & Valerie Moran

PLACINGS: 6/31411/3120-				RPR **154**h
Starts	1st	2nd	3rd	4th	Win & Pl
10	4	1	2	1	£41,073
12/20	Limk	2m Gd2 Hdl 4yo heavy	£17,500
2/20	Wwck	2m Cls4 Hdl 4yo heavy	£4,549
1/20	Fknm	2m Mdn Hdl gd-sft	£6,628
12/19	Winc	1m7¹/₂f Cls5 NHF 3yo gd-sft	£2,274

Bought for £400,000 after winning three times

for Nicky Henderson in 2019-20 but made only a modest dent in that investment last season, with sole win coming in a Grade 2 at Limerick; finished in mid-division when favourite for the Coral Cup on handicap debut.

Grand Sancy (Fr)
7 b g Diamond Boy - La Courtille (Risk Seeker)

Paul Nicholls   Martin Broughton Racing Partners

PLACINGS: 114210/F23341/13934-   RPR **155+c**

Starts	1st	2nd	3rd	4th	Win & Pl
25	6	6	4	5	£149,285
	10/20	Chep	2m3¹/₂f Cls1 Nov List Ch good		£11,546
	2/20	Font	2m3¹/₂f Cls3 Ch soft		£9,068
	2/19	Winc	1m7¹/₂f Cls1 Gd2 Hdl good		£34,170
	11/18	Hayd	1m7¹/₂f Cls1 Nov List Hdl good		£14,238
	11/18	Winc	1m7¹/₂f Cls3 Nov Hdl 4-6yo good		£6,498
125	10/18	Chep	2m Cls2 121-132 Hdl 4yo Hcap good		£12,996

Former Kingwell Hurdle winner who ran well at a similar level in novice chases before winning small-field events at Fontwell and Chepstow; struggled when switched to competitive handicaps in the spring but eased 7lb for those three runs.

Grangeclare West (Ire)
5 b g Presenting - Hayabusa (Sir Harry Lewis)

Willie Mullins (Ire)   Cheveley Park Stud

PLACINGS: 1-1   RPR **115+h**

Starts	1st	2nd	3rd	4th	Win & Pl
1	1	-	-	-	£5,267
	5/21	Punc	2m¹/₂f NHF 4-7yo soft		£5,268

Bought for £430,000 after winning sole point-to-point last season and made a winning start under rules at Punchestown in May, hacking up by nine lengths; bred to be a staying chaser and should be one for good novice hurdles when stepped up in trip.

Greaneteen (Fr)
7 b g Great Pretender - Manson Teene (Mansonnien)

Paul Nicholls   Chris Giles

PLACINGS: 3/611/01114/12341-   RPR **171+c**

Starts	1st	2nd	3rd	4th	Win & Pl
14	7	1	2	2	£193,918
	4/21	Sand	1m7¹/₂f Cls1 Gd1 Ch good		£65,493
151	11/20	Extr	2m1¹/₂f Cls1 Gd2 138-158 Ch Hcap good		£32,329
	2/20	Fknm	2m¹/₂f Cls3 Nov Ch soft		£8,058
138	2/20	Muss	2m Cls3 124-140 Ch Hcap gd-sft		£13,256
132	12/19	Asct	2m1f Cls3 Nov 119-132 Ch Hcap heavy		£10,007
	1/19	Font	2m1¹/₂f Cls4 Nov Hdl gd-sft		£4,094
	1/19	Extr	2m2¹/₂f Cls4 Mdn Hdl gd-sft		£4,549

Developed into a top-class chaser last season

as he learned to settle; had been particularly keen when disappointing in the Game Spirit but looked unlucky when a close fourth in the Champion Chase and backed that up when comfortably beating Altior at Sandown.

Grumpy Charley
6 gr g Shirocco - Whisky Rose (Old Vic)

Chris Honour   G Thompson

PLACINGS: 13/69/251116-   RPR **145+h**

Starts	1st	2nd	3rd	4th	Win & Pl
9	3	1	1	-	£19,286
132	2/21	Chep	2m Cls3 117-132 Hdl Hcap soft		£5,913
	2/21	Chep	2m Cls4 Nov Hdl 4-7yo heavy		£4,419
	1/21	Chep	2m Cls4 Nov Hdl heavy		£3,769

Out of his depth when a distant sixth in last season's Supreme Novices' Hurdle at Cheltenham but had flourished at a lower level prior to that; won three in a row over 2m at Chepstow, all on soft or heavy ground, though raised 11lb for final victory on handicap debut.

Guard Your Dreams
5 b g Fame And Glory - Native Sunrise (Definite Article)

Nigel Twiston-Davies   Graham & Alison Jelley

PLACINGS: 2/1411673-   RPR **144h**

Starts	1st	2nd	3rd	4th	Win & Pl
8	3	1	1	1	£28,998
128	1/21	Sand	2m Cls2 119-145 Hdl Hcap heavy		£10,010
	11/20	Bang	2m¹/₂f Cls4 Nov Hdl soft		£3,769
	9/20	Bang	2m¹/₂f Cls4 Mdn Hdl gd-sft		£4,029

Won three times over hurdles last season and went on to acquit himself well in much stronger company; finished sixth and seventh in the Betfair and County Hurdles before a fine third in a Grade 1 novice hurdle at Aintree; effective at 2m-2m5f.

Gypsy Island (Ire)
7 b m Jeremy - Thieving Gypsy (Presenting)

Peter Fahey (Ire)   John P McManus

PLACINGS: 1211/1/1   RPR **123+h**

Starts	1st	2nd	3rd	4th	Win & Pl
6	5	1	-	-	£66,995
	5/21	Tipp	2m Mdn Hdl good		£5,268
	5/19	Punc	2m¹/₂f Gd3 NHF 4-7yo yield		£26,577
	4/19	Fair	2m List NHF 4-7yo gd-yld		£19,392
	3/19	Naas	2m NHF 4-7yo yield		£6,382
	8/18	Baln	2m NHF 4yo yield		£5,996

High-class bumper performer three seasons ago, winning four times including black-type races at Fairyhouse and Punchestown; missed more than two years through injury before making a winning start over hurdles in May, beating subsequent Galway winner Annie G.

Haut En Couleurs (Fr)

4 b g Saint Des Saints - Sanouva (Muhtathir)

Willie Mullins (Ire)   Mrs J Donnelly

PLACINGS: 13-3   RPR **146**h

Starts	1st	2nd	3rd	4th	Win & Pl
3	1	-	2	-	£36,287
	10/20	Autl	2m2f Hdl 3yo heavy		£18,305

Thrown in at the deep end in last season's Triumph Hurdle on just his second run over hurdles (and stable debut) but ran a huge race in

third behind Quilixios before filling the same spot in another Grade 1 at Punchestown; very keen both times and open to significant improvement.

Heather Rocco (Ire)

6 ch g Shirocco - Liss A Chara (Presenting)

Henry de Bromhead (Ire)   Mustafa Elatrash

PLACINGS: 1141-F   RPR **135+**h

Starts	1st	2nd	3rd	4th	Win & Pl
4	2	-	-	1	£18,910
	3/21	Limk	2m Nov Hdl heavy		£8,429
	12/20	Limk	2m5f Mdn Auct Hdl heavy		£10,000

Fine chasing type who produced a real mixed bag of form in novice hurdles last season but

showed quality when twice winning by wide margins; finished last of four in between and ran another poor race when favourite on final run at Punchestown (fell at the last when well beaten).

Heaven Help Us (Ire)

7 b m Yeats - Spare The Air (Trans Island)

Paul Hennessy (Ire)   J Turner

PLACINGS: 8/0134237/21754411-0   RPR **149+**h

Starts	1st	2nd	3rd	4th	Win & Pl
21	5	4	2	2	£146,928

138	3/21	Chel	2m5f Cls1 Gd3 130-155 Hdl Hcap gd-sft........£42,203
126	2/21	Leop	2m2f 119-158 Hdl Hcap st-hvy.....................£52,679
	10/20	Fair	2m Ch yield...£5,500
	10/19	Chel	2m¹/₂f Cls3 Mdn Hdl gd-sft...........................£9,384
	1/19	Navn	2m NHF 4-7yo yield.....................................£6,105

Spent much of last season struggling over fences but switched back to hurdles to devastating effect, running away with the Coral Cup at Cheltenham by nine lengths to follow up a narrow victory at Leopardstown; well beaten when stepped up to Grade 1 level at Punchestown.

Hitman (Fr)

5 b g Falco - Tercah Girl (Martaline)

Paul Nicholls   Mason, Hogarth, Ferguson & Done

PLACINGS: 201/12F13-   RPR **160+**c

Starts	1st	2nd	3rd	4th	Win & Pl
8	3	2	1	-	£52,884

3/21	Newb	2m4f Cls3 Nov Ch good................................£7,798
11/20	Ffos	2m Cls3 Ch soft...£7,791
1/20	Pau	2m¹/₂f Hdl 4yo v soft.................................£12,203

Among last season's leading novice chasers despite both wins coming in moderate company; had other three runs at Grade 1 level, doing best when second behind Allmankind at Sandown; outstayed when third over 2m4f at Aintree (had raced keenly); still only five and open to further improvement.

Hometown Boy (Ire)

6 ch g Curtain Time - Mercy Mission (Karinga Bay)

Stuart Edmunds   The Garratt Family

PLACINGS: 1/433127/11-   RPR **146+**h

Starts	1st	2nd	3rd	4th	Win & Pl
8	3	1	2	1	£47,866

137	4/21	Aint	3m¹/₂f Cls1 Gd3 132-149 Hdl Hcap gd-sft........£31,511
130	2/21	Kemp	2m5f Cls3 118-139 Hdl Hcap good..................£5,913
114	12/19	MRas	2m2¹/₂f Cls4 100-121 Hdl Hcap gd-sft £6,498

Won both starts last season in handicap hurdles, shrugging off a long absence with knee trouble and looking a much-improved performer; successfully stepped up to 3m for the first time when winning at Aintree's Grand National meeting; likely to go novice chasing.

Hometown Boy comes home in good style over 3m at Aintree

Honest Vic (Ire)

8 b g Kalanisi - Miss Vic Lovin (Old Vic)

Henry Daly   Carole Daly & Partners

PLACINGS: 155/6425205/1415/15-   RPR **154+**h

Starts	1st	2nd	3rd	4th	Win & Pl
19	5	2	-	2	£66,797

141	10/20	Chel	3m Cls2 126-152 Hdl Hcap good £12,512
132	12/19	Kemp	2m5f Cls3 117-141 Hdl Hcap soft £12,996
126	10/19	MRas	2m4¹/₂f Cls3 122-135 Hdl Hcap gd-sft £12,996
	11/17	Strf	2m¹/₂f Cls3 Nov Hdl 4-6yo good £6,498
	5/17	Towc	1m7¹/₂f Cls5 Mdn NHF 4-5yo gd-fm................£2,599

Progressive for much of the last two seasons, making it three victories in last five races when winning well at Cheltenham last term on first run over 3m; fair fifth when stepped up in class behind Thyme Hill at Newbury but well beaten on only subsequent run in an all-weather bumper.

Honeysuckle

7 b m Sulamani - First Royal (Lando)

Henry de Bromhead (Ire)   Kenneth Alexander

PLACINGS: 1/1111/1111/111-1   RPR **166+**h

Starts	1st	2nd	3rd	4th	Win & Pl
12	12	-	-	-	£781,035

4/21	Punc	2m Gd1 Hdl yield £131,646
3/21	Chel	2m1¹/₂f Cls1 Gd1 Hdl soft £189,911
2/21	Leop	2m Gd1 Hdl sft-hvy...................................£75,000
11/20	Fair	2m4f Gd1 Hdl soft £50,000
3/20	Chel	2m4f Cls1 Gd1 Hdl soft...............................£67,524
2/20	Leop	2m Gd1 Hdl yield £94,915
12/19	Fair	2m4f Gd1 Hdl yld-sft..................................£66,441
11/19	Fair	2m4f Hdl heavy..£9,318
4/19	Fair	2m4f Nov Gd1 Hdl gd-yld............................£53,153
1/19	Fair	2m2f Nov Gd3 Hdl yield..............................£19,392
12/18	Thur	2m Nov List Hdl good.................................£17,688
11/18	Fair	2m4f Mdn Hdl good £5,996

Phenomenal mare who has won all 12 races under rules, eight at Grade 1 level; stepped up to take on the boys in last season's Champion Hurdle at Cheltenham and hacked up ahead of Sharjah to supplement two Irish Champion Hurdle wins; stays over hurdles.

I Am Maximus (Fr)

5 b g Authorized - Polysheba (Poliglote)

Nicky Henderson   Claudio Michael Grech

PLACINGS: 1-   RPR **125+**b

Starts	1st	2nd	3rd	4th	Win & Pl
1	1	-	-	-	£8,758

10/20	Chel	2m¹/₂f Cls2 NHF 4-6yo soft.............................£8,758

Impressive winner of sole start in a bumper at Cheltenham last October; form worked out really well, with runner-up My Drogo proving the best novice hurdler in Britain; held back for a novice hurdling campaign this season and could go to the top.

Ibleo (Fr)

8 b g Dick Turpin - Mahendra (Next Desert)

Venetia Williams   The Bellamy Partnership

PLACINGS: 719/8/112/221138-   RPR **159+**c

Starts	1st	2nd	3rd	4th	Win & Pl
13	5	3	1	-	£69,499

147	1/21	Donc	2m¹/₂f Cls2 122-147 Ch Hcap soft	....................£12,512
140	1/21	Sand	1m7¹/₂f Cls2 117-147 Ch Hcap soft	................£11,574
118	2/20	Hntg	2m¹/₂f Cls4 Nov 117-118 Ch Hcap heavy	..........£6,498
112	1/20	Winc	1m7¹/₂f Cls4 Nov 95-117 Ch Hcap soft	.............£7,473
	6/16	Comp	2m1f Hdl 3yo v soft	....£7,765

Progressive chaser who won good 2m handicaps at Sandown and Doncaster last season and was placed in three more, including when third in the Grand Annual; longer trip no apparent issue despite finishing only eighth in the Topham (stayed on after getting detached early).

If The Cap Fits (Ire)

9 b g Milan - Derravaragh Sayra (Sayarshan)

Harry Fry   Simon Munir & Isaac Souede

PLACINGS: 111/21321/15/123290-   RPR **157**c

Starts	1st	2nd	3rd	4th	Win & Pl
19	9	4	2	1	£311,591

10/20	Ffos	2m5f Cls3 Nov Ch gd-sft	...............................£7,018
11/19	Asct	2m3¹/₂f Cls1 Gd2 Hdl soft	...........................£56,950
4/19	Aint	3m¹/₂f Cls1 Gd1 Hdl good	..........................£101,034
11/18	Asct	2m3¹/₂f Cls1 Gd2 Hdl gd-sft	........................£56,950
12/17	Kemp	2m Cls2 Nov Hdl gd-sft	.............................£12,512
11/17	Bang	2m¹/₂f Cls4 Nov Hdl soft	..............................£3,249
10/17	Extr	2m2¹/₂f Cls4 Nov Hdl good	...........................£3,899
2/17	Tntn	2m¹/₂f Cls5 Am NHF 4-6yo good	.....................£3,184
11/16	Plum	2m1¹/₂f Cls6 NHF 4-5yo gd-sft	.......................£1,625

High-class staying hurdler who won a Grade 1 at Aintree in 2019 in between successive victories in the Ascot Hurdle; failed to reach that level in four runs over fences last season, not looking a natural, though fared even worse when reverting to hurdles for final two runs.

Imperial Alcazar (right): could be an interesting contender for novice chases this season

Impact Factor (Ire)

9 b g Flemensfirth - Hello Kitty (Houmayoun)

Jessica Harrington (Ire) Robcour

PLACINGS: 22120/0F8322251/2/1-					RPR **152**+c
Starts	1st	2nd	3rd	4th	Win & Pl
18	3	8	2	-	£90,608

141	11/20	Fair	2m¹/₂f 125-148 Ch Hcap soft	£20,000
134	4/19	Fair	2m¹/₂f Nov 118-139 Ch Hcap gd-yld	£26,577
	1/18	Punc	2m Mdn Hdl sft-hvy	£7,359

Plagued by injury since a useful novice chase campaign in 2018-19, running just once in that time, but made it count with a runaway handicap win at Fairyhouse last season on return from long absence; capable of better if getting a full campaign.

Imperial Alcazar (Ire)

7 b g Vinnie Roe - Maddy's Supreme (Supreme Leader)

Fergal O'Brien Imperial Racing Partnership

PLACINGS: 423/1221/910-					RPR **150**+h
Starts	1st	2nd	3rd	4th	Win & Pl
10	3	3	1	1	£40,121

139	1/21	Wwck	3m1f Cls2 123-149 Hdl Hcap heavy	£10,010
	1/20	Leic	2m4¹/₂f Cls3 Nov Hdl 4-7yo heavy	£8,058
	10/19	Aint	2m4f Cls4 Mdn Hdl soft	£5,198

Useful staying hurdler who impressed in winning a Pertemps qualifier at Warwick last season; fluffed his lines in two more valuable races, including the final at Cheltenham (first run on ground quicker than soft since 2019); likely to go novice chasing.

Imperial Aura (Ire)

8 b g Kalanisi - Missindependence (Executive Perk)

Kim Bailey   Imperial Racing Partnership

PLACINGS: 31/11/31221/11UP-   RPR **167**+c

Starts		1st	2nd	3rd	4th	Win & Pl
13		7	2	2	-	£123,689
	11/20	Asct	2m5f Cls1 Gd2 Ch soft			£26,427
	11/20	Carl	2m4f Cls1 List Ch heavy			£13,668
143	3/20	Chel	2m4f Cls1 Nov List 138-145 Ch Hcap soft			£39,389
	11/19	Fknm	3m Cls3 Ch good			£13,666
	2/19	Newc	2m4¹/₂f Cls3 Nov Hdl gd-sft			£5,718
	10/18	Carl	2m3¹/₂f Cls4 Nov Hdl good			£4,874
	4/18	Ludl	2m Cls4 NHF 4-6yo soft			£3,899

Sharply progressive for much of the last two seasons, following up his victory at the 2020 Cheltenham Festival by winning his first two races last term, including a Grade 2 at Ascot; big disappointment when well fancied for the Ryanair (bled from the nose).

Indefatigable (Ire)

8 b m Schiaparelli - Spin The Wheel (Kalanisi)

Paul Webber   Philip Rocher

PLACINGS: 712251/522311/36472-   RPR **149**h

Starts		1st	2nd	3rd	4th	Win & Pl
19		5	5	3	1	£126,880
145	3/20	Chel	2m4¹/₂f Cls2 136-145 Cond Hdl Hcap soft			£43,330
	2/20	Wwck	2m5f Cls1 List Hdl gd-sft			£14,238
	4/19	Chel	2m4¹/₂f Cls1 Nov List Hdl good			£14,068
	11/18	Uttx	2m Cls4 Nov Hdl gd-sft			£4,094
	4/18	Sthl	1m7¹/₂f Cls5 NHF 4-6yo good			£1,471

Won the Martin Pipe at Cheltenham in 2020 and again did well last spring after a poor start to the season (perhaps helped by wind surgery);

finished a close fourth in the Mares' Hurdle at Cheltenham and beaten just half a length by Younevercall in a Grade 2 at Sandown.

Israel Champ (Ire)

6 b g Milan - La Dariska (Take Risks)

David Pipe   John White & Anne Underhill

PLACINGS: 1/6110/   RPR **133**b

Starts		1st	2nd	3rd	4th	Win & Pl
4		2	-	-	-	£29,614
	12/19	Asct	1m7¹/₂f Cls1 List NHF 4-6yo heavy			£17,085
	11/19	Chel	2m1¹/₂f Cls1 List NHF 4-6yo soft			£12,529

Missed last season through injury but had been the shortest-priced British runner when well beaten in the 2020 Champion Bumper at Cheltenham on his last run; won two Listed bumpers that season, impressing when defying a penalty at Ascot; big horse who looks made for jumping.

Itchy Feet (Fr)

7 b g Cima De Triomphe - Maeva Candas (Brier Creek)

Olly Murphy   Kate & Andrew Brooks

PLACINGS: 2/111234/411U/32253-   RPR **162**+c

Starts		1st	2nd	3rd	4th	Win & Pl
16		5	4	3	2	£129,455
	2/20	Sand	2m4f Cls1 Nov Gd1 Ch soft			£31,323
	12/19	Leic	2m4f Cls3 Nov Ch soft			£8,382
	10/18	Kemp	2m Cls1 Nov List Hdl good			£11,390
	10/18	Sthl	1m7¹/₂f Cls4 Nov Hdl good			£4,094
	9/18	Strf	2m1¹/₂f Cls5 NHF 4-6yo good			£2,599

Among the best novice chasers two seasons ago

(won the Scilly Isles) but couldn't quite make the step up to open company last term despite several good runs; disappointing back over hurdles on first run over 3m before a fair third on final run in the Melling Chase at Aintree.

J'Ai Froid (Ire)

8 b g Flemensfirth - Park Wave (Supreme Leader)

Laura Morgan · Mrs K Bromley

PLACINGS: 52/95471/411112-				RPR **149+**h

Starts	1st	2nd	3rd	4th	Win & Pl
13	5	2	-	2	£38,773
130	3/21	Wwck	3m2f Cls3 116-132 Hdl Hcap soft £5,913
124	2/21	Asct	2m7¹/₂f Cls3 113-126 Hdl Hcap soft £7,635
113	1/21	Donc	3m¹/₂f Cls4 97-113 Hdl Hcap soft £3,769
106	1/21	Ayr	3m¹/₂f Cls5 79-106 Hdl Hcap heavy................£2,794
108	3/19	Extr	2m7f Cls4 95-115 Hdl Hcap soft £4,874

Massive improver in handicap hurdles last season, winning four times in a row before a fine second at Aintree's Grand National meeting; began winning run off 106 and was 37lb higher at Aintree (coped well with good to soft ground but ideally suited by a stiff test on softer).

James Du Berlais (Fr)

5 ch g Muhtathir - King's Daughter (King's Theatre)

Willie Mullins (Ire) · Simon Munir & Isaac Souede

PLACINGS: F996212/1212129-2				RPR **160**h

Starts	1st	2nd	3rd	4th	Win & Pl
15	4	6	-	-	£322,051
	10/20	Autl	2m3¹/₂f Gd3 Hdl 4yo heavy.....................£36,038
	7/20	Autl	2m3¹/₂f Gd3 Hdl 4yo v soft.....................£36,038
0	5/20	Autl	2m2f List Hdl 4yo Hcap v soft..................£34,322
0	11/19	Autl	2m2f List Hdl 3yo Hcap heavy...................£47,027

High-class French recruit who was thrown in at the deep end on his only two runs for current connections, finishing ninth in the Champion Hurdle and second in a 3m Grade I at Punchestown (third runner-up finish at the top level); likely to go novice chasing.

Janidil (Fr)

7 b g Indian Daffodil - Janidouce (Kaldounevees)

Willie Mullins (Ire) · John P McManus

PLACINGS: 5/422/1115/13F1-2				RPR **160+**c

Starts	1st	2nd	3rd	4th	Win & Pl
13	5	3	1	1	£187,098
	4/21	Fair	2m4f Nov Gd1 Ch yield......................£42,143
	11/20	Naas	2m3f Ch sft-hvy..............................£6,250
135	12/19	Fair	2m 118-144 Hdl Hcap yld-sft................£53,153
125	11/19	DRoy	2m¹/₂f 116-139 Hdl Hcap soft £26,577
	10/19	Tipp	2m Mdn Hdl yield £5,857

Won a Grade I novice chase at Fairyhouse last

season, though perhaps dropped lucky in a weak race for that level (market principals Asterion Forlonge and Andy Dufresne below par); well beaten in three other runs in Grade I company.

Jason The Militant (Ire)

7 b g Sans Frontieres - Rock Angel (Desert King)

Henry de Bromhead (Ire) · Peter Michael

PLACINGS: 3/2151/331U-7				RPR **160+**h

Starts	1st	2nd	3rd	4th	Win & Pl
10	3	1	3	-	£62,368
	2/21	Fair	2m Gd3 Hdl soft.............................£14,487
	2/20	Naas	2m Nov Gd2 Hdl sft-hvy.....................£23,250
	12/19	Limk	2m Mdn Hdl heavy..........................£7,188

Disappointed on final run at Punchestown but had been progressive prior to that; hacked up in the Red Mills Trial Hurdle on first run since a half-length third in the Morgiana Hurdle and was sent off favourite for the Aintree Hurdle only to unseat rider when in front.

Jeff Kidder (Ire)

4 b g Hallowed Crown - Alpine (Rail Link)

Noel Meade (Ire) · Albert Dravins & Eamonn Scanlon

PLACINGS: 221711-1				RPR **147**h

Starts	1st	2nd	3rd	4th	Win & Pl
7	4	2	-	-	£113,420
	5/21	Punc	2m Gd1 Hdl 4yo gd-yld......................£52,679
	4/21	Fair	2m Gd2 Hdl 4yo yield........................£18,438
125	3/21	Chel	2m¹/₂f Cls1 Gd3 123-141 Hdl 4yo gd-sft..£33,762
	11/20	Fair	2m Mdn Hdl 3yo soft........................£5,000

Came from nowhere to emerge as a top-class juvenile hurdler last spring, completing a hat-trick of spring festival wins; had been an 80-1 shot when landing the Fred Winter at Cheltenham but went from strength to strength, beating Zanahiyr to win a Grade I at Punchestown.

Jersey Bean (Ire)

8 b g Court Cave - Jennifers Diary (Supreme Leader)

Oliver Sherwood · A Taylor

PLACINGS: /112P5P/2278/311341-				RPR **143**c

Starts	1st	2nd	3rd	4th	Win & Pl
22	7	4	3	1	£62,094
133	4/21	Chel	3m1¹/₂f Cls3 Nov 122-133 Ch Hcap good £6,066
125	11/20	Extr	3m Cls3 116-130 Ch Hcap good £7,018
120	10/20	NAbb	3m2f Cls4 Nov 99-122 Ch Hcap gd-sft.........£4,394
127	11/18	Newb	3m Cls2 125-143 Hdl Hcap gd-sft..............£9,747
122	2/18	Font	2m4¹/₂f Cls3 115-134 Hdl Hcap good............£12,996
	10/18	MRas	2m4¹/₂f Cls4 Nov Hdl gd-sft...................£4,094
	11/17	Asct	1m7¹/₂f Cls4 NHF 4-6yo good...................£4,549

Flourished as a second-season novice last term, jumping better and winning three of his last five

---

Jeff Kidder: sprang a huge surprise when winning at the Cheltenham Festival but showed that to be no flash in the pan when following up at Fairyhouse and Punchestown

races; signed off with a terrific win at Cheltenham in April; best on good ground and expected to stay longer trips (has won up to 3m2f).

Johnbb (Ire)

7 b g Stowaway - Flemins Evening (Flemensfirth)

Tom Lacey   C Boultbee-Brooks

PLACINGS: 2313/316/1F2-   RPR **144**c

Starts	1st	2nd	3rd	4th	Win & Pl
10	3	2	3	-	£38,311
130	11/20	Weth	2m3¹/₂f Cls3 124-139 Ch Hcap soft		£9,877
124	12/19	Sand	1m7¹/₂f Cls3 105-125 Ch Hcap gd-sft		£9,384
	1/19	Ayr	2m4¹/₂f Cls5 Mdn Hdl soft		£3,379

Progressive chaser who won at Wetherby last season and put a fall at the same track behind him to finish a fine second on Grand National day at Aintree, relishing step up to 3m1f; open to further improvement after just six runs over fences.

Jon Snow (Fr)

6 br g Le Havre - Saroushka (Westerner)

Willie Mullins (Ire)   Mrs S Ricci

PLACINGS: 3321/11-   RPR **156**h

Starts	1st	2nd	3rd	4th	Win & Pl
6	3	1	2	-	£29,899
	8/20	Klny	2m7f Nov Hdl soft		£8,750
	7/20	Gway	2m4¹/₂f Nov Hdl yield		£10,000
	3/20	Leop	2m2f Mdn Hdl soft		£6,750

Missed much of last season just as the penny seemed to have dropped in the summer with wins at Galway and Killarney; had long had a big reputation but was beaten in three maiden hurdles (twice when favourite) before finding his feet; fine prospect if resuming progress.

Kilcruit: winner of three of his five starts, including when scoring at Punchestown

Jonbon (Fr)
5 b g Walk In The Park - Star Face (Saint Des Saints)

Nicky Henderson   John P McManus

PLACINGS: 11-				RPR **124+**b
Starts	1st	2nd	3rd	4th	Win & Pl
1	1	-	-	-	£4,520

3/21 Newb 2m¹/₂f Cls3 NHF 4-6yo gd-sft £4,520

Full brother to Douvan who was bought for £570,000 after winning sole point by 15 lengths last season; made a winning start under rules in a Newbury bumper last spring; looks a fine prospect.

Journey With Me (Ire)
5 ch g Mahler - Kilbarry Demon (Bob's Return)

Henry de Bromhead (Ire)   Robcour

PLACINGS: 11-				RPR **131+**b
Starts	1st	2nd	3rd	4th	Win & Pl
1	1	-	-	-	£5,267

3/21 Gowr 2m2f NHF 4-7yo heavy £5,268

Bought after winning a point-to-point by 12 lengths and made a winning start under rules in similarly impressive fashion last spring, running away with the same bumper as stablemate Bob Olinger 12 months earlier; more of a galloper than that horse on racecourse evidence.

Jungle Boogie (Ire)
7 b g Gold Well - A Better Excuse (Moscow Society)

Willie Mullins (Ire)   Malcolm C Denmark

PLACINGS: 11-				RPR **135+**h
Starts	1st	2nd	3rd	4th	Win & Pl
2	2	-	-	-	£10,821

2/21 Punc 2m4f Mdn Hdl soft............................ £6,321
11/20 Clon 2m¹/₂f NHF 5-7yo heavy £4,500

Won both races last season, following up bumper debut with a comfortable 30-length victory in a maiden hurdle at Punchestown; lacks experience having missed spring targets (had been entered in the Ballymore and Albert Bartlett) but could go straight over fences given his age.

Kalooki (Ger)
7 gr g Martaline - Karuma (Surumu)

Philip Hobbs   Andrew L Cohen

PLACINGS: 0325/4112/13P32-				RPR **148+**c
Starts	1st	2nd	3rd	4th	Win & Pl
13	3	3	3	1	£34,886

11/20 Newb 2m6¹/₂f Cls3 Ch good.................... £6,498
2/20 Weth 2m5¹/₂f Cls4 Nov Hdl soft.................... £4,534
1/20 Ludl 2m5f Cls4 Mdn Hdl soft.................... £4,224

Found out in Graded novice chases last season but bookended campaign with two fine runs at Newbury, winning easily first time out and

finishing a head second on handicap debut; better than bare form of latter run having thrown away victory by jumping and hanging left.

Kemboy (Fr)
9 b g Voix Du Nord - Vitora (Victory Note)

Willie Mullins (Ire)   Kemboy, Brett Graham & Ken Sharp Syndicate

PLACINGS: F11/11U1/1427/2219-4				RPR **169**c
Starts	1st	2nd	3rd	4th	Win & Pl
23	9	5	-	3	£684,374

2/21	Leop	3m¹/₂f Gd1 Ch soft	£100,000
5/19	Punc	3m¹/₂f Gd1 Ch yld-sft	£159,459
4/19	Aint	3m1f Cls1 Gd1 Ch gd-sft....................	£112,260
12/18	Leop	3m Gd1 Ch good....................	£91,372
11/18	Clon	2m4f Gd2 Ch good	£26,106
147	4/18	Punc	2m5f Nov 126-147 Ch Hcap soft....................	£52,212
4/18	Limk	3m Nov Gd3 Ch heavy	£22,190
1/18	Fair	2m5¹/₂f Ch heavy....................	£7,632
12/16	Limk	2m3f Mdn Hdl yield	£4,522

Gained sole win in the last two seasons when landing the Irish Gold Cup last term, belatedly adding a fourth Grade 1 after a stellar 2018-19 campaign; has been a nearly horse in that time otherwise, including when second in last season's Savills Chase.

Kilcruit (Ire)
6 b g Stowaway - Not Broke Yet (Broken Hearted)

Willie Mullins (Ire)   Miss M A Masterson

PLACINGS: 2/112-1				RPR **142+**b
Starts	1st	2nd	3rd	4th	Win & Pl
5	3	2	-	-	£123,477

4/21 Punc 2m¹/₂f Gd1 NHF 4-7yo yield £52,679
2/21 Leop 2m Gd2 NHF 4-7yo sft-hvy.................... £52,679
12/20 Navn 2m NHF 4-7yo soft £4,500

Last season's top bumper horse according to Racing Post Ratings, achieving a mark of 142 when winning by 12 lengths at the Dublin Racing Festival; narrowly beaten at Cheltenham but made amends when winning well at Punchestown; should stay well over hurdles.

Kildisart (Ire)
9 b g Dubai Destination - Princess Mairead (Blueprint)

Ben Pauling   Simon Munir & Isaac Souede

PLACINGS: 2519/21141/36652/37-				RPR **151**c
Starts	1st	2nd	3rd	4th	Win & Pl
19	5	5	2	1	£172,080

148	4/19	Aint	3m1f Cls1 Gd3 127-148 Ch Hcap good	£42,203
141	1/19	Chel	2m4¹/₂f Cls2 Nov 120-146 Ch Hcap gd-sft	£17,034
12/18	Asct	2m5f Cls2 Ch soft	£31,280
135	3/18	Kemp	2m5f Cls2 122-135 Hdl Hcap soft....................	£21,896
11/17	Asct	2m3¹/₂f Cls3 Mdn Hdl gd-sft....................	£6,498

Got closer and closer in top handicap chases two seasons ago and went down by just a neck behind The Conditional in the Ultima at Cheltenham; ran only twice last season, finishing seventh when 8-1 for the Ladbrokes Trophy after a seemingly ideal prep run over hurdles.

Killer Clown (Ire)

7 b g Getaway - Our Soiree (Milan)

Emma Lavelle   Tim Syder

PLACINGS: 1/2553/U63123-   RPR **144 +** c

Starts	1st	2nd	3rd	4th	Win & Pl
10	1	2	3	-	£25,834
123	12/20 Kemp	2m4½f Cls3 Nov 123-140 Ch Hcap gd-sft			£10,722

Largely progressive in novice chases last season; impressed when getting off the mark on fourth run at Kempton and finished a length second when favourite for the Greatwood Gold Cup; below par when a well-beaten third at Sandown on final run (favourite again).

Kimberlite Candy (Ire)

9 b g Flemensfirth - Mandys Native (Be My Native)

Tom Lacey   John P McManus

PLACINGS: 531P431/1935P/21/2P-   RPR **145** c

Starts	1st	2nd	3rd	4th	Win & Pl
20	6	2	3	1	£144,631
140	1/20 Wwck	3m5f Cls1 Gd3 122-148 Ch Hcap soft			£42,713
133	11/18 Ayr	3m Cls3 108-134 Ch Hcap heavy			£9,292
125	4/18 Chep	2m7½f Cls3 Nov 110-126 Ch Hcap heavy			£7,343
123	12/17 MRas	2m5½f Cls3 Nov 106-125 Ch Hcap soft			£7,798
	12/16 Newc	2m6f Cls4 Nov Hdl soft			£4,549
	11/16 Asct	2m3½f Cls3 Mdn Hdl gd-sft			£5,848

Has finished second in the last two runnings of the Becher Chase at Aintree, though beaten 24 lengths by Vieux Lion Rouge last season after being hit hard by the handicapper for winning the Classic Chase at Warwick in between; pulled up on only subsequent run in the Grand National.

King D'Argent (Fr)

6 ch g Kendargent - Ephigenie (Groom Dancer)

Dan Skelton   Andrew Dick And John Stevenson

PLACINGS: 1324/550835/231F112-   RPR **150** c

Starts	1st	2nd	3rd	4th	Win & Pl
17	4	3	3	1	£37,519
135	3/21 Wwck	2m Cls3 124-140 Ch Hcap good			£5,882
125	3/21 Sthl	2m Cls3 Nov 125-131 Ch Hcap gd-sft			£7,018
	2/21 Newc	2m4f Cls5 NHF std-slw			£2,729
114	12/20 Wwck	2m Cls4 Nov 99-121 Ch Hcap soft			£4,289
	10/18 Weth	2m Cls4 Hdl 3yo good			£4,159

Thrived when sent chasing midway through last season and won first three completed starts over fences (fell when in front on other occasion); beaten favourite on final run at Ayr but lost little in defeat when sharply up in class for a Listed 2m handicap, finishing second.

Kimberlite Candy (right): talented staying handicapper remains relatively lightly raced

Kitty's Light

5 b g Nathaniel - Daraiyna (Refuse To Bend)

Christian Williams   R J Bedford & All Stars Sports Racing

PLACINGS: 9/75312113712-   RPR **145+c**

Starts	1st	2nd	3rd	4th	Win & Pl
12	4	2	2	-	£68,040

135	3/21	Kels	3m2f Cls2 125-142 Ch Hcap gd-sft............£18,159
123	10/20	Extr	3m Cls3 119-132 Ch Hcap gd-fm.................£9,747
117	9/20	Wwck	3m Cls4 Nov 97-117 Ch Hcap good................£4,289
109	8/20	Sthl	2m4¹/₂f Cls4 Nov 97-118 Ch Hcap good........£3,964

Quickly developed into a very useful staying chaser last season, winning four times during a busy novice campaign; also ran well in top handicaps, notably when desperately unlucky not to win the bet365 Gold Cup (badly hampered on run-in).

Klassical Dream (Fr)

7 b g Dream Well - Klassical Way (Septieme Ciel)

Willie Mullins (Ire)   Mrs Joanne Coleman

PLACINGS: P324P/111/135/1   RPR **171+h**

Starts	1st	2nd	3rd	4th	Win & Pl
12	5	1	2	1	£376,524

	4/21	Punc	3m Gd1 Hdl yield...£131,696
	4/19	Punc	2m¹/₂f Nov Gd1 Hdl yield.................................£53,153
	3/19	Chel	2m¹/₂f Cls1 Nov Gd1 Hdl soft............................£70,338
	2/19	Leop	2m Nov Gd1 Hdl good.......................................£66,441
	12/18	Leop	2m Mdn Hdl 4yo gd-yld......................................£8,177

Brilliant winner of a 3m Grade 1 hurdle at Punchestown in April, re-emerging as a top-class horse following a long time in the wilderness after winning three Grade 1 novice hurdles three seasons ago; had been set to go chasing last season until suffering a setback.

Knappers Hill (Ire)

5 b g Valirann - Brogella (King's Theatre)

Paul Nicholls   P K Barber & P J Vogt

PLACINGS: 111-   RPR **134+h**

Starts	1st	2nd	3rd	4th	Win & Pl
3	3	-	-	-	£32,062

	4/21	Aint	2m1f Cls2 Gd2 NHF 4-6yo gd-sft.....................£19,132
	12/20	Asct	1m7¹/₂f Cls1 List NHF 4-6yo soft........................£9,682
	10/20	Chep	2m Cls4 NHF 4-6yo good...................................£3,249

Unbeaten in three runs in bumpers last season, completing a hat-trick in a Grade 2 at Aintree's Grand National meeting; had also beaten the same rivals in a Listed race at Ascot just before Christmas, battling to narrow wins both times; should make a smart novice hurdler.

Lalor (Ger)

9 b g It's Gino - Laviola (Waky Nao)

Paul Nicholls   D G Staddon

PLACINGS: 1/23201/13P6/433/P-P   RPR **159c**

Starts	1st	2nd	3rd	4th	Win & Pl
18	5	3	4	1	£135,848

	11/18	Chel	2m Cls1 Nov Gd2 Ch good................................£19,695
	4/18	Aint	2m¹/₂f Cls1 Nov Gd1 Hdl soft..............................£56,130
	4/17	Aint	2m1f Cls1 Gd2 NHF 4-6yo good........................£25,322
	3/17	Winc	1m7¹/₂f Cls6 Mdn NHF 4-6yo heavy......................£1,949
	12/16	Winc	1m7¹/₂f Cls6 NHF 4-6yo soft...............................£1,625

Looked to have the world at his feet when winning first time out over fences in late 2018, following up Grade 1 hurdles win, but hasn't won since despite sporadic glimmers of form; left Kayley Woollacott for Paul Nicholls after twice being pulled up this spring.

Langer Dan (Ire)

5 b g Ocovango - What A Fashion (Milan)

Dan Skelton   Colm Donlon

PLACINGS: 11226/95412-   RPR **144+h**

Starts	1st	2nd	3rd	4th	Win & Pl
10	3	3	-	1	£65,255

130	3/21	Sand	2m Cls1 Gd3 121-146 Hdl Hcap soft.................£28,230
	11/19	Weth	2m Cls1 List Hdl 3yo soft..................................£14,238
	10/19	Ludl	2m Cls4 Mdn Hdl 3yo good.................................£5,263

Massive improver last spring after wind surgery, easily winning the Imperial Cup on second run back; unlucky not to follow up in the Martin Pipe at Cheltenham, bumping into subsequent Grade 1 winner Galopin Des Champs when nine lengths clear of the third.

Latest Exhibition (Ire)

8 b g Oscar - Aura About You (Supreme Leader)

Paul Nolan (Ire)   Toberona Partnership

PLACINGS: 21/12112/12224-   RPR **160c**

Starts	1st	2nd	3rd	4th	Win & Pl
12	5	6	-	1	£205,883

	10/20	Punc	2m6¹/₂f Ch yld-sft..£6,250
	2/20	Leop	2m6f Nov Gd1 Hdl yield.....................................£75,000
	12/19	Navn	2m4f Nov Gd2 Hdl soft.....................................£22,590
	10/19	Gway	2m¹/₂f Mdn Hdl soft...£7,454
	1/19	Naas	2m3f NHF 5-7yo yield...£5,550

Very smart stayer who has been unlucky to bump into Monkfish several times, finishing second to that rival in the 2020 Albert Bartlett and twice more in Grade 1 novice chases last season; made a bold effort under top weight when fourth in the Irish Grand National.

Knappers Hill: unbeaten in bumpers last season and is now a bright prospect for novice hurdles

Lisnagar Oscar (Ire)

8 b g Oscar - Asta Belle (Astarabad)

Rebecca Curtis — Racing For Fun

PLACINGS: 221153/239F31/472F8- — RPR **156**h

Starts	1st	2nd	3rd	4th	Win & Pl
18	3	4	4	1	£245,567

3/20	Chel	3m Cls1 Gd1 Hdl soft	£182,878
2/19	Hayd	3m¹/₂f Cls1 Nov Gd2 Hdl good	£16,938
1/19	Chep	2m3¹/₂f Cls4 Nov Hdl gd-sft	£4,094

Shock winner of the Stayers' Hurdle in 2020 but suspicion he was the best of a bad bunch largely borne out last season; did slightly better after wind surgery, finishing second in the Rendlesham Hurdle, but fell in the Stayers' Hurdle and only eighth at Aintree.

Livelovelaugh (Ire)

11 b g Beneficial - Another Evening (Saddlers' Hall)

Willie Mullins (Ire) — Mrs S Ricci

PLACINGS: P200/2008/6372321-P0 — RPR **158+**c

Starts	1st	2nd	3rd	4th	Win & Pl
32	5	5	6	2	£166,630

145	4/21	Aint	2m5f Cls1 Gd3 131-157 Ch Hcap gd-sft	£58,937
	1/18	Cork	2m4f Ch heavy	£7,904
	2/17	Thur	2m4f Nov Hdl soft	£9,477
	5/16	Baln	2m5f Mdn Hdl soft	£4,748
	12/14	Punc	2m NHF 4yo gd-yld	£4,888

Spectacular winner of last season's Topham Chase at Aintree (had also relished the fences when failing to stay in the 2019 Grand National); hasn't won in more than three years otherwise and disappointed this summer, though was placed in two big handicaps at Leopardstown last term.

Llandinabo Lad

6 ch g Malinas - Hot Rhythm (Haafhd)

Tom Symonds   Celia & Michael Baker

PLACINGS: 4/22/1125P-   RPR **144**h

Starts	1st	2nd	3rd	4th	Win & Pl
8	2	3	-	1	£23,474

11/20	Hayd	1m7½f Cls1 Nov List Hdl soft	£11,444
10/20	Bang	2m1½f Cls4 Nov Hdl soft	£3,769

Looked an exciting prospect early last season, winning two novice hurdles including a Listed race at Haydock before pushing subsequent Grade 1 winner My Drogo close at Ascot; bitterly disappointing on final two runs, stopping quickly both times.

Longhouse Poet (Ire)

7 b g Yeats - Moscow Madame (Moscow Society)

Martin Brassil (Ire)   Sean & Bernardine Mulryan

PLACINGS: 1/121338/6231-   RPR **148+**c

Starts	1st	2nd	3rd	4th	Win & Pl
10	3	2	3	-	£46,320

12/20	Punc	3m1f Ch heavy	£6,250
12/19	Navn	2m4f Mdn Hdl soft	£7,188
5/19	Punc	2m2f NHF 5-7yo gd-yld	£8,324

Lord Du Mesnil: heading to victory at Haydock, where he has now scored three times

Missed second half of last season but had been a steady improver since being sent chasing, winning at the fourth attempt when stepped up beyond 3m for the first time; twice finished third in Grade I novice hurdles in 2019-20 but trainer sees his future in handicaps.

Lord Du Mesnil (Fr)

8 b g Saint Des Saints - Ladies Choice (Turgeon)

Richard Hobson   Paul Porter

PLACINGS: F3/642211122/4991P-U				RPR **159+**c

Starts	1st	2nd	3rd	4th	Win & Pl
34	4	6	6	4	£193,503

149	2/21	Hayd	3m4¹/₂f Cls1 Gd3 132-152 Ch Hcap soft £42,713
137	12/19	Hayd	3m4¹/₂f Cls2 132-140 Ch Hcap soft £16,314
127	12/19	Hayd	3m1¹/₂f Cls2 127-146 Ch Hcap heavy £31,280
122	11/19	Newc	2m7¹/₂f Cls3 Nov 118-129 Ch Hcap heavy £7,083

Dour stayer who has a particularly good record at Haydock and gained a third win there in last

season's Grand National Trial after finishing second in the race 12 months earlier; pulled up in the Grand National at Aintree, with good to soft ground reportedly too quick.

Lord Royal (Fr)

6 gr g Lord Du Sud - Tinoroyale (Karinga Bay)

Willie Mullins (Ire)   Paul Connell & Alan McGonnell

PLACINGS: 12/F527-				RPR **146+**c

Starts	1st	2nd	3rd	4th	Win & Pl
6	1	2	-	-	£14,096

1/20	Clon	2m4f Mdn Hdl heavy £5,509

Largely disappointing since runaway win on Irish debut in January 2020, failing to win again; sent off odds-on three times and even just 10-1 when seventh in last season's National Hunt Chase; big horse who could yet come good as a second-season novice as he strengthens up.

Lostintranslation (Ire)

9 b g Flemensfirth - Falika (Hero's Honor)

Colin Tizzard   Taylor & O'Dwyer

PLACINGS: 72/231221/11P3/3P5P-   RPR **155**c

Starts	1st	2nd	3rd	4th	Win & Pl
20	5	6	3	-	£372,621

11/19	Hayd	3m1½f Cls1 Gd1 Ch gd-sft	£112,540
11/19	Carl	2m4f Cls1 List Ch soft	£17,085
4/19	Aint	3m1f Cls1 Nov Gd1 Ch soft	£56,394
1/19	Chel	2m4½f Cls1 Nov Gd2 Ch gd-sft	£19,695
12/17	Newb	2m½f Cls3 Mdn Hdl soft	£6,498

Proved himself a top-class staying chaser two seasons ago, winning the Betfair Chase and finishing third in the Gold Cup; well below that level in all four runs last season, faring slightly better after wind surgery when fifth in the Denman Chase only to be pulled up in the Gold Cup.

M C Muldoon (Ire)

6 gr g Mastercraftsman - Alizaya (Highest Honor)

Willie Mullins (Ire)   Mrs Mullins, David Manasseh & Robert Brown

PLACINGS: 412-31   RPR **138**+h

Starts	1st	2nd	3rd	4th	Win & Pl
5	2	1	1	1	£24,808

7/21	Gway	2m4½f Nov Hdl good	£10,536
2/21	Fair	2m Mdn Hdl heavy	£6,321

Improved when stepped up in trip this summer, producing career-best efforts on the Flat and over hurdles; finished a short-head second in the Ascot Stakes before narrowly landing a second hurdles win at Galway; acts on any ground.

Magic Daze (Ire)

5 b m Doyen - Magic Maze (Gamut)

Henry de Bromhead (Ire)   Robcour

PLACINGS: 1312-4   RPR **137**+h

Starts	1st	2nd	3rd	4th	Win & Pl
4	1	1	1	1	£21,564

1/21	Clon	2m Mdn Hdl heavy	£5,268

Point-to-point winner who did well over hurdles last season despite tendency to race keenly in front; made all by nine lengths at Clonmel before doing really well to hang on for second in the Mares' Novices' Hurdle at the Cheltenham Festival; below par when fourth at Punchestown.

Magic Saint (Fr)

7 b g Saint Des Saints - Magic Poline (Trempolino)

Paul Nicholls   Mr & Mrs J D Cotton

PLACINGS: /2510F2/517/61445P2-   RPR **160**c

Starts	1st	2nd	3rd	4th	Win & Pl
22	7	3	1	2	£196,613

152	11/20	Chel	2m Cls2 128-152 Ch Hcap gd-sft	£22,522
147	11/19	Newb	2m½f Cls2 126-150 Ch Hcap gd-sft	£25,024
142	2/19	Winc	1m7½f Cls2 125-152 Ch Hcap good	£15,784
	3/18	Autl	2m2f Ch 4yo v soft	£22,088
	11/17	Autl	2m1½f Ch 3yo v soft	£21,744
	10/17	Autl	2m1½f Hdl 3yo v soft	£19,692
	9/17	Autl	2m2f Hdl 3yo heavy	£26,667

Claimed a second valuable 2m handicap chase when winning at Cheltenham in November; just came up short over higher marks subsequently, though did manage a good second in the Silver

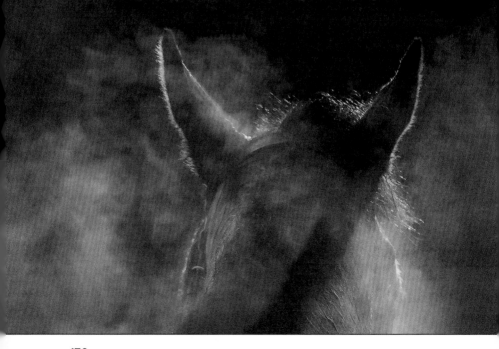

Trophy back at Cheltenham over 2m4f having struggled over that trip in previous years.

Malone Road (Ire)

7 b g Kalanisi - Zaffarella (Zaffaran)

Henry de Bromhead (Ire)   Cheveley Park Stud

PLACINGS: 1/11/13-				RPR **133+h**
Starts	1st	2nd	3rd	4th	Win & Pl
4			1	-	£20,742
	8/20	Kbgn	2m Mdn Hdl soft..£5,000
	11/18	Punc	2m NHF 4yo good..£6,269
	11/18	DRoy	2m¹/₂f NHF 4-7yo gd-yld..................................£8,177

Long held in high regard but has run just twice since two impressive bumper wins in late 2018, suffering another setback last season; had already had his bubble burst slightly when narrowly beaten at 2-5 in a novice hurdle at Listowel, jumping poorly.

Manofthemountain (Ire)

8 b g Mahler - Womanofthemountain (Presenting)

Emma Lavelle   Paul G Jacobs

PLACINGS: 3/742/11U1/14P21-				RPR **144+c**
Starts	1st	2nd	3rd	4th	Win & Pl
12	5	2	-	2	£54,301
137	4/21	Chel	2m4¹/₂f Cls1 Gd2 137-157 Ch Hcap good.......£21,527
130	9/20	Bang	3m Cls3 118-137 Ch Hcap good......................£7,018
120	12/19	Tntn	2m7f Cls4 Nov 94-120 Ch Hcap soft................£7,083
114	10/19	Sthl	3m Cls4 Nov 95-114 Ch Hcap good..................£4,604
110	8/19	NAbb	3m2f Cls4 Nov 87-110 Ch Hcap good...............£5,946

Won first four completed starts over fences and belatedly built on that last spring, returning to form with a second at Kempton before winning the Silver Trophy at Cheltenham; connections feel those trips of around 2m4f are key despite victories up to 3m2f.

Marown (Ire)

7 b g Milan - Rosie Suspect (Presenting)

Nicky Richards   Trevor Hemmings

PLACINGS: 1/11/312219-				RPR **144+c**
Starts	1st	2nd	3rd	4th	Win & Pl
9	5	2	1	-	£29,741
	3/21	Weth	3m Cls3 Nov Ch gd-sft.....................................£7,190
	12/20	Ayr	2m4¹/₂f Cls4 Nov Ch heavy..............................£4,289
	3/20	Ayr	2m4¹/₂f Cls4 Nov Ch soft.................................£4,159
	1/20	Ayr	2m4¹/₂f Cls5 Mdn Hdl soft...............................£3,184
	3/19	Newc	2m Cls5 NHF 4-6yo heavy................................£2,274

Held in high regard by connections and began to make his mark over fences last season, winning twice and finishing second twice; hacked up at Wetherby when stepped up to 3m for the first time but well beaten when favourite for a valuable novice handicap at Ayr on final run.

Master Tommytucker

10 b g Kayf Tara - No Need For Alarm (Romany Rye)

Paul Nicholls   A G Fear

PLACINGS: 11/F/1FF/2117126-				RPR **165c**
Starts	1st	2nd	3rd	4th	Win & Pl
13	6	2	-	-	£96,223
	1/21	Kemp	2m4¹/₂f Cls1 Gd2 Ch gd-sft............................£22,316
	11/20	Hayd	2m5¹/₂f Cls2 Ch soft......................................£25,371
	11/20	Hntg	2m4f Cls4 Ch good..£4,289
	11/19	Kemp	2m2f Cls4 Ch gd-sft...£4,809
	4/18	Extr	2m5¹/₂f Cls4 Nov Hdl soft................................£4,224
	2/18	Extr	2m2¹/₂f Cls4 Nov Hdl soft................................£4,549

Plagued by jumping problems through his career (fell in three of first four runs over fences spanning two seasons) but finally able to show his true colours last term, winning three times and finishing second in the Ascot Chase; struggled in toughest tests at Cheltenham and Aintree.

McFabulous (Ire)

7 b g Milan - Rossavon (Beneficial)

Paul Nicholls   Giraffa Racing

PLACINGS: 1711/2411/13128-				RPR **159+h**
Starts	1st	2nd	3rd	4th	Win & Pl
13	7	2	1	1	£131,856
	1/21	Kemp	2m5f Cls1 Gd2 Hdl soft...................................£17,085
	10/20	Chep	2m3¹/₂f Cls1 Nov Gd2 Hdl good.......................£17,085
132	3/20	Kemp	2m5f Cls1 Nov Gd3 123-134 Hdl 4-7yo Hcap gd-sft..£39,389
	2/20	MRas	2m4¹/₂f Cls3 Nov Hdl 4-7yo gd-sft....................£6,498
	4/19	Aint	2m1f Cls1 Gd2 NHF 4-6yo soft........................£25,322
	3/19	Newb	2m1¹/₂f Cls3 NHF 4-6yo gd-sft...........................£2,599
	10/18	Chep	2m Cls4 NHF 4-6yo gd-sft.................................£3,899

Long held in very high regard (sent off favourite for ten of last 12 races) and went some way to justifying that last season without fully delivering; won Grade 2s at Chepstow and Kempton but was beaten at odds-on in that grade at Fontwell and disappointed in the Aintree Hurdle; built to go chasing.

Melon

9 ch g Medicean - Night Teeny (Platini)

Willie Mullins (Ire)   Mrs J Donnelly

PLACINGS: F/442F/702142/335P-P				RPR **168c**
Starts	1st	2nd	3rd	4th	Win & Pl
23	3	6	3	3	£368,112
	12/19	Leop	2m1f Ch soft..£9,318
	11/17	DRoy	2m Gd2 Hdl soft..£25,214
	1/17	Leop	2m Mdn Hdl good..£6,833

Has won just once since 2017 yet has run several big races, notably when beaten a nose in the Marsh Novices' Chase in 2020 to finish second at a fourth successive Cheltenham Festival; just found out in open Grade 1 chases last season before losing his way when pulled up the last twice.

McFabulous: dual Grade 2 winner over hurdles is a promising recruit to the novice chase ranks this season

Messire Des Obeaux (Fr)

9 b g Saddler Maker - Madame Lys (Sheyrann)

Alan King   Simon Munir & Isaac Souede

PLACINGS: 5637/111233/4/114P-   RPR **159**+c

Starts	1st	2nd	3rd	4th	Win & Pl
15	5	1	3	2	£111,659

	1/21	Winc	2m4f Cls1 Nov Gd2 Ch gd-sft	£13,668
138	12/20	Winc	2m4f Cls3 Nov 122-138 Ch Hcap soft	£7,018
	12/16	Newb	2m4¹/₂f Cls1 Nov Gd1 Hdl gd-sft	£22,780
	12/16	Sand	2m4f Cls1 Nov Gd2 Hdl gd-sft	£17,085
128	11/16	Bang	2m3¹/₂f Cls2 122-135 Hdl Hcap gd-sft	£14,271

Enjoyed a fairytale renaissance last season having been nursed back to health after three years off the track; won a novice handicap chase at Wincanton (first victory since the 2016 Challow Hurdle) and followed up in the rearranged Dipper Chase, though disappointed on last two runs.

Metier (Ire)

5 b g Mastercraftsman - We'll Go Walking (Authorized)

Harry Fry   G C Stevens

PLACINGS: 1117-   RPR **150**+h

Starts	1st	2nd	3rd	4th	Win & Pl
4	3	-	-	-	£36,062

	1/21	Sand	2m Cls1 Nov Gd1 Hdl heavy	£19,933
	11/20	Asct	1m7¹/₂f Cls2 Hdl soft	£11,696
	10/20	NAbb	2m2¹/₂f Cls4 Nov Hdl heavy	£3,769

Won first three races over hurdles last season, including an authoritative 12-length victory in the Tolworth at Sandown; shortest-priced British contender for the Supreme Novices' Hurdle at Cheltenham only to trail home a distant seventh, possibly unsuited by drying ground.

Midnight River
6 ch g Midnight Legend - Well Connected (Presenting)

Dan Skelton · Frank McAleavy

PLACINGS: 33/12141F- · RPR **142+**h

Starts	1st	2nd	3rd	4th	Win & Pl
8	3	1	2	1	£25,579
	2/21	Asct	2m3¹/₂f Cls2 Nov Hdl soft		£10,989
	11/20	Leic	2m4¹/₂f Cls3 Nov Hdl soft		£5,913
	10/20	Uttx	2m4f Cls4 Mdn Hdl gd-sft		£3,769

Won three novice hurdles last season at around 2m4f, most notably at Ascot, though only fourth on sole completed start at Graded level; seen as a future stayer but fell three out when stepped up to 3m in a Grade 1 at Aintree (still in contention); likely to go novice chasing.

Midnight Shadow
8 b g Midnight Legend - Holy Smoke (Statoblest)

Sue Smith · Mrs Aafke Clarke

PLACINGS: 71/20110/3F2126/02P- · RPR **154**c

Starts	1st	2nd	3rd	4th	Win & Pl
24	6	8	1	-	£196,180
	1/20	Chel	2m4¹/₂f Cls1 Nov Gd2 Ch soft		£20,026
	1/19	Chel	2m4¹/₂f Cls1 Gd2 Hdl gd-sft		£28,135
141	12/18	Aint	2m4f Cls2 122-143 Hdl Hcap soft		£18,570
134	4/18	Ayr	2m Cls1 Gd2 134-154 Hdl Hcap good		£59,798
	10/17	Uttx	2m Cls4 Nov Hdl 4-6yo soft		£3,899
	12/16	Newc	1m6¹/₂f Cls6 NHF 3yo soft		£1,884

Very lightly raced last season and ran just once (disappointing over hurdles) after a fine second in the Caspian Caviar Gold Cup at Cheltenham (no match for easy winner but 12 lengths clear of rest); has gained last two wins at that track, including a Grade 2 novice chase in 2020.

Mighty Thunder
8 b g Malinas - Cool Island (Turtle Island)

Lucinda Russell · Allson Sparkle

PLACINGS: 5133/218142/9116121- · RPR **153**c

Starts	1st	2nd	3rd	4th	Win & Pl
26	8	5	4	1	£174,691
144	4/21	Ayr	4m Cls3 Gd3 129-155 Ch Hcap good		£84,405
129	2/21	Muss	4m1f Cls2 117-134 Ch Hcap soft		£19,028
	11/20	Hexm	3m Cls4 Nov Ch soft		£4,549
	10/20	Hexm	2m4f Cls4 Nov Ch soft		£4,394
120	12/19	Muss	3m Cls3 105-132 Hdl Hcap gd-sft		£6,888
115	9/19	Prth	3m Cls3 114-128 Hdl Hcap gd-sft		£9,487
	12/18	Kels	2m6¹/₂f Cls4 Mdn Hdl good		£4,224
	6/17	Prth	2m Cls5 NHF 4-6yo good		£2,599

Capped an outstanding first campaign over fences when running down Dingo Dollar close home in last season's Scottish National; had already won three times and particularly flourished when

sent over marathon trips, winning the Edinburgh National and finishing second in the Midlands National.

Milkwood (Ire)
7 b g Dylan Thomas - Tropical Lake (Lomond)

Neil Mulholland · Ms J Bridel

PLACINGS: 7/521/132/143031-2 · RPR **151**h

Starts	1st	2nd	3rd	4th	Win & Pl
14	4	3	3	1	£93,941
142	4/21	Ayr	2m Cls1 Gd2 130-146 Hdl Hcap good		£22,780
	10/20	Ffos	2m Cls4 Hdl gd-sft		£3,769
	10/19	Hrfd	2m Cls4 Mdn Hdl good		£4,159
	4/19	Font	1m5¹/₂f Cls5 NHF 4-6yo good		£2,274

Has done well in good 2m handicap hurdles over the last year, especially since the spring, winning the Scottish Champion Hurdle in between third in the County Hurdle at Cheltenham and second in the Galway Hurdle; most effective on good ground; likely to go novice chasing, though not bred for it.

Millers Bank
7 b g Passing Glance - It Doesn't Matter (Karinga Bay)

Alex Hales · Millers Bank Partnership

PLACINGS: 5/211/98113- · RPR **154**h

Starts	1st	2nd	3rd	4th	Win & Pl
9	4	2	1		£43,128
137	3/21	Newb	2m¹/₂f Cls3 122-140 Hdl Hcap good		£7,507
133	1/21	Kemp	2m Cls3 120-141 Hdl Hcap soft		£5,913
	12/19	MRas	2m¹/₂f Cls4 Nov Hdl gd-sft		£4,549
	11/19	Bang	2m¹/₂f Cls4 Nov Hdl heavy		£4,094

Hugely progressive in second half of last season, winning handicap hurdles at Kempton and Newbury (by ten lengths on second occasion) before a stunning 80-1 third behind Abacadabras when stepped up to 2m4f in the Aintree Hurdle; likely to go novice chasing.

Minella Drama (Ire)
6 b g Flemensfirth - Midsummer Drama (King's Theatre)

Donald McCain · Green Day Racing

PLACINGS: 22/211212- · RPR **144**h

Starts	1st	2nd	3rd	4th	Win & Pl
6	3	3			£39,791
	2/21	MRas	2m4¹/₂f Cls1 Nov List Hdl soft		£10,402
	12/20	Bang	2m¹/₂f Cls4 Nov Hdl heavy		£3,769
	11/20	Sedg	2m1f Cls4 Nov Hdl good		£3,769

Progressive and very useful novice hurdler last season; won three of last five races and twice finished second when stepped up in class,

Minella Drama: heading to success at Sedgefield last November – the first of three wins in novice hurdles

including behind My Drogo in a 2m4f Grade 1 at Aintree; likely to go novice chasing and could get 3m.

Minella Indo (Ire)

8 b g Beat Hollow - Carrigeen Lily (Supreme Leader)
Henry de Bromhead (Ire)   Barry Maloney

PLACINGS: 13/321/1212/11F41-   RPR **179+**c

Starts	1st	2nd	3rd	4th	Win & Pl
13	6	3	2	1	£498,038

3/21	Chel	3m2½f Cls1 Gd1 Ch gd-sft	£263,766
11/20	Navn	3m Gd2 Ch soft	£30,000
10/20	Wxfd	2m7f Gd3 Ch soft	£13,750
1/20	Navn	3m Ch sft-hvy	£7,262
5/19	Punc	3m Nov Gd1 Hdl yield	£53,153
3/19	Chel	3m Cls1 Nov Gd1 Hdl gd-sft	£73,506

Tremendous winner of last season's Cheltenham Gold Cup when beating A Plus Tard, extending fine festival record having come first and second previously; had fallen in the Savills Chase over Christmas before a disappointing fourth when favourite for the Irish Gold Cup.

Gold Cup ace: Minella Indo

Minella Melody (Ire)
7 b m Flemensfirth - Cottage Theatre (King's Theatre)
Henry de Bromhead (Ire)   Kenneth Alexander

PLACINGS: 112/31110/2227-2   RPR **148**h

Starts	1st	2nd	3rd	4th	Win & Pl
12	4	5	1	-	£101,578
	1/20	Fair	2m2f Nov Gd3 Hdl yield.............................		£17,000
	12/19	Punc	2m3¹/₂f Nov List Hdl soft............................		£14,617
	11/19	Cork	2m4f Mdn Hdl sft-hvy................................		£6,922
	3/19	Gowr	2m2f NHF 4-7yo soft.................................		£5,550

Perennial bridesmaid last season, finishing second in four Graded races, including twice behind Concertista; had been a prolific novice in 2019-20, winning first three races before losing unbeaten hurdle record at Cheltenham.

Minella Times (Ire)
8 b g Oscar - Triptoshan (Anshan)
Henry de Bromhead (Ire)   John P McManus

PLACINGS: 147283/9242120/1221-   RPR **158+**c

Starts	1st	2nd	3rd	4th	Win & Pl
18	4	6	1	3	£484,607
146	4/21	Aint	4m2¹/₂f Cls1 Gd3 145-167 Ch Hcap gd-sft.....		£375,000
130	9/20	List	2m6f 118-130 Ch Hcap soft........................		£10,500
122	12/19	Navn	2m4f 122-150 Ch Hcap soft........................		£26,577
	5/18	Kbgn	2m Mdn Hdl 4-5yo soft.............................		£6,289

Famous winner of last season's Grand National at Aintree when partnering Rachael Blackmore to a comfortable victory; had been progressive in other big handicaps, including when second in the Paddy Power Chase, but handicapper has now taken drastic action.

Miranda (Ire)
6 b m Camelot - Great Artist (Desert Prince)
Paul Nicholls   Owners Group

PLACINGS: 11P/813/1415-   RPR **145+**h

Starts	1st	2nd	3rd	4th	Win & Pl
10	5	-	1	1	£58,011
	1/21	Donc	2m¹/₂f Cls1 Gd2 Hdl soft............................		£19,933
136	12/20	Ludl	2m Cls2 119-138 Hdl Hcap gd-sft...............		£9,747
124	12/19	Kemp	2m Cls3 115-135 Hdl Hcap soft...................		£12,996
	3/19	Winc	1m7¹/₂f Cls4 Nov Hdl gd-sft........................		£4,224
	2/19	Ludl	2m Cls4 Hdl 4yo gd-sft.............................		£4,938

Useful dual-purpose mare who won twice last season, taking tally to five over hurdles in all, most notably in a Grade 2 mares' hurdle at Doncaster; struggled under top weight in the Imperial Cup at Sandown, finishing a well-beaten fifth.

Mister Coffey (Fr)
6 b g Authorized - Mamitador (Anabaa)
Nicky Henderson   Lady Bamford & Alice Bamford

PLACINGS: 1/12/1374-   RPR **142**h

Starts	1st	2nd	3rd	4th	Win & Pl
7	3	1	1	1	£25,782
128	11/20	Sand	2m Cls3 117-130 Hdl Hcap soft		£9,747
	12/19	Newb	2m¹/₂f Cls4 Hdl soft.................................		£4,484
	4/19	Hntg	2m Cls5 NHF 4-6yo good		£2,274

Ran well in top handicaps last season without quite living up to expectations after first-time-out

win; made the frame in good races at Sandown and Aintree (favourite both times) either side of finishing seventh in the Betfair Hurdle; still very lightly raced.

Mister Fisher (Ire)
7 b g Jeremy - That's Amazing (Marignan)
Nicky Henderson   James & Jean Potter

PLACINGS: 10/2118/72114/P1PU2-   RPR **168+**c

Starts	1st	2nd	3rd	4th	Win & Pl
16	3	3	-	1	£112,166
	12/20	Chel	2m4f Cls1 Gd2 Ch soft..............................		£21,356
	1/20	Chel	2m¹/₂f Cls1 Nov Gd2 Ch gd-sft...................		£19,933
	12/19	Chel	2m4¹/₂f Cls2 Nov Ch soft...........................		£15,698
	1/19	Hayd	1m7¹/₂f Cls1 Nov Gd2 Hdl gd-sft.................		£17,085
	12/18	Kemp	2m Cls2 Nov Hdl gd-sft.............................		£12,512
	3/18	Kemp	2m Cls5 Mdn NHF 4-6yo soft.......................		£3,119

Smart novice chaser in 2019-20 and stepped forward last season to win the rearranged Peterborough Chase at Cheltenham on soft ground; twice found out by his jumping in Grade 1 company in the spring but bounced back with a close second behind Frodon at Sandown.

Mister Fogpatches (Ire)
7 gr g Fairly Ransom - Jenniferjo (Witness Box)
Pat Fahy (Ire)   J B Fahy

PLACINGS: 25218577/232263543-1   RPR **137**c

Starts	1st	2nd	3rd	4th	Win & Pl
25	2	5	5	2	£65,724
128	5/21	Punc	3m7f 121-145 Ch Hcap gd-yld....................		£21,071
110	11/19	Navn	2m6f 95-125 Hdl Hcap soft........................		£8,785

Big improver when stepped up to marathon trips at end of last season, finishing third in the Scottish Grand National before winning over 3m7f at Punchestown; produced both those performances on good ground but won a big-field handicap hurdle on soft.

Mister Malarky
8 ch g Malinas - Priscilla (Teenoso)
Colin Tizzard   Wendy & Malcolm Hezel

PLACINGS: 131142/06P1P/6U173P-   RPR **161**c

Starts	1st	2nd	3rd	4th	Win & Pl
27	6	2	5	1	£174,166
150	12/20	Asct	3m Cls1 List 137-157 Ch Hcap heavy..............		£34,170
147	2/20	Kemp	3m Cls1 Gd3 133-159 Ch Hcap gd-sft.............		£56,950
	2/19	Asct	3m Cls1 Nov Gd2 Ch gd-sft		£22,780
130	1/19	Newb	2m7¹/₂f Cls3 120-130 Ch Hcap good..............		£7,343
126	11/18	Plum	2m3¹/₂f Cls3 Nov 126-136 Ch Hcap good		£7,522
	11/17	Kemp	2m Cls4 Nov Hdl 4-6yo gd-sft......................		£3,899

Inconsistent but capable staying chaser who has won valuable 3m handicaps in each of the last two seasons, most recently in the Silver Cup at Ascot on heavy ground (had been felt to want it quicker); has otherwise made the first five just twice since April 2019.

Molly Ollys Wishes

7 b m Black Sam Bellamy - September Moon (Bustino)

Dan Skelton   West Mercia Fork Trucks

PLACINGS: 34/P24212/371113-   RPR **152**+h

Starts		1st	2nd	3rd	4th	Win & Pl
14		4	3	3	2	£40,109
	2/21	Wwck	2m5f Cls1 List Hdl heavy			£9,441
130	12/20	Kemp	3m¹/₂f Cls2 120-135 Hdl Hcap soft			£10,010
124	11/20	Hrfd	2m3¹/₂f Cls3 106-124 Hdl Hcap soft			£5,913
	1/20	Wwck	2m5f Cls4 Nov Hdl soft			£4,549

Big improver last season, winning three races in a row on soft or heavy ground; completed the hat-trick by 15 lengths in a Listed mares' hurdle at Warwick and backed that up with a fine third against geldings in a Grade 2 at Fontwell behind Brewin'upastorm.

Monalee (Ire)

10 b g Milan - Tempest Belle (Glacial Storm)

Henry de Bromhead (Ire)   Barry Maloney

PLACINGS: 4/1F12F/3214/P324/3-   RPR **161**c

Starts		1st	2nd	3rd	4th	Win & Pl
21		5	7	3	3	£317,220
	2/19	Gowr	2m4f Gd2 Ch yld-sft			£31,892
	2/18	Leop	2m5f Nov Gd1 Ch soft			£52,212
	11/17	Punc	2m4f Ch sft-hvy			£7,371
	2/17	Clon	3m Nov Gd1 Hdl heavy			£19,712
	11/16	Punc	2m6f Mdn Hdl soft			£6,331

Has won just once outside novice company but took form to a new level when stepped back up in trip two seasons ago, finishing second behind Delta Work in the Savills Chase and fourth (beaten less than two lengths) in the Cheltenham Gold Cup; missed nearly all of last season through injury.

Monkfish (Ire)

7 ch g Stowaway - Martovic (Old Vic)

Willie Mullins (Ire)   Mrs S Ricci

PLACINGS: P/1/22111/1111-2   RPR **170**+c

Starts		1st	2nd	3rd	4th	Win & Pl
10		7				£295,324
	3/21	Chel	3m¹/₂f Cls1 Nov Gd1 Ch gd-sft			£75,164
	2/21	Leop	2m5¹/₂f Nov Gd1 Ch soft			£65,848
	12/20	Leop	3m Nov Gd1 Ch yield			£40,000
	11/20	Fair	2m5f Ch soft			£6,250
	3/20	Chel	3m Cls1 Nov Gd1 Hdl soft			£73,506
	1/20	Thur	2m6¹/₂f Nov Hdl yield			£7,262
	12/19	Fair	2m7f Mdn Hdl heavy			£5,857

Won last season's Brown Advisory Chase to make it back-to-back Cheltenham Festival victories, though not at his best to win at 1-4 in a weak renewal and beaten next time at Punchestown; had been imperious earlier in the season, notably in a 2m5f Grade 1 at Leopardstown; ruled out for season as guide went to press.

Monmiral (Fr)

4 bl g Saint Des Saints - Achere (Mont Basile)

Paul Nicholls   Sir A Ferguson G Mason J Hales & L Hales

PLACINGS: 1/1111-   RPR **151**+h

Starts		1st	2nd	3rd	4th	Win & Pl
5		5	-	-	-	£105,338
	4/21	Aint	2m1f Cls1 Gd1 Hdl 4yo gd-sft			£42,203
	2/21	Hayd	1m7¹/₂f Cls2 Hdl 4yo soft			£9,747
	12/20	Donc	2m1f Cls1 Gd2 Hdl 3yo gd-sft			£28,468
	11/20	Extr	2m1f Cls4 Hdl 3yo soft			£3,769
	3/20	Autl	1m7f Hdl 3yo heavy			£21,153

Unbeaten in five races over hurdles and completed a tremendous season when winning the Grade 1 juvenile hurdle at Aintree (had bypassed Cheltenham); looks a future chaser but trainer considering another season over hurdles first, potentially starting in the Fighting Fifth.

Monte Cristo (Fr)

5 b g Montmartre - Rylara Des Brosses (Rapid Man)

Nicky Henderson   Simon Munir & Isaac Souede

PLACINGS: 662141/8109-   RPR **148**+h

Starts		1st	2nd	3rd	4th	Win & Pl
10		3	1	-	1	£41,437
133	12/20	Kemp	2m5f Cls3 116-138 Hdl Hcap gd-sft			£9,747
	2/20	Newb	2m¹/₂f Cls4 Hdl 4yo soft			£3,769
	10/19	Autl	2m2f Hdl 3yo Hcap v soft			£21,892

Patchy profile but won a 2m5f handicap hurdle at Kempton last season to serve a reminder of formerly sky-high reputation (had been sent off odds-on in a Grade 2 at Cheltenham on British debut); disappointed at Cheltenham and Aintree in the spring; likely to go novice chasing.

Moonlighter

8 b g Midnight Legend - Countess Camilla (Bob's Return)

Nick Williams   Huw & Richard Davies & Friends Racing

PLACINGS: 6/31F7/U2U142/2F51P-   RPR **151**+c

Starts		1st	2nd	3rd	4th	Win & Pl
17		4	3	1	1	£48,020
144	2/21	Sand	1m7¹/₂f Cls2 132-158 Ch Hcap heavy			£11,886
137	1/20	Newb	2m¹/₂f Cls3 Nov 131-140 Ch Hcap heavy			£7,343
	11/18	Asct	2m3¹/₂f Cls3 Mdn Hdl good			£6,758
	12/17	Bang	2m1¹/₂f Cls6 NHF 4-6yo soft			£2,053

Ran well in a couple of good handicap chases at around 2m last season, beating Dolos at Sandown after running Greaneteen to a neck in the Haldon Gold Cup at Exeter; pulled up in the Grand Annual at Cheltenham after racing prominently to three out.

Mount Ida (Ire)
7 b m Yeats - Jolivia (Dernier Empereur)

Gordon Elliott (Ire)   Ktda Racing

PLACINGS: 4121/1230/31213-   RPR **160+**c

Starts	1st	2nd	3rd	4th	Win & Pl
11	4	3	3	-	£82,909

142	3/21	Chel	3m2f Cls2 132-142 Ch Hcap gd-sft	£32,498
	12/20	Cork	2m¹/₂f Nov Gd3 Ch sft-hvy	£17,500
	10/19	Gway	2m Mdn Hdl soft	£7,454
	4/19	Wxfd	2m NHF 4-7yo yield	£6,105

Expertly laid out for last season's Kim Muir at Cheltenham, justifying strong favouritism in remarkable fashion (had been all but tailed off early) when stepped sharply up in trip for the first time; well below that level otherwise, including when only third at Fairyhouse on final run.

Mr Incredible (Ire)
5 b g Westerner - Bartlemy Bell (Kalanisi)

Henry de Bromhead (Ire)   Stephen E McCarthy

PLACINGS: 221-   RPR **139+**h

Starts	1st	2nd	3rd	4th	Win & Pl
2	1	1	-	-	£9,833

	1/21	Naas	2m3f Mdn Hdl heavy	£7,902

Big chasing type who was quietly campaigned over hurdles last season, easily winning a maiden after finishing second behind subsequent Grade 1 winner Gaillard Du Mesnil; should come into his own over fences.

Mrs Milner (Ire)
6 b m Flemensfirth - Thegirlonthehill (Oscar)

Paul Nolan (Ire)   Softco

PLACINGS: 5/51702/1324F1-   RPR **145+**h

Starts	1st	2nd	3rd	4th	Win & Pl
12	3	2	1	1	£74,902

134	3/21	Chel	3m Cls1 Gd3 126-151 Hdl Hcap gd-sft	£42,203
116	7/20	Gway	2m¹/₂f 99-125 Hdl Hcap good	£15,000
	11/19	Thur	2m Mdn Hdl yld-sft	£5,857

Impressive five-length winner of last season's Pertemps Final at Cheltenham; had been unexposed at staying trips, losing by a neck over course and distance among just two previous runs over 3m; suffered a setback when set to step up to Grade 1 level at Punchestown.

My Drogo
6 b g Milan - My Petra (Midnight Legend)

Dan Skelton   Mr & Mrs R Kelvin-Hughes

PLACINGS: 21111-   RPR **156+**h

Starts	1st	2nd	3rd	4th	Win & Pl
5	4	1	-	-	£88,408

	4/21	Aint	2m4f Cls1 Nov Gd1 Hdl gd-sft	£42,239
	3/21	Kels	2m2f Cls1 Nov Gd2 Hdl gd-sft	£22,780
	12/20	Asct	1m7¹/₂f Cls1 Nov Gd2 Hdl good	£14,305
	11/20	Newb	2m¹/₂f Cls3 Mdn Hdl good	£6,498

Last season's leading novice hurdler in Britain, making it four wins out of four over timber with a runaway victory in a 2m4f Grade 1 at Aintree;

had purposely missed Cheltenham, instead targeting a second Grade 2 win at Kelso (form worked out well), to prioritise future chasing career.

Native River (Ire)
11 ch g Indian River - Native Mo (Be My Native)

Colin Tizzard   Brocade Racing

PLACINGS: 1113/11/234/11/3143-   RPR **174**c

Starts	1st	2nd	3rd	4th	Win & Pl
30	14	3	8	2	£1,085,003

	2/21	Sand	3m Cls1 Gd2 Ch heavy	£28,268
	2/20	Newb	2m7¹/₂f Cls1 Gd2 Ch good	£28,475
	12/19	Aint	3m1f Cls1 Gd2 Ch gd-sft	£34,822
	3/18	Chel	3m2¹/₂f Cls1 Gd1 Ch soft	£369,822
	2/18	Newb	2m7¹/₂f Cls1 Gd2 Ch soft	£28,475
	2/17	Newb	2m7¹/₂f Cls1 Gd2 Ch soft	£28,475
155	12/16	Chep	3m5¹/₂f Cls1 Gd3 139-155 Ch Hcap soft	£85,425
155	11/16	Newb	3m2f Cls1 Gd3 140-166 Ch Hcap gd-sft	£113,900
	4/16	Aint	3m1f Cls1 Nov Gd1 Ch gd-sft	£56,319
	11/15	Newb	2m7¹/₂f Cls1 Nov Gd2 Ch gd-sft	£20,284
	11/15	Extr	3m Cls2 Nov Ch soft	£12,974
	2/15	Extr	2m1f Cls1 Nov List Hdl gd-sft	£11,390
	11/14	Newc	2m6f Cls2 Nov Hdl soft	£11,261
	10/14	Strf	2m6f Cls5 Mdn Hdl good	£2,599

Bold front-running chaser who enjoyed his finest hour when winning the Gold Cup in 2018; lightly raced since then but showed he retains plenty of ability last term, winning a third Grade 2 across the last two seasons in the Cotswold Chase (moved to Sandown) and finishing fourth in the Gold Cup.

Natural History
6 b g Nathaniel - Film Script (Unfuwain)

Gary Moore   Hail Sargent Evans

PLACINGS: 22162-   RPR **135+**h

Starts	1st	2nd	3rd	4th	Win & Pl
5	1	3	-	-	£11,311

116	3/21	Plum	2m Cls3 111-121 Hdl Hcap good	£6,173

Smart Flat horse who qualified for a very low opening handicap mark over hurdles last season by comparison and duly hacked up at Plumpton; finished a poor sixth when favourite for the Imperial Cup next time and beaten at 2-7 on final run, albeit hindered by final-flight error.

Navajo Pass
5 b g Nathaniel - Navajo Charm (Authorized)

Donald McCain   T G Leslie

PLACINGS: 1214/57512-   RPR **157**h

Starts	1st	2nd	3rd	4th	Win & Pl
9	4	2	1	1	£83,692

	1/21	Hayd	1m7¹/₂f Cls1 Gd2 Hdl heavy	£26,909
142	1/21	Muss	2m4f Cls3 116-142 Hdl Hcap soft	£8,837
	12/19	Donc	2m¹/₂f Cls1 Gd2 Hdl 3yo good	£28,135
	11/19	Bang	2m¹/₂f Cls4 Mdn Hdl 3yo heavy	£4,094

Did well last season, running away with a 2m4f handicap hurdle at Musselburgh before dropping back in trip to land the Champion Hurdle Trial at Haydock; had a big fitness edge over main rival Buveur D'Air in a three-runner race that day and subsequent handicap rise might flatter him.

Next Destination (Ire)

9 b g Dubai Destination - Liss Alainn (Flemensfirth)

Paul Nicholls   Malcolm C Denmark

PLACINGS: 1/142/11131/2112-   RPR **156**c

Starts	1st	2nd	3rd	4th	Win & Pl
12	7	3	1	1	£209,886

1/21	Wwck	3m Cls1 Nov Gd2 Ch soft	£13,668
11/20	Newb	2m7¹/₂f Cls1 Nov Gd2 Ch good	£17,085
4/18	Punc	3m Nov Gd1 Hdl yield	£52,212
1/18	Naas	2m4f Nov Gd1 Hdl sft-hvy	£46,991
12/17	Navn	2m4f Nov Gd2 Hdl heavy	£21,432
11/17	Naas	2m3f Mdn Hdl sft-hvy	£6,844
1/17	Fair	2m NHF 5-7yo soft	£4,070

Did brilliantly last season after more than two and a half years off the track; won his first two races over fences, both at Grade 2 level, before running another huge race when second in the National Hunt Chase at Cheltenham; won on good ground last season but felt to prefer softer.

No Ordinary Joe (Ire)

5 b g Getaway - Shadow Dearg (Beneficial)

Nicky Henderson   John P McManus

PLACINGS: 14-11   RPR **132**h

Starts	1st	2nd	3rd	4th	Win & Pl
4	2	-	-	1	£10,965

5/21	Worc	2m4f Cls4 Nov Hdl gd-sft	£3,159
5/21	Sthl	2m4¹/₂f Cls4 Nov Hdl good	£3,159
11/20	Sand	2m Cls4 NHF 4-6yo soft	£3,249

Impressive Sandown bumper winner who was thrown in at the deep end on hurdling debut last season (fourth in a Grade 2 at Ascot) and benefited from that experience when next seen in May, winning at odds-on at Southwell and Worcester; could take high rank among novice hurdlers.

Not So Sleepy

9 ch g Beat Hollow - Papillon De Bronze (Marju)

Hughie Morrison   Lady Blyth

PLACINGS: 415/110P/U157-   RPR **159**h

Starts	1st	2nd	3rd	4th	Win & Pl
11	4	-	-	1	£176,287

12/20	Asct	1m7¹/₂f Cls1 Gd3 128-148 Hdl Hcap heavy	£56,950
12/19	Asct	1m7¹/₂f Cls1 Gd3 127-150 Hdl Hcap heavy	£85,425
11/19	Asct	1m7¹/₂f Cls2 122-143 Hdl Hcap soft	£18,768
2/19	Winc	1m7¹/₂f Cls4 Nov Hdl good	£4,224

Has won the last two runnings of the valuable Betfair Exchange Trophy at Ascot, both times making all on heavy ground and in impressive fashion last season off a 15lb higher mark; unable to dominate at Cheltenham or Aintree but still ran well to be fifth in the Champion Hurdle.

Notachance (Ire)

7 b g Mahler - Ballybrowney Hall (Saddlers' Hall)

Alan King   David J S Sewell & Tim Leadbeater

PLACINGS: 2/23351/2152/11PP-   RPR **152**+c

Starts	1st	2nd	3rd	4th	Win & Pl
13	4	3	2	-	£67,504

139	1/21	Wwck	3m5f Cls1 Gd3 134-160 Ch Hcap soft	£28,475
132	11/20	Bang	3m Cls2 124-149 Ch Hcap soft	£11,617
121	11/19	Extr	3m Cls3 Nov 121-134 Ch Hcap soft	£16,245
115	3/19	Newb	3m Cls4 100-116 Hdl Hcap gd-sft	£4,549

Big improver in first half of last season, following up reappearance win at Bangor by landing the Classic Chase at Warwick; pulled up subsequently in the Grand National Trial at Haydock and the Scottish Grand National but found to be lame both times.

Notebook (Ger)

8 b g Samum - Nova (Winged Love)

Henry de Bromhead (Ire)   Gigginstown House Stud

PLACINGS: 122120/211116/12377-   RPR **169**+c

Starts	1st	2nd	3rd	4th	Win & Pl
16	6	5	1	-	£245,266

11/20	Naas	2m Gd2 Ch sft-hvy	£30,000
2/20	Leop	2m1f Nov Gd1 Ch yield	£75,000
12/19	Leop	2m1f Nov Gd1 Ch yield	£53,153
11/19	Punc	2m Nov Gd2 Ch soft	£23,653
10/19	Punc	2m Ch gd-yld	£7,720
1/19	Tram	2m Mdn Hdl soft	£6,659

Dual Grade 1 winner as a novice chaser in 2019-20 but just found wanting in open company last season; best run in four efforts at the top level when second to Chacun Pour Soi over Christmas but regressed in three subsequent runs, including when seventh in the Champion Chase.

Nube Negra (Spa)

7 br g Dink - Manly Dream (Highest Honor)

Dan Skelton   T Spraggett

PLACINGS: 12135/8B36/1122/12-3   RPR **168**c

Starts	1st	2nd	3rd	4th	Win & Pl
16	5	4	3	-	£189,751

12/20	Kemp	2m Cls1 Gd2 Ch soft	£46,364
10/19	Fknm	2m Cls3 Nov Ch good	£8,058
10/19	Wwck	2m Cls4 Ch good	£5,198
1/18	Donc	2m¹/₂f Cls4 Nov Hdl good	£4,094
11/17	MRas	2m7¹/₂f Cls4 Hdl 3yo gd-sft	£3,899

Big improver last season, developing into one of the top 2m chasers in Britain; sprang a 20-1 surprise when beating Altior first time out at Kempton and backed that up with an unlucky half-length second in the Champion Chase; disappointed on final run at Punchestown.

Nuts Well

10 b g Dylan Thomas - Renada (Sinndar)

Ann Hamilton   Ian Hamilton

PLACINGS: 62F446/5441113/1126-				RPR **160** +c

Starts	1st	2nd	3rd	4th	Win & Pl
40	11	9	3	7	£221,928

155	10/20	Aint	2m4f Cls1 Gd2 138-155 Ch Hcap soft	£36,013
152	10/20	Kels	2m1f Cls2 135-157 Ch Hcap gd-sft	£15,698
146	2/20	Weth	2m3¹/₂f Cls2 123-148 Ch Hcap soft	£11,574
140	1/20	Muss	2m4¹/₂f Cls2 114-140 Ch Hcap gd-sft	£18,768
130	12/19	Weth	1m7f Cls3 118-140 Ch Hcap soft	£7,538
136	10/18	Kels	2m1f Cls2 132-158 Ch Hcap good	£24,760
	11/17	Carl	2m Cls2 Ch soft	£12,820
131	4/17	Newc	2m Cls3 118-131 Hdl Hcap good	£5,393
129	4/16	Newc	2m Cls3 120-136 Hdl Hcap soft	£7,148
122	3/16	Newc	2m Cls3 115-130 Hdl Hcap heavy	£9,747
	11/15	Hexm	2m Cls5 Mdn Hdl gd-sft	£3,080

Hugely progressive during the last two seasons, making it five wins in six races when landing last year's Old Roan Chase at Aintree; ran another big race when second in the Melling Chase (unlucky in running) but outpaced back at 2m in the Celebration Chase.

O'Toole (Ire)

5 ch g Mahler - On Galley Head (Zaffaran)

Stuart Crawford (Ire)   Simon Munir & Isaac Souede

PLACINGS: 1-2				RPR **131**b

Starts	1st	2nd	3rd	4th	Win & Pl
2	1	1	-	-	£22,232

	2/21	Fair	2m NHF 5-7yo soft	£5,268

Outperformed market expectations in two bumper runs last season; made a winning debut at 25-1 at Fairyhouse and proved that was no fluke with a 33-1 second behind Kilcruit at Punchestown, staying on well; good prospect for novice hurdles.

One For Rosie

8 gr g Getaway - Whisky Rose (Old Vic)

Kim Bailey   A Bottle On Ice For Rosie

PLACINGS: 1/13123/6/11-				RPR **156** +c

Starts	1st	2nd	3rd	4th	Win & Pl
9	5	1	2	-	£49,638

	3/21	Carl	2m Cls3 Nov Ch soft	£7,018
	2/21	Leic	2m Cls3 Nov Ch heavy	£7,018
	2/19	Wwck	2m3f Cls4 Nov Hdl 4-7yo good	£4,419
	11/18	Carl	2m4f Cls4 Nov Hdl good	£4,549
	10/17	Bang	2m¹/₂f Cls6 NHF 4-6yo good	£1,949

Looked an exciting young chaser when winning both races last season on return from a long absence, albeit in ordinary company at Leicester and Carlisle; had previously been a useful novice hurdler three seasons ago (second in the EBF Final and third in a Grade 1 at Aintree).

One More Fleurie (Ire)

7 b g Mustameet - Auburn Cherry (Treasure Hunter)

Ian Williams   K McKenna

PLACINGS: 452/52358/F05611F11-				RPR **144** +c

Starts	1st	2nd	3rd	4th	Win & Pl
17	4	2	1	1	£41,964

128	4/21	Ayr	3m Cls2 Nov 125-142 Ch Hcap good	£26,015
122	4/21	Wwck	3m Cls4 Nov 100-122 Ch Hcap good	£3,594
112	3/21	Donc	3m Cls4 Nov 105-120 Ch Hcap good	£4,289
105	2/21	Wwck	2m4f Cls5 Nov 79-107 Ch Hcap soft	£2,989

Massive improver since being sent chasing at the turn of the year, winning last four completed starts over fences; began winning run off just 105 at Warwick and ended by easily landing a valuable novice handicap at Ayr to earn another 10lb rise to 138.

Oscar Elite (Ire)

6 b g Oscar - Lady Elite (Lord Americo)

Colin Tizzard   Mrs Mary-Ann Middleton

PLACINGS: 581/119323-				RPR **142**h

Starts	1st	2nd	3rd	4th	Win & Pl
6	2	1	2		£38,074

	12/20	Chep	2m7¹/₂f Cls4 Nov Hdl heavy	£3,769
	11/20	Chep	2m3¹/₂f Cls4 Mdn Hdl heavy	£3,769

Very useful staying novice hurdler last season, finishing second in the Albert Bartlett at Cheltenham; had suffered a mid-season blip (stable out of form) after first two runs but backed up festival run with another solid third at Aintree; likely to go novice chasing.

Paisley Park (Ire)

9 b g Oscar - Presenting Shares (Presenting)

Emma Lavelle   Andrew Gemmell

PLACINGS: 1220/11111/117/213P-				RPR **164** +h

Starts	1st	2nd	3rd	4th	Win & Pl
17	9	4	1	-	£507,991

	12/20	Asct	3m¹/₂f Cls1 Gd1 Hdl heavy	£45,560
	1/20	Chel	3m Cls1 Gd2 Hdl soft	£33,762
	11/19	Newb	3m Cls1 Gd2 Hdl gd-sft	£28,810
	3/19	Chel	3m Cls1 Gd1 Hdl gd-sft	£182,878
	1/19	Chel	3m Cls1 Gd2 Hdl soft	£33,762
	12/18	Asct	3m¹/₂f Cls1 Gd1 Hdl soft	£56,950
147	11/18	Hayd	3m¹/₂f Cls1 Gd3 125-147 Hdl Hcap good	£56,950
140	10/18	Aint	2m4f Cls2 116-140 Hdl Hcap good	£17,204
	12/17	Hrfd	2m3¹/₂f Cls4 Nov Hdl good	£4,549

Brilliant staying hurdler who won seven races in a row including the 2019 Stayers' Hurdle before suffering heart issues in that race the following year; not far off his best last season, winning the Long Walk and finishing third in the Stayers' Hurdle, though pulled up on final run at Aintree.

Pay The Piper (Ire)

6 b g Court Cave - Regal Holly (Gildoran)

Ann Hamilton — Ian Hamilton

PLACINGS: 223/U311112- — RPR **142+**h

Starts	1st	2nd	3rd	4th	Win & Pl
4	3	1	-	-	£15,187
129	3/21	Weth	2m Cls3 113-137 Hdl Hcap gd-sft		£5,913
	2/21	Carl	2m1f Cls4 Nov Hdl heavy		£3,769
	12/20	Sedg	2m1f Cls4 Mdn Hdl soft		£3,769

Beaten only once in four races over hurdles last season and emerged with plenty of credit even when losing unbeaten record at Newcastle, going down by a neck under top weight after late jumping errors; point-to-point winner and now likely to go novice chasing.

Pencilfulloflead (Ire)

7 b g Shantou - Quaspia (Fragrant Mix)

Gordon Elliott (Ire) — Robcour

PLACINGS: 14214/1123- — RPR **159+**c

Starts	1st	2nd	3rd	4th	Win & Pl
9	4	2	1	2	£59,395
	11/20	Punc	2m6½f Nov Gd2 Ch heavy		£17,500
	10/20	Gway	2m6½f Ch soft		£7,750
	2/20	Punc	2m6f Mdn Hdl heavy		£6,750
	11/19	DRoy	2m½f NHF 4-7yo soft		£7,986

Smart novice chaser last season; impressed in a Grade 2 win over Latest Exhibition at Punchestown and was beaten just half a length by Colreevy in a Grade 1 at Limerick; didn't jump well enough when third (sent off favourite) at Naas on first run over 3m.

Politologue: 2020 Champion Chase winner highly likely to continue proving a force at the top level

Pentland Hills (Ire)

6 b g Motivator - Elle Galante (Galileo)

Nicky Henderson — Owners Group

PLACINGS: 111/529/ — RPR **157**h

Starts	1st	2nd	3rd	4th	Win & Pl
6	3	1	-	-	£150,337
	4/19	Aint	2m1f Cls1 Gd1 Hdl 4yo gd-sft		£56,155
	3/19	Chel	2m1f Cls1 Gd1 Hdl 4yo gd-sft		£70,338
	2/19	Plum	2m Cls4 Mdn Hdl good		£4,094

Top-class juvenile hurdler three seasons ago, winning the Triumph Hurdle and following up at Aintree; slightly disappointing during the following season, still looking a work in progress, and hasn't run since finishing only ninth in the 2020 Champion Hurdle.

Petit Mouchoir (Fr)

10 gr g Al Namix - Arnette (Denham Red)

Gordon Elliott (Ire) — Bective Stud

PLACINGS: 6304/442235/233522F- — RPR **161**h

Starts	1st	2nd	3rd	4th	Win & Pl
34	5	9	8	5	£457,222
	10/17	Punc	2m Ch yld-sft		£7,634
	1/17	Leop	2m Gd1 Hdl good		£55,470
	12/16	Leop	2m Gd1 Hdl yield		£43,382
	11/15	Thur	2m Mdn Hdl 4yo soft		£5,349
	4/15	Punc	2m NHF 4-5yo gd-yld		£45,736

Dual Grade 1 winner five seasons ago and

remains highly capable despite failing to win since 2017; has finished second or third in four Grade 1 hurdles across the last two seasons and run well in top handicaps, notably when second in the County Hurdle in March.

Pic D'Orhy (Fr)

6 b g Turgeon - Rose Candy (Roli Abi)

Paul Nicholls   Mrs Johnny De La Hey

PLACINGS: 11/21U220/F61/2F424-   RPR **154+h**

Starts	1st	2nd	3rd	4th	Win & Pl
16	4	5	-	2	£271,475

146	2/20	Newb	2m¹/₂f Cls1 Gd3 130-153 Hdl Hcap good.........£87,219
	9/18	Autl	2m2f Hdl 3yo v soft £25,487
	4/18	Autl	1m7f Hdl 3yo v soft £23,363
	3/18	Autl	1m7f Hdl 3yo heavy £22,088

Won the Betfair Hurdle in 2020 but failed to live up to high expectations as a novice chaser last season; had wind surgery after a tame fourth at Ascot and did better back over hurdles at Taunton, finishing a head second under top weight, though well beaten at Sandown on final run.

Pistol Whipped (Ire)

7 b g Beneficial - Holiday Time (Turtle Island)

Nicky Henderson   A Speelman & M Speelman

PLACINGS: S231P/1F50/2011-2   RPR **160c**

Starts	1st	2nd	3rd	4th	Win & Pl
12	4	2	1	-	£48,560

144	4/21	Prth	2m4f Cls2 118-144 Ch Hcap good £10,556
137	4/21	Plum	2m3¹/₂f Cls2 120-147 Ch Hcap good...........£10,406
128	12/19	Leic	2m6¹/₂f Cls3 Nov 122-135 Ch Hcap gd-sft £8,058
	2/19	Fknm	2m4f Cls3 Nov Hdl 4-7yo good.......................£8,058

Progressive chaser who thrived last spring, winning handicaps at Plumpton and Perth before a fine effort when a nose second behind subsequent Summer Plate winner Francky Du Berlais under top weight in an 18-runner race at Uttoxeter; best on good ground.

Politologue (Fr)

10 gr g Poliglote - Scarlet Row (Turgeon)

Paul Nicholls   J Hales

PLACINGS: 11241/14422/251/124-   RPR **173+c**

Starts	1st	2nd	3rd	4th	Win & Pl
29	12	8	-	5	£999,373

	12/20	Sand	1m7¹/₂f Cls1 Gd1 Ch soft £68,340
	3/20	Chel	2m Cls1 Gd1 Ch soft.................................£225,080
	11/18	Asct	2m5f Cls1 Gd2 Ch gd-sft...........................£39,865
	4/18	Aint	2m4f Cls1 Gd1 Ch soft £140,985
	12/17	Kemp	2m Cls1 Gd2 Ch soft..................................£52,854
	12/17	Kemp	1m7¹/₂f Cls1 Gd2 Ch soft £85,827
154	11/17	Extr	2m1¹/₂f Cls1 Gd2 142-162 Ch Hcap soft £37,192
	2/17	Kemp	2m4¹/₂f Cls2 Ch gd-sft £12,512
	12/16	Asct	2m5f Cls1 Nov Gd2 Ch gd-sft.....................£18,224
	11/16	Hayd	2m5¹/₂f Cls2 Nov Ch soft.............................£16,245
	2/16	Extr	2m1f Cls1 Nov List Hdl heavy £11,524
	6/15	Autl	2m2f Hdl 4yo soft £17,860

Four-time Grade 1 winner over fences, adding a second Tingle Creek last season to his 2020 Champion Chase crown; missed his Cheltenham defence with a last-minute setback and broke

blood vessels when fourth in the Melling Chase; had won that race in 2019 but seems most effective back at 2m.

Porlock Bay (Fr)

10 b g Kayf Tara - Exolthir (Muhtathir)

Will Biddick   John Studd

PLACINGS: 2431/21/4122/21/121-   RPR **147+c**

Starts	1st	2nd	3rd	4th	Win & Pl
19	6	7	1	3	£187,772

	3/21	Chel	3m2¹/₂f Cls2 Am Hunt Ch gd-sft £21,114
	6/19	Nant	2m3¹/₂f Hdl soft...£12,973
	9/18	Nant	2m3¹/₂f Hdl v soft...£12,743
	6/17	Claf	2m2f Hdl v soft..£19,692
	12/15	Pau	2m1¹/₂f Hdl 4yo soft £33,140
	3/15	Mars	2m1¹/₂f Hdl 4yo gd-sft £7,814

Bought from France to go hunter chasing last season and won in thrilling fashion at the Cheltenham Festival, edging out Billaway by a short head; stamina barely lasted home having run only once beyond 2m4f previously when a close second on British rules debut at Wincanton.

Port Of Mars (Ire)

7 b g Westerner - Sarahall (Saddlers' Hall)

Olly Murphy   Bective Stud

PLACINGS: 1/213/321P-   RPR **149+c**

Starts	1st	2nd	3rd	4th	Win & Pl
7	2	2	2	-	£14,827

	1/21	Hrfd	3m1f Cls4 Ch good £4,289
	1/20	Chep	2m7¹/₂f Cls4 Mdn Hdl heavy £3,769

Pulled up on final run last season but had been quietly progressive in novice chases prior to that; won at the third attempt at Hereford when relishing step up to 3m (had also gained sole win over hurdles around that trip); yet to run on ground quicker than soft.

Potterman

8 b g Sulamani - Polly Potter (Kayf Tara)

Alan King   James & Jean Potter

PLACINGS: 52/1131125/02122U1-P   RPR **150c**

Starts	1st	2nd	3rd	4th	Win & Pl
25	9	6	3	1	£138,798

147	4/21	Sand	3m5f Cls1 Gd3 124-150 Ch Hcap good £64,711
137	8/20	MRas	3m Cls2 120-144 Ch Hcap good £9,747
	9/19	Strf	2m3¹/₂f Cls4 Nov Ch good............................£4,809
	8/19	Worc	2m7f Cls4 Nov Ch good...............................£4,289
	6/19	Worc	2m4f Cls3 Nov Ch good...............................£7,343
126	5/19	Wwck	2m3f Cls3 117-140 Hdl Hcap good £6,498
	6/18	Bang	2m3¹/₂f Cls4 Nov Hdl good £5,296
	5/18	Hntg	2m4¹/₂f Cls5 Mdn Hdl good £3,249
	5/17	Hntg	2m Cls6 NHF 4-6yo good £1,819

Controversial winner of last season's bet365 Gold Cup at Sandown having been only third past the post; perhaps deserved good fortune after a short-head second in the Badger Beers Trophy on previous run, two races punctuated by normal winter break (kept away from soft ground).

RACING POST

Proschema (Ire)

6 ch g Declaration Of War - Notable (Zafonic)

Dan Skelton — Empire State Racing Partnership

PLACINGS: 314/2P51-1 — RPR **142+h**

Starts		1st	2nd	3rd	4th	Win & Pl
8		3	1	1	1	£25,543
140	5/21	Aint	2m4f Cls2 119-141 Hdl Hcap good			£8,169
129	4/21	Chel	2m4¹/₂f Cls2 114-140 Hdl Hcap good			£8,195
	2/21	Newc	2m¹/₂f Cls4 NHF std-slw			£4,549
	1/21	Newc	2m¹/₂f Cls4 NHF std-slw			£4,679
	11/19	Weth	2m Cls3 Nov Hdl soft			£6,173

Smart Flat horse who proved a slow learner over hurdles but flourished during the spring, winning handicaps at Cheltenham and Aintree to add to all-weather bumper successes; looked a strong stayer when stepped up to 2m4f and should get further.

Protektorat (Fr)

6 b g Saint Des Saints - Protektion (Protektor)

Dan Skelton — Sir A Ferguson, G Mason, J Hales & L Hales

PLACINGS: 2U57/22130/11221- — RPR **160+c**

Starts		1st	2nd	3rd	4th	Win & Pl
14		4	5	1	-	£115,783
	4/21	Aint	2m4f Cls1 Nov Gd1 Ch gd-sft			£42,285
	11/20	Chel	2m4f Cls2 Nov Ch gd-sft			£12,820
	10/20	Carl	2m Cls3 Ch good			£7,018
	1/20	Chel	2m4¹/₂f Cls1 Nov List Hdl soft			£14,238

Impressive winner of the 2m4f Grade 1 novice chase at Aintree last season, undergoing a remarkable transformation after successive defeats at 1-2 (had wind surgery in between); had also looked very smart when winning at Cheltenham earlier in the season.

Put The Kettle On (Ire)

7 b m Stowaway - Name For Fame (Quest For Fame)

Henry de Bromhead (Ire) — One For Luck Racing Syndicate

PLACINGS: 52153/31111211/1314- — RPR **162c**

Starts		1st	2nd	3rd	4th	Win & Pl
17		9	2	3	1	£401,511
	3/21	Chel	2m Cls1 Gd1 Ch gd-sft			£168,810
	11/20	Chel	2m Cls1 Gd2 Ch soft			£35,236
	3/20	Chel	2m Cls1 Nov Gd1 Ch soft			£98,764
	11/19	Chel	2m Cls1 Nov Gd2 Ch soft			£19,933
	9/19	Wxfd	2m4f Nov Ch good			£10,649
	7/19	Tipp	2m3¹/₂f Nov Ch good			£8,785
113	6/19	Dpat	2m3f 102-115 Hdl Hcap yield			£13,851
	5/19	Kbgn	2m4f Ch yield			£6,937
	11/18	Navn	2m Mdn Auct Hdl good			£10,903

Wonderfully game mare who ran out a narrow winner of last season's Champion Chase; has now won all four races at Cheltenham, including another festival success in the Arkle, though didn't prove as effective in defeats at Leopardstown and Sandown last season.

Quilixios

4 b g Maxios - Quilita (Lomitas)

Henry de Bromhead (Ire) — Cheveley Park Stud

PLACINGS: 1/1111-7 — RPR **149+h**

Starts		1st	2nd	3rd	4th	Win & Pl
6		5	-	-	-	£151,440
	3/21	Chel	2m1f Cls1 Gd1 Hdl 4yo gd-sft			£52,753
	2/21	Leop	2m Gd1 Hdl 4yo sft-hvy			£65,848
	10/20	DRoy	2m¹/₂f Hdl 3yo soft			£5,750
	10/20	Punc	2m Hdl 3yo yield			£6,750
	3/20	Comp	2m Hdl 3yo heavy			£20,339

Completed a five-timer when storming to an impressive win in last season's Triumph Hurdle at Cheltenham; had looked equally effective on softer ground when much too good for some smart rivals in Ireland; well below par when losing unbeaten record in seventh at Punchestown.

Ramses De Teillee (Fr)

9 gr g Martaline - Princesse D'Orton (Saint Cyrien)

David Pipe — John White & Anne Underhill

PLACINGS: /5122P/14110/517049- — RPR **157c**

Starts		1st	2nd	3rd	4th	Win & Pl
29		4	7	2	3	£179,665
149	11/20	Chel	3m3¹/₂f Cls1 Gd3 142-156 Ch Hcap soft			£25,748
	2/20	Hayd	3m¹/₂f Cls1 Nov Gd2 Hdl heavy			£16,938
	1/20	Donc	3m¹/₂f Cls1 Nov Gd2 Hdl gd-sft			£17,085
	10/19	Chel	3m Cls2 Nov Hdl heavy			£9,384
140	12/18	Chep	2m7¹/₂f Cls2 127-142 Ch Hcap heavy			£12,660
	1/18	Chep	2m7¹/₂f Cls3 Nov Ch heavy			£7,343
122	11/17	Chep	2m7¹/₂f Cls4 Nov 103-122 Ch Hcap heavy			£3,899

Did well in novice hurdles in 2019-20 and successfully returned to fences last season, winning a big staying handicap at Cheltenham; struggled subsequently, with best run coming when fourth in the Grand National Trial at Haydock (had been second in that race two years earlier).

Rath An luir (Ire)

8 b g Flemensfirth - Amathea (Exit To Nowhere)

Rose Dobbin — Mr & Mrs Duncan Davidson

PLACINGS: 3/31/4122/11- — RPR **144+c**

Starts		1st	2nd	3rd	4th	Win & Pl
6		3	2	-	1	£23,909
129	11/20	Carl	3m¹/₂f Cls3 120-130 Ch Hcap soft			£7,473
123	11/20	Carl	2m4f Cls3 Nov 120-127 Ch Hcap heavy			£7,018
	12/19	Newc	2m6f Cls4 Nov Hdl soft			£3,769

Lightly raced stayer who was a big improver when sent chasing last season despite missing most of the campaign after fracturing a pedal bone in a freak accident; had won first two runs over fences, including by ten lengths when stepped up to 3m at Carlisle.

Real Steel (Fr)

8 ch g Loup Breton - Kalimina (Monsun)

Paul Nicholls   Mrs Kathy Stuart & Sullivan Bloodstock

PLACINGS: P4/F1162/1141P6/3PP-   RPR **163**c

Starts	1st	2nd	3rd	4th	Win & Pl
21	6	2	1	2	£176,005

1/20	Thur	2m4¹/₂f Gd2 Ch yield	£22,500
11/19	DRoy	2m3¹/₂f Gd2 Ch soft	£26,577
151	5/19	Punc	2m5f Nov 130-151 Ch Hcap gd-yld	£53,153
2/19	Thur	2m2f Ch good	£14,405
1/19	Fair	2m5¹/₂f Ch yield	£7,769
11/17	Thur	2m Mdn Hdl 4yo soft	£5,791

Formerly high-class chaser for Willie Mullins in Ireland, winning two Grade 2 chases and finishing sixth in the Gold Cup two seasons ago; failed to hit those heights for Paul Nicholls last term and was even pulled up on final two runs at Kempton and Aintree.

Remastered

8 ch g Network - Cathodine Cayras (Martaline)

David Pipe   Brocade Racing

PLACINGS: /21/152/052P33/1115-   RPR **152+**c

Starts	1st	2nd	3rd	4th	Win & Pl
17	5	4	2	-	£50,905

2/21	Asct	3m Cls1 Nov Gd2 Ch soft	£16,819
12/20	Weth	3m Cls4 Nov Ch heavy	£4,289
11/20	Carl	2m4f Cls3 Nov Ch heavy	£7,018
11/18	Ffos	2m Cls4 Nov Hdl heavy	£4,159
2/18	Chep	2m Cls5 NHF 4-6yo heavy	£2,274

Proved a smart staying chaser in testing conditions last season, completing a hat-trick with a dour all-the-way win in the Reynoldstown at Ascot on soft ground (all four previous wins under rules on heavy); fifth on quicker ground in the National Hunt Chase at Cheltenham.

Ribble Valley (Ire)

8 b g Westerner - Miss Greinton (Greinton)

Nicky Richards   David Wesley Yates

PLACINGS: 161/112/13-   RPR **147**h

Starts	1st	2nd	3rd	4th	Win & Pl
8	5	1	1	-	£34,138

10/20	Carl	2m1f Cls4 Hdl soft	£3,769
11/19	Weth	2m Cls4 Nov Hdl soft	£4,224
11/19	Hexm	2m Cls4 Nov Hdl heavy	£4,419
1/19	Ayr	2m Cls5 NHF 4-6yo gd-sft	£2,274
11/18	Ayr	2m Cls5 Am Mdn NHF 4-6yo good	£2,395

Has won five out of eight races under rules, though all at Class 4 level or below and well beaten on all three runs at a higher level; still fared well enough when third in the Fighting Fifth Hurdle last season on ground perhaps quicker than ideal; likely to go novice chasing.

Road To Respect (Ire)

10 ch g Gamut - Lora Lady (Lord Americo)

Noel Meade (Ire)   Gigginstown House Stud

PLACINGS: 2211/12143/13235/13/   RPR **170**c

Starts	1st	2nd	3rd	4th	Win & Pl
26	8	6	7	2	£584,114

11/19	DRoy	3m Gd1 Ch soft	£79,730
11/18	DRoy	3m Gd1 Ch gd-yld	£73,097
12/17	Leop	3m Gd1 Ch yield	£75,641
10/17	Punc	3m1f Gd3 Ch soft	£20,171
4/17	Fair	2m4f Nov Gd1 Ch gd-yld	£50,427
145	3/17	Chel	2m5f Cls1 Gd3 133-158 Ch Hcap good	£59,798
11/16	Naas	2m3f Ch yld-sft	£6,105
2/16	Thur	2m6¹/₂f Mdn Hdl heavy	£4,522

Hasn't run since finishing third in the Savills Chase at Leopardstown at the end of 2019; had just won a fourth Grade 1 in Ireland at that time at Down Royal, though has always tended to come up short in the very best races.

Roksana (Ire)

9 b m Dubai Destination - Talktothetail (Flemensfirth)

Dan Skelton   Mrs Sarah Faulks

PLACINGS: 1112/312/2524/13132-   RPR **155**h

Starts	1st	2nd	3rd	4th	Win & Pl
18	6	5	4	2	£280,849

1/21	Asct	2m7¹/₂f Cls1 Gd2 Hdl soft	£19,933
10/20	Weth	3m Cls1 Gd2 Hdl soft	£19,933
3/19	Chel	2m4f Cls1 Gd1 Hdl soft	£70,563
130	3/18	Newb	2m4¹/₂f Cls1 Nov Gd2 115-135 Hdl Hcap soft	£22,780
12/17	Font	2m3f Cls4 Nov Hdl heavy	£3,249
11/17	Plum	2m4¹/₂f Cls4 Nov Hdl good	£3,249

Won the Mares' Hurdle at Cheltenham in 2019 but has proved best over 3m and benefited from running more regularly at that trip last season; won two Grade 2 races, including against geldings at Wetherby, and was a close second in the 3m Grade 1 at Aintree for the second time.

Ronald Pump

8 ch g Schiaparelli - Fruit Yoghurt (Hernando)

Matthew J Smith (Ire)   Laois Limerick Syndicate

PLACINGS: 04911411/12242/F2-35   RPR **158**h

Starts	1st	2nd	3rd	4th	Win & Pl
25	5	4	2	6	£205,827

11/19	Fair	2m5f Ch heavy	£6,389
136	4/19	Fair	3m Nov 112-136 Hdl Hcap gd-yld	£29,234
123	3/19	Cork	3m 108-130 Hdl Hcap soft	£9,989
108	1/19	Fair	3m 81-108 Hdl Hcap good	£6,659
102	12/18	Cork	2m4f Nov 80-102 Hdl Hcap sft-hvy	£5,996

Finished second in the Stayers' Hurdle at Cheltenham in 2020; backed that up with a close second behind Honeysuckle in last season's Hatton's Grace Hurdle but then suffered injury problems and was third and fifth on only subsequent runs in the spring.

Roseys Hollow (Ire)

7 b m Beat Hollow - Saoirse's Sister (Hubbly Bubbly)

Jonathan Sweeney (Ire)   John P McManus

PLACINGS: 1/3/4117-					RPR **139+**h
Starts	1st	2nd	3rd	4th	Win & Pl
6	3	-	1	1	£28,239

2/21	Fair	2m2f Nov Gd3 Hdl heavy...............................£14,487
1/21	Fair	2m2½f Mdn Hdl heavy......................................£6,321
3/19	Cork	2m NHF 4-7yo soft..£5,550

Won two mares' novice hurdles last season, most notably a Grade 3 at Fairyhouse over Royal Kahala; only seventh on a much quicker surface at the Cheltenham Festival (both wins had come on heavy) and withdrawn due to similar ground conditions subsequently.

Rouge Vif (Fr)

7 b g Sageburg - Rouge Amour (Cadoudal)

Paul Nicholls   Kate & Andrew Brooks

PLACINGS: /5212113/14213/1349-					RPR **167+**c
Starts	1st	2nd	3rd	4th	Win & Pl
17	7	3	3	2	£165,297

10/20	Chel	2m Cls2 135-161 Ch Hcap good £30,029
2/20	Wwck	2m Cls1 Nov Gd2 Ch gd-sft.......................£22,780
10/19	MRas	2m1f Cls3 Nov Ch gd-sft...............................£7,988
3/19	Kels	2m2f Cls1 Nov Gd2 Hdl gd-sft £28,475
1/19	Newc	2m Cls4 Nov Hdl soft £4,094
12/18	Sthl	1m7½f Cls4 Mdn Hdl gd-sft..........................£4,094
3/18	Ludl	2m Cls4 NHF 4-6yo soft...................................£4,809

Smart novice chaser in 2019-20 and made a sparkling return last season, running away with a handicap at Cheltenham on good ground; unsuited by a softer surface the next twice but no real excuses when last of nine in the Champion Chase (beaten when badly hampered three out); has since left Harry Whittington.

Royal Kahala (Ire)

6 ch m Flemensfirth - Leading Lady (Fraam)

Peter Fahey (Ire)   Winning Ways Starlet Syndicate

PLACINGS: 2/511129-					RPR **141+**h
Starts	1st	2nd	3rd	4th	Win & Pl
7	3	2	-	-	£25,297

1/21	Fair	2m2½f Hdl heavy...£7,112
11/20	Fair	2m4f Mdn Hdl sft-hvy......................................£6,500
11/20	Fair	2m NHF 4-7yo soft...£5,000

Sent off favourite for the Mares' Novices' Hurdle at the Cheltenham Festival last season but found to be lame after finishing only ninth; had won three in a row earlier in the season, including first two races over hurdles, before a narrow defeat by Roseys Hollow at Fairyhouse.

Royal Rendezvous (Ire)

9 b g King's Theatre - Novacella (Beyssac)

Willie Mullins (Ire)   Dr S P Fitzgerald

PLACINGS: 4F1/5111/P1351/2-011					RPR **161**c
Starts	1st	2nd	3rd	4th	Win & Pl
13	7	1	1	-	£223,658

7/21	Gway	2m6½f 140-158 Ch Hcap good £131,696
5/21	Baln	2m2f Hdl sft-hvy...£6,058
3/20	Naas	2m4f Nov Gd3 Ch soft....................................£16,250
11/19	Thur	2m2f Ch soft...£6,389
10/18	Gway	2m1½f Mdn Hdl yield.......................................£7,632
10/18	Tipp	2m NHF 4-7yo good...£7,087
8/18	Dpat	2m3f NHF 4-7yo gd-yld...................................£5,451

Late developer who won the Galway Plate this summer on just his seventh run over fences, making up for a near miss in the race 12 months earlier (sent off favourite both times); still improving according to his trainer.

Royale Pagaille (Fr)
7 b g Blue Bresil - Royale Cazoumaille (Villez)

Venetia Williams · Mrs S Ricci

PLACINGS: 661326/F5U2/23/1116- · RPR **171+**c

Starts	1st	2nd	3rd	4th	Win & Pl
16	4	3	2	-	£132,098

156	1/21	Hayd	3m1¹/₂f Cls1 Gd2 136-156 Ch Hcap heavy	£27,036
140	12/20	Kemp	3m Cls2 129-147 Ch Hcap soft	£25,024
	12/20	Hayd	2m5¹/₂f Cls2 Nov Ch heavy	£12,021
	1/18	Pau	2m¹/₂f Hdl 4yo heavy	£13,593

Massive improver last season, ending up in the Gold Cup having begun as an eight-race maiden over fences; won three times on soft/heavy ground, most notably in the Peter Marsh Chase under top weight, but well beaten in sixth on much quicker going at Cheltenham.

Run Wild Fred (Ire)
7 ch g Shantou - Talkin Madam (Talkin Man)

Gordon Elliott (Ire) · Gigginstown House Stud

PLACINGS: 1d3161/31F1/3455222- · RPR **151+**c

Starts	1st	2nd	3rd	4th	Win & Pl
15	4	3	3	1	£130,186

2/20	Punc	3m Nov Gd3 Hdl heavy	£17,500
12/19	Navn	2m4f Mdn Hdl soft	£7,188
3/19	Limk	2m NHF 5-7yo heavy	£6,382
1/19	Fair	2m¹/₂f NHF 4-7yo good	£5,827

Still a maiden over fences but was unlucky not to bag a big handicap chase last season, finishing second in the Thyestes and the Irish Grand National (didn't jump the last two fences cleanly); strong stayer who has proved effective on any ground.

Saint Calvados (Fr)
8 b g Saint Des Saints - Lamorrese (Pistolet Bleu)

Paul Nicholls · Kate & Andrew Brooks

PLACINGS: 6/1114/1336/1422/4U- · RPR **164**c

Starts	1st	2nd	3rd	4th	Win & Pl
18	8	2	2	3	£296,339

155	10/19	Chel	2m Cls2 129-155 Ch Hcap heavy	£37,164
	11/18	Naas	2m Gd3 Ch yield	£17,688
	2/18	Wwck	2m Cls1 Nov Gd2 Ch soft	£22,780
147	1/18	Newb	2m¹/₂f Cls3 Nov 135-147 Ch Hcap soft	£7,343
143	12/17	Newb	2m¹/₂f Cls3 Nov 127-143 Ch Hcap heavy	£8,656
	3/17	Autl	2m2f Hdl 4yo v soft	£28,718
	12/16	Cagn	2m1¹/₂f Hdl 3yo soft	£15,882
	11/16	Fnth	2m2f Hdl 3yo heavy	£8,118

Developed into a top-class chaser two seasons ago, finishing a neck second in the Ryanair, but couldn't build on that in just two runs last term; finished a fair fourth in the King George but in rear when unseating at Sandown and pulled out of the Ryanair (ground too quick); has since left Harry Whittington.

Royal Kahala: had shown progressive form before finishing lame at the Cheltenham Festival

Saint Roi (Fr)
6 br g Coastal Path - Sainte Vigne (Saint Des Saints)

Willie Mullins (Ire) · John P McManus

PLACINGS: 3/511/1244- · RPR **159**h

Starts	1st	2nd	3rd	4th	Win & Pl
8	3	1	1	2	£112,020

	10/20	Tipp	2m Gd3 Hdl good	£17,500
137	3/20	Chel	2m1f Cls1 Gd3 133-150 Hdl Hcap soft	£56,270
	1/20	Tram	2m Mdn Hdl soft	£5,760

Began last season among the Champion Hurdle favourites but didn't even get to Cheltenham after a disappointing campaign, with trainer blaming "one or two niggles"; beaten just a neck by Abacadabras in the Morgiana Hurdle but regressed in two subsequent Grade I outings.

Saint Sam (Fr)
4 b g Saint Des Saints - Ladeka (Linda's Lad)

Willie Mullins (Ire) · Edward Ware

PLACINGS: 9112422-5 · RPR **143**h

Starts	1st	2nd	3rd	4th	Win & Pl
8	2	3		1	£60,566

7/20	Claf	2m1f Hdl 3yo soft	£10,983
6/20	Diep	2m1f Hdl 3yo soft	£8,258

Dual French hurdles winner who ran several fine races in defeat following switch to Ireland, notably when second behind Jeff Kidder in the Fred Winter at Cheltenham; also finished second behind high-class pair Zanahiyr and Quilixios and fifth on final run in a Grade I at Punchestown.

Saldier (Fr)
7 b g Soldier Hollow - Salve Evita (Monsun)

Willie Mullins (Ire) · Mrs S Ricci

PLACINGS: 1531/F/1/667-81 · RPR **161**h

Starts	1st	2nd	3rd	4th	Win & Pl
11	4		1	-	£255,570

155	7/21	Gway	2m 132-155 Hdl Hcap good	£131,696
	11/19	Punc	2m1¹/₂f Gd1 Hdl soft	£53,153
	4/18	Punc	2m Gd1 Hdl 4yo yld-sft	£52,212
	2/18	Gowr	2m Mdn Hdl 4yo heavy	£7,359

Plagued by injury since looking potentially top class as a youngster but bounced back this summer with a brilliant win under top weight in the Galway Hurdle; had been slow to regain form last season after latest long absence but did better when seventh in the Champion Hurdle.

Sam Brown
9 b g Black Sam Bellamy - Cream Cracker (Sir Harry Lewis)

Anthony Honeyball · T C Frost

PLACINGS: 11/41/11P/3-7 · RPR **158**c

Starts	1st	2nd	3rd	4th	Win & Pl
9	5	-	1	1	£33,733

1/20	Hayd	2m4f Cls1 Nov Gd2 Ch heavy	£18,793
1/20	Ling	2m7¹/₂f Cls4 Nov Ch heavy	£4,289
12/17	Plum	2m4¹/₂f Cls4 Nov Hdl soft	£3,249
3/17	Newb	2m1¹/₂f Cls5 NHF 4-6yo soft	£2,599
2/17	Winc	1m7¹/₂f Cls6 NHF 4-6yo heavy	£1,949

Plagued by injury but has continued to hint at real

potential in rare appearances; won two novice chases in 2019-20, including a Grade 2, and was a good third behind Imperial Aura first time out at Carlisle last term; ground possibly too quick on only subsequent run at Punchestown.

Sam's Adventure

9 b g Black Sam Bellamy - My Adventure (Strong Gale)

Brian Ellison   Julie & Phil Martin

PLACINGS: 302415/42271/P51U1U-   **RPR 153+c**

Starts	1st	2nd	3rd	4th	Win & Pl
21	7	4	1	2	£151,003
139	2/21	Newc	4m1½f Cls2 124-150 Ch Hcap soft		£43,792
133	12/20	Hayd	3m1½f Cls2 124-141 Ch Hcap heavy		£25,024
129	3/20	Uttx	3m Cls2 Nov 129-138 Ch Hcap heavy		£25,024
118	3/19	Newc	2m6f Cls2 Nov 110-126 Hdl Hcap heavy		£12,512
	1/17	Ayr	2m Cls6 NHF 4-6yo heavy		£1,949
	3/16	Newb	2m1½f Cls2 NHF 4-5yo soft		£29,505
	2/16	Weth	2m Cls6 NHF 4-6yo heavy		£1,949

Progressive staying chaser who proved his stamina for marathon trips when winning last

season's Eider Chase over 4m1f; twice unseated his rider either side of that but had also won good handicaps at Haydock and Uttoxeter in the previous 12 months.

Samcro (Ire)

9 ch g Germany - Dun Dun (Saddlers' Hall)

Gordon Elliott (Ire)   Gigginstown House Stud

PLACINGS: 11F/225/1F21/3PP-160   **RPR 159c**

Starts	1st	2nd	3rd	4th	Win & Pl
21	10	3	1	-	£340,451
5/21	Klny	2m4f Gd3 Ch gd-yld			£14,487
3/20	Chel	2m4f Cls1 Nov Gd1 Ch soft			£84,405
11/19	DRoy	2m3½f Ch soft			£7,986
3/18	Chel	2m5f Cls1 Nov Gd1 Hdl soft			£71,188
2/18	Leop	2m Nov Gd1 Hdl soft			£52,212
11/17	Navn	2m4f Nov Gd3 Hdl sft-hvy			£21,432
10/17	Punc	2m Mdn Hdl yld-sft			£6,844
4/17	Fair	2m NHF 4-7yo gd-yld			£8,424
12/16	Navn	2m List NHF 4-7yo sft-hvy			£12,436
11/16	Punc	2m NHF 4yo soft			£4,522

Once seen as the next big thing but has become

hugely disappointing; bounced back to land a second Cheltenham Festival win in the 2020 Marsh Novices' Chase but was out of sorts last term and again failed to build on a comeback win at Killarney this summer, flopping in the Galway Plate.

Sams Profile
7 b g Black Sam Bellamy - Lucylou I (Bob Back)

Mouse Morris (Ire)   Michael O'Flynn & John F O'Flynn

PLACINGS: 13/1225/2/F31-   RPR **157+**h

Starts	1st	2nd	3rd	4th	Win & Pl
9	2	3	2	-	£69,417
	1/21	Gowr	3m Gd2 Hdl heavy.............................£18,438
	11/18	Cork	2m Mdn Hdl 4yo yield..........................£7,359

Smart novice hurdler three seasons ago (dual Grade 1 runner-up) prior to long layoff; struggled over fences upon return last season but bounced back when reverting to hurdles, winning the Galmoy Hurdle.

Santini
9 b g Milan - Tinagoodnight (Sleeping Car)

Polly Gundry   Mr & Mrs R Kelvin-Hughes

PLACINGS: 1/1131/132/112/253P-   RPR **165**c

Starts	1st	2nd	3rd	4th	Win & Pl
14	6	3	3	-	£394,463
	1/20	Chel	3m1¹/₂f Cls1 Gd2 Ch soft.......................£57,268
	11/19	Sand	3m Cls1 List Ch soft..............................£17,085
	12/18	Newb	2m7¹/₂f Cls1 Nov Gd2 Ch soft..............£22,780
	4/18	Aint	3m1¹/₂f Cls1 Nov Gd1 Hdl soft...............£56,224
	1/18	Chel	2m4¹/₂f Cls1 Nov Gd2 Hdl heavy...........£18,224
	12/17	Newb	2m4¹/₂f Cls3 Nov Hdl soft......................£6,498

High-class stayer who ran a huge race when finishing a neck second in the Gold Cup in 2020 on just his sixth run over fences; bitterly disappointing last season, though, regressing with every run and pulled up around halfway in the Gold Cup after jumping badly; has since left Nicky Henderson.

Scaramanga (Ire)
6 b g Mastercraftsman - Herboriste (Hernando)

Paul Nicholls   Malcolm C Denmark

PLACINGS: 3212/8170/311-   RPR **151+**h

Starts	1st	2nd	3rd	4th	Win & Pl
11	4	2	2	-	£44,635
144	4/21	Sand	2m4f Cls2 119-144 Hdl Hcap good........£11,967
139	3/21	Newb	2m¹/₂f Cls3 117-139 Hdl Hcap gd-sft.......£5,913
132	12/19	Winc	1m7¹/₂f Cls1 107-132 Hdl Hcap gd-sft......£10,072
	3/19	Tntn	2m¹/₂f Cls4 Nov Hdl gd-sft.....................£5,133

Smart dual-purpose performer who flourished when back over hurdles last spring, winning handicaps at Newbury and Sandown; better than bare form of latest victory (struggled to last longer 2m4f trip having eased clear); likely type for a big 2m handicap hurdle on good ground.

Scarlet And Dove (Ire)
7 b m Jeremy - Dark Mimosa (Bahri)

Joseph O'Brien (Ire)   Gigginstown House Stud

PLACINGS: 1/514/221F115-2   RPR **147**c

Starts	1st	2nd	3rd	4th	Win & Pl
12	5	3	-	1	£80,474
	3/21	Limk	2m6¹/₂f Nov Gd2 Ch heavy...................£22,388
	3/21	Navn	2m Nov Gd3 Ch soft..............................£18,438
	12/20	Limk	2m3¹/₂f Ch heavy.................................£6,250
	3/20	Navn	2m Mdn Hdl heavy................................£6,750
	11/18	Limk	2m NHF 4-7yo yield................................£5,451

Among last season's leading mares over fences, winning three times including two clearcut Graded victories; found out against the boys at Grade 1 level at Fairyhouse behind Janidil but bounced back with a neck second in a mares' handicap chase at Punchestown.

Sceau Royal (Fr)
9 b g Doctor Dino - Sandside (Marchand De Sable)

Alan King   Simon Munir & Isaac Souede

PLACINGS: 14232/6325/1124F153-   RPR **168+**c

Starts	1st	2nd	3rd	4th	Win & Pl
37	14	7	4	3	£481,894
	2/21	Newb	2m1¹/₂f Cls3 Gd2 Ch gd-sft..................£25,628
	11/20	Winc	1m7¹/₂f Cls1 Gd2 Hdl good...................£27,336
150	10/20	Ffos	2m Cls2 134-154 Hdl Hcap gd-sft..........£25,024
	11/18	Chel	2m Cls2 Ch good.................................£42,203
	1/18	Donc	2m1¹/₂f Cls1 Nov Gd2 Ch soft...............£19,933
	12/17	Sand	1m7¹/₂f Cls1 Nov Gd1 Ch gd-sft............£29,810
	11/17	Wwck	2m Cls3 Nov Ch 4-5yo gd-sft..................£9,384
	10/17	Wwck	2m Cls4 Nov Ch good............................£5,198
149	11/16	Winc	2m Cls2 133-149 Hdl Hcap good.........£35,772
	10/16	Chel	2m1¹/₂f Cls2 Hdl 4yo good...................£21,977
	1/16	Hntg	2m Cls2 Hdl 4yo soft...........................£12,512
	12/15	Chel	2m1f Cls2 Hdl 3yo soft.........................£12,628
	11/15	Wwck	2m Cls2 Hdl 3yo gd-sft..........................£3,249
	3/15	Bord	2m1¹/₂f Hdl 3yo v soft............................£7,814

Produced arguably the best form of his career last season, winning the Game Spirit Chase and unlucky not to go close when fifth in the Champion Chase (badly squeezed up); had reverted to hurdles earlier in the season, winning the Welsh Champion Hurdle and Elite Hurdle.

Secret Reprieve (Ire)
7 b g Flemensfirth - Oscar's Reprieve (Oscar)

Evan Williams   Mr & Mrs William Rucker

PLACINGS: 515/522/F11-   RPR **146+**c

Starts	1st	2nd	3rd	4th	Win & Pl
9	3	2	-	-	£107,451
134	1/21	Chep	3m6¹/₂f Cls1 Gd3 133-159 Ch Hcap soft.........£85,425
130	12/20	Chep	2m7¹/₂f Cls2 125-143 Ch Hcap heavy..........£12,660
	12/18	Chep	2m3¹/₂f Cls4 Nov Hdl heavy.....................£4,159

Sharply progressive staying chaser who won last season's Welsh Grand National at Chepstow (5-2 favourite) to follow up victory in the trial at the same course; subsequently laid out for the Grand National only to narrowly miss the cut.

Sam's Adventure: tough staying handicapper who loves a thorough test of stamina

Shan Blue (Ire)

7 b g Shantou - Lady Roberta (Bob Back)

Dan Skelton · Colm Donlon

PLACINGS: 13/2F1326/111252- · **RPR 157+c**

Starts	1st	2nd	3rd	4th	Win & Pl
13	4	4	2	-	£100,537

12/20	Kemp	3m Cls1 Nov Gd1 Ch gd-sft	£45,774
10/20	Weth	3m Cls4 Nov Ch gd-sft	£4,289
10/20	Weth	2m3¹/₂f Cls4 Nov Ch gd-sft	£4,289
12/19	Sthl	1m7¹/₂f Cls5 Mdn Hdl heavy	£2,794

Electric jumper who took really well to fences last season, winning a 3m Grade 1 at Kempton; disappointed in the spring, going for home too soon when only fifth at Cheltenham but faring even worse under restraint when a distant second behind Chantry House at Aintree.

Sharjah (Fr)

8 b g Doctor Dino - Saaryeh (Royal Academy)

Willie Mullins (Ire) · Mrs S Ricci

PLACINGS: 46/31311B/4162/132-2 · **RPR 168h**

Starts	1st	2nd	3rd	4th	Win & Pl
21	7	3	3	2	£648,182

	12/20	Leop	2m Gd1 Hdl soft	£50,000
	12/19	Leop	2m Gd1 Hdl yield	£66,441
	12/18	Leop	2m Gd1 Hdl gd-yld	£65,265
	11/18	Punc	2m Gd1 Hdl good	£52,212
146	8/18	Gway	2m 135-146 Hdl Hcap soft	£156,637
	11/17	Gowr	2m Nov Hdl 4yo heavy	£8,161
	9/17	Gowr	2m Mdn Hdl 4yo heavy	£6,844

Top-class hurdler who has won the last three runnings of the Grade 1 Matheson Hurdle at Leopardstown over Christmas; hasn't won elsewhere in that time but has finished second in the last two Champion Hurdles and pushed Honeysuckle closer at Punchestown in April.

Shewearsitwell (Ire)

6 b m Shirocco - Ware It Vic (Old Vic)

Willie Mullins (Ire) · Closutton Racing Club

PLACINGS: 111- · **RPR 147+h**

Starts	1st	2nd	3rd	4th	Win & Pl
3	3	-	-	-	£23,750

10/20	Tipp	2m Nov Gd3 Hdl good	£13,750
8/20	Slig	2m1¹/₂f Mdn Hdl good	£5,000
7/20	Gway	2m1¹/₂f NHF 4-7yo gd-yld	£5,000

Missed much of last season but had made a big impact during the summer and autumn, winning all three races; hacked up by eight lengths in a 2m Grade 3 at Tipperary on final run; ought to stay further.

Shishkin (Ire)

7 b g Sholokhov - Labarynth (Exit To Nowhere)

Nicky Henderson · Mrs J Donnelly

PLACINGS: 3/11/F111/11111- · **RPR 174+c**

Starts	1st	2nd	3rd	4th	Win & Pl
10	9	-	-	-	£249,146

4/21	Aint	2m Cls1 Nov Gd1 Ch gd-sft	£42,701
3/21	Chel	2m Cls1 Nov Gd1 Ch soft	£73,854
1/21	Donc	2m¹/₂f Cls1 Nov Gd2 Ch soft	£14,682
12/20	Kemp	2m Cls1 Nov Gd2 Ch soft	£18,224
11/20	Kemp	2m2f Cls4 Ch good	£4,394
3/20	Chel	2m¹/₂f Cls1 Nov Gd1 Hdl soft	£70,338
2/20	Hntg	2m3¹/₂f Cls1 Nov List Hdl gd-sft	£17,286
1/20	Newb	2m¹/₂f Cls4 Nov Hdl heavy	£4,549
3/19	Kemp	2m Cls5 Mdn NHF 4-6yo gd-sft	£3,119

Brilliant winner of the Supreme Novices' Hurdle

and the Arkle Chase at the Cheltenham Festival in the last two seasons; has won his last eight races and would surely be unbeaten under rules but for falling on his hurdles debut in 2019; clear favourite for the Champion Chase.

Silver Hallmark

7 bg g Shirocco - Gaye Sophie (Environment Friend)

Fergal O'Brien Mr & Mrs William Rucker

PLACINGS: 13/17/21-					RPR **150**+c
Starts	1st	2nd	3rd	4th	Win & Pl
5	2	1	1		£20,305
	1/21	Hayd	2m4f Cls1 Nov Gd2 Ch heavy		£14,094
	11/19	Chep	2m Cls4 Mdn Hdl soft		£3,769

Very lightly raced youngster who won a 2m4f Grade 2 novice chase at Haydock last season (main rival Allart fell early) on just his second run over fences and fifth under rules; had been beaten a head by Fiddlerontheroof first time out despite suffering a knock; should stay further.

Silver Streak (Ire)

8 gr g Dark Angel - Happy Talk (Hamas)

Evan Williams L Fell

PLACINGS: 1122235/1326/1C2166-					RPR **164**+h
Starts	1st	2nd	3rd	4th	Win & Pl
27	8	7	3	2	£443,176
	12/20	Kemp	2m Cls1 Gd1 Hdl gd-sft		£59,798
	10/20	Kemp	2m Cls1 List Hdl good		£18,224
	10/19	Kemp	2m Cls1 List Hdl good		£23,048
139	10/18	Ffos	2m Cls2 139-159 Hdl Hcap gd-sft		£28,152
132	5/18	Hayd	1m7¹/₂f Cls1 Gd3 130-156 Hdl Hcap good		£56,950
122	10/17	Chep	2m Cls2 109-135 Hdl 4yo Hcap gd-sft		£12,996
116	3/17	Muss	1m7¹/₂f Cls4 100-122 Hdl Hcap good		£4,549
96	12/16	Tntn	2m¹/₂f Cls5 74-102 Hdl Hcap good		£3,899

Has finished second or third six times in Grade 1 or Grade 2 races but finally broke through in last season's Christmas Hurdle, making the most of facing a below-par Epatante; shortcomings exposed again when sixth in the Champion Hurdle before failing to stay 2m4f in the Aintree Hurdle.

Simply The Betts (Ire)

8 b g Arcadio - Crimson Flower (Soviet Lad)

Paul Nicholls Kate & Andrew Brooks

PLACINGS: 13420/1184/11211/6-					RPR **156**c
Starts	1st	2nd	3rd	4th	Win & Pl
15	7	2	1	2	£114,996
149	3/20	Chel	2m4¹/₂f Cls1 Gd3 140-157 Ch Hcap soft		£61,897
140	1/20	Chel	2m4¹/₂f Cls2 Nov 121-147 Ch Hcap soft		£17,204
132	11/19	Newc	2m¹/₂f Cls3 Nov 125-132 Ch Hcap heavy		£7,018
125	11/19	Chep	2m Cls3 Nov 109-127 Ch Hcap soft		£7,018
	10/18	Hexm	2m Cls4 Nov Hdl soft		£4,159
	5/18	Wwck	2m Cls5 Mdn Hdl good		£3,249
	9/17	MRas	2m¹/₂f Cls6 NHF 4-6yo good		£1,560

Missed nearly all of last season, running just once when sixth in the Paddy Power Gold Cup; had

---

gone from strength to strength in the previous campaign and won four out of five, including the Plate at Cheltenham having beaten fast-improving Imperial Aura at the track in January; has since left Harry Whittington.

Sir Gerhard (Ire)

6 b g Jeremy - Faanan Aldaar (Authorized)

Willie Mullins (Ire) Cheveley Park Stud

PLACINGS: 1/111-3					RPR **138**+b
Starts	1st	2nd	3rd	4th	Win & Pl
4	3	-	1	-	£55,937
	3/21	Chel	2m¹/₂f Cls1 Gd1 NHF 4-6yo gd-sft		£31,652
	12/20	Navn	2m List NHF 4-7yo sft-hvy		£11,250
	10/20	DRoy	2m¹/₂f NHF 4-7yo soft		£5,000

Won last season's Champion Bumper at Cheltenham, completing a hat-trick as he made all the running and just held off strong-finishing Kilcruit (pair clear); below best when only third behind that rival at Punchestown; likely type for top 2m novice hurdles.

Sire Du Berlais (Fr)

9 b g Poliglote - Royale Athenia (Garde Royale)

Gordon Elliott (Ire) John P McManus

PLACINGS: 0/248/8618/4941/132-					RPR **165**h
Starts	1st	2nd	3rd	4th	Win & Pl
18	4	2	3	3	£212,806
	11/20	Navn	2m4f Gd2 Hdl sft-hvy		£17,500
152	3/20	Chel	3m Cls1 Gd3 131-152 Hdl Hcap soft		£56,270
145	3/19	Chel	3m Cls1 Gd3 134-148 Hdl Hcap gd-sft		£56,270
	5/16	Comp	2m1f Hdl 4yo v soft		£7,765

Cheltenham specialist who won successive runnings of the Pertemps Final in 2019 and 2020 before a terrific second behind Flooring Porter in last season's Stayers' Hurdle; generally less effective elsewhere, though did start last term by winning a Grade 2 at Navan.

Siruh Du Lac (Fr)

8 b g Turgeon - Margerie (Le Balafre)

David Pipe John White & Anne Underhill

PLACINGS: 324/P113/1111/PF/U-					RPR **154**c
Starts	1st	2nd	3rd	4th	Win & Pl
14	6	1	2	1	£145,397
141	3/19	Chel	2m4¹/₂f Cls1 Gd3 135-156 Ch Hcap gd-sft		£61,897
134	1/19	Chel	2m4¹/₂f Cls1 Gd3 131-151 Ch Hcap soft		£42,203
129	12/18	Extr	2m3f Cls3 124-137 Ch Hcap soft		£16,245
123	11/18	Newb	2m4f Cls3 116-137 Ch Hcap good		£8,058
118	12/17	Extr	2m3f Cls4 100-120 Ch Hcap soft		£7,148
112	11/17	Bang	2m4¹/₂f Cls4 93-122 Ch Hcap soft		£3,899

Unseated at the first on only run last season in the Paddy Power Gold Cup, making it three non-completions since winning the 2019 Plate at Cheltenham; had been hugely progressive up to that point, winning four in a row, and still in front in that race in 2020 when falling two out.

Shan Blue: talented chaser who is much better than he showed at the big spring meetings

Sixshooter (Ire)

6 ch g Well Chosen - Lobinstown Girl (Luso)

Noel Meade (Ire) — Gigginstown House Stud

PLACINGS: 1/11342/13343- — RPR **152**h

Starts 11	1st 4	2nd 1	3rd 4	4th 2	Win & Pl £48,608
10/20 Punc	2m2½f Hdl yield				£8,500
10/19 Punc	2m4f Mdn Hdl gd-yld				£7,188
5/19 Punc	2m NHF 4-7yo gd-yld				£9,712
3/19 Leop	2m NHF 4yo yld-sft				£6,382

Developed into a smart staying hurdler early last season, winning at Punchestown and finishing a close third behind Sire Du Berlais in the Lismullen Hurdle; regressed subsequently and beaten much further when third twice more at Grade 2 level; likely to go novice chasing.

Sizing Pottsie (Fr)

7 b/br g Kapgarde - Line Salsa (Kingsalsa)

Jessica Harrington (Ire) — Ann & Alan Potts Limited

PLACINGS: 14/53/33U11F/521F5P- — RPR **159+**c

Starts 16	1st 4	2nd 1	3rd 3	4th 1	Win & Pl £72,598
149					
12/20 Fair	2m 132-156 Ch Hcap sft-hvy				£20,000
3/20 Navn	2m Nov Gd3 Ch heavy				£21,250
2/20 Fair	2m1½f Ch heavy				£8,500
3/18 Leop	2m NHF 4yo soft				£6,269

Smart novice chaser in early 2020 and began last season in similar vein, finishing second behind Felix Desjy at Punchestown and winning a good handicap at Fairyhouse; form tailed off subsequently and jumping not up to the task in the Grand Annual at Cheltenham.

Sky Pirate
8 b g Midnight Legend - Dancingwithbubbles (Supreme Leader)

Jonjo O'Neill | M Tedham

PLACINGS: 31322F47/F22/251121- | RPR **159+c**

Starts	1st	2nd	3rd	4th	Win & Pl
20	5	7	3	1	£114,040

152	3/21	Chel	2m Cls1 Gd3 136-158 Ch Hcap gd-sft	£46,423
145	1/21	Wwck	2m Cls2 120-146 Ch Hcap soft	£12,021
134	12/20	Chel	2m¹/₂f Cls2 134-159 Ch Hcap soft	£15,014
123	6/18	Worc	2m7f Cls3 122-159 Hdl Hcap good	£6,758
	10/17	Worc	2m4f Cls4 Nov Hdl good	£4,431

Remarkable success story last season, winning three of his last four races, including the Grand Annual at Cheltenham, having gone ten races without a win over fences dating back to 2018; key to improvement seems to be a fast pace over 2m, though does stay much further.

Skyace (Ire)
6 b m Westerner - Graigace (Milan)

John Joseph Hanlon (Ire) | Birdinthehand Syndicate

PLACINGS: 233/11206F1141-FP | RPR **140+h**

Starts	1st	2nd	3rd	4th	Win & Pl
15	5	4	2	1	£103,918

	4/21	Fair	2m4f Nov Gd1 Hdl yield	£52,679
	12/20	Punc	2m Nov List Hdl heavy	£11,250
	10/20	DRoy	2m¹/₂f Nov Gd3 Hdl yld-sft	£17,500
	7/20	Gowr	2m4f Hdl good	£6,750
	6/20	Tipp	3m Mdn Hdl gd-yld	£5,000

Remarkable mare who cost just £600 in November 2019 and progressed into a Grade 1 winner last season, winning at Fairyhouse after managing fourth in the stronger mares' novice hurdle at the Cheltenham Festival; pulled up in the Galway Hurdle this summer.

Soaring Glory (Ire)
6 b g Fame And Glory - Hapeney (Saddlers' Hall)

Jonjo O'Neill | P Hickey

PLACINGS: 112/12F314- | RPR **146+h**

Starts	1st	2nd	3rd	4th	Win & Pl
9	4	2	1	1	£96,528

133	2/21	Newb	2m¹/₂f Cls1 Gd3 129-152 Hdl Hcap gd-sft	£70,338
	10/20	Chep	2m Cls4 Nov Hdl good	£3,769
	11/19	Asct	2m Cls4 NHF 4-6yo soft	£4,549
	10/19	Wwck	2m Cls5 NHF 4-6yo good	£2,599

Impressive winner of last season's Betfair Hurdle on sole handicap run, leaving previous form in novice hurdles well behind; couldn't make any impact when up in class for the Supreme Novices' Hurdle at Cheltenham, finishing a well-beaten fourth (raced keenly).

Sojourn (Ire)
8 b g Getaway - Toscar (Oscar)

Anthony Honeyball | Jon & Jacqueline Hughes

PLACINGS: 4/133/12/12P- | RPR **148c**

Starts	1st	2nd	3rd	4th	Win & Pl
9	3	2	2	1	£35,437

129	11/20	Carl	3m2f Cls3 109-137 Ch Hcap heavy	£12,512
117	11/19	MRas	3m Cls4 Nov 107-122 Ch Hcap heavy	£7,656
	11/18	Aint	2m1f Cls4 NHF 4-6yo good	£4,549

Very lightly raced chaser who progressed in good staying handicaps last season; hacked up at Carlisle on just his third run over fences before finishing second in the Tommy Whittle at Haydock; suffered a wound when pulled up in the Grand National Trial at Haydock.

Solo (Fr)
5 b g Kapgarde - Flameche (Balko)

Paul Nicholls | Mrs Johnny De La Hey

PLACINGS: 2118/45040- | RPR **143h**

Starts	1st	2nd	3rd	4th	Win & Pl
9	2	1	-	2	£55,319

	2/20	Kemp	2m Cls1 Gd2 Hdl 4yo gd-sft	£17,085
	11/19	Autl	2m1¹/₂f Hdl 3yo heavy	£19,459

Wide-margin Grade 2 winner on British debut as a juvenile two seasons ago but paid the price with a very stiff handicap mark and struggled last term; could still have been expected to do better, managing no better than fourth in five runs; likely to go novice chasing.

Song For Someone (Ger)
6 ch g Medicean - Sweni Hill (Danehill Dancer)

Tom Symonds | Sir Peter & Lady Gibbings

PLACINGS: 3122116/1321/112P- | RPR **160+h**

Starts	1st	2nd	3rd	4th	Win & Pl
15	7	4	2	-	£170,496

	12/20	Chel	2m1f Cls1 Gd2 Hdl soft	£63,784
	11/20	Asct	2m3¹/₂f Cls1 Gd2 Hdl soft	£22,780
	2/20	Kemp	2m Cls1 Gd2 Hdl gd-sft	£25,748
136	11/19	Font	2m1¹/₂f Cls3 108-136 Hdl Hcap soft	£7,216
	2/19	Wwck	2m Cls4 Hdl 4yo good	£4,419
	12/18	Newb	2m1¹/₂f Cls3 Hdl 3yo gd-sft	£6,238
	7/18	Le L	2m1¹/₂f Hdl 3yo gd-sft	£8,496

Very smart hurdler who mopped up three Grade 2 races during 2020, including last season's Ascot Hurdle and International Hurdle; struggled later in the season, trailing home a long way behind Goshen in the Kingwell and being pulled up in the Aintree Hurdle.

Song For Someone: progressive over hurdles last season before pulling up on final start

Spiritofthegames (Ire)

9 b g Darsi - Lucy Walters (King's Ride)

Dan Skelton | N W Lake

PLACINGS: /14335/P0226/248283- | RPR **154**c

Starts	1st	2nd	3rd	4th	Win & Pl
25	4	6	4	3	£165,944

	10/18	Chep	2m3¹/₂f Cls1 Nov List Ch good	£16,465
129	11/17	Ling	2m3¹/₂f Cls3 112-132 Hdl Hcap soft	£7,596
	3/17	Tntn	2m1¹/₂f Cls5 Mdn Hdl gd	£4,549
	10/16	Ayr	2m4¹/₂f Cls5 Mdn Hdl gd-sft	£2,729

Without a win since chasing debut in October 2018 but has run well in several good handicaps, especially at Cheltenham; was placed at the track for the fifth time when second in last season's Paddy Power Gold Cup; struggled subsequently but did better when third at Aintree on final run.

Sporting John (Ire)

6 b/br g Getaway - Wild Spell (Oscar)

Philip Hobbs | John P McManus

PLACINGS: 1/1117/31FP- | RPR **160**+c

Starts	1st	2nd	3rd	4th	Win & Pl
8	4	-	1	-	£47,983

2/21	Sand	2m4f Cls1 Nov Gd1 Ch heavy	£20,026
2/20	Asct	2m3¹/₂f Cls2 Nov Hdl soft	£15,640
12/19	Extr	2m1f Cls4 Nov Hdl 4-6yo soft	£4,224
11/19	Extr	2m1f Cls3 Nov Hdl soft	£6,238

Won last season's Scilly Isles Novices' Chase, powering home after getting detached early as heavy ground brought stamina to the fore; stepped up to 3m subsequently but let down by poor jumping, falling when well beaten at Cheltenham and being pulled up at Aintree.

Star Gate (Ire)

5 b g Imperial Monarch - Supreme Judge (Brian Boru)

Evan Williams | Mr & Mrs William Rucker

PLACINGS: 1/112- | RPR **146**+h

Starts	1st	2nd	3rd	4th	Win & Pl
3	2	1	-	-	£27,052

12/20	Sand	2m4f Cls1 Nov Gd2 Hdl heavy	£13,668
10/20	Chep	2m3¹/₂f Cls4 Mdn Hdl soft	£3,769

Missed the second half of last season but had looked a very exciting novice hurdler earlier in the campaign; easily won first two races over hurdles, including a Grade 2 at Sandown on heavy ground; well beaten by Bravemansgame in the Challow, though still a fair second.

Stattler (Ire)

6 br g Stowaway - Our Honey (Old Vic)

Willie Mullins (Ire) | R A Bartlett

PLACINGS: 132/3134-3 | RPR **147**h

Starts	1st	2nd	3rd	4th	Win & Pl
8	2	1	4	1	£38,111

12/20	Leop	2m4f Mdn Hdl soft	£6,000
1/20	Fair	2m NHF 5-7yo heavy	£5,008

Smart novice hurdler last season, though didn't quite live up to expectations having been sent off

favourite for the Albert Bartlett at Cheltenham; only fourth that day and ran to a similar level when third behind Galopin Des Champs at Punchestown; likely to go novice chasing.

Stoner's Choice

6 br g Great Pretender - High Benefit (Beneficial)

Fergal O'Brien | Mrs Carolyn Kendrick

PLACINGS: 21/57/2111214- | RPR **143**+h

Starts	1st	2nd	3rd	4th	Win & Pl
11	5	3	-	1	£26,496

	3/21	Asct	2m5¹/₂f Cls3 116-139 Cond Hdl Hcap good	£5,174
139	11/20	MRas	2m4f Cls4 Nov Hdl good	£3,769
	10/20	Carl	2m1f Cls4 Nov Hdl good	£3,769
	9/20	Prth	2m Cls4 Nov Hdl gd-sft	£3,769
	4/19	Wwck	2m Cls5 NHF 4-6yo good	£2,599

Largely progressive hurdler last season, winning four times, most notably by six lengths on handicap debut at Ascot; had finished second in a Listed novice at Market Rasen but disappointed when favourite back in that grade at Perth on final run.

Stormy Ireland (Fr)

7 b m Motivator - Like A Storm (Ultimately Lucky)

Willie Mullins (Ire) | FB Racing Club

PLACINGS: 31222/261115/22921-1 | RPR **154**+h

Starts	1st	2nd	3rd	4th	Win & Pl
23	8	9	1	-	£292,616

5/21	Punc	2m4f Gd1 Hdl gd-yld	£63,214
4/21	Fair	2m4f Gd2 Hdl yield	£26,339
1/20	Naas	2m Gd3 Hdl yld-sft	£17,000
12/19	Leop	2m1¹/₂f Gd3 Hdl yield	£21,261
11/19	Punc	2m2f List Hdl soft	£15,946
11/18	Punc	2m2f List Hdl good	£16,327
5/18	Klny	2m1f List Hdl yield	£16,327
12/17	Fair	2m Mdn Hdl 3yo heavy	£6,055

Enjoyed a remarkable renaissance last spring, storming to her biggest ever wins at Fairyhouse and Punchestown while showing career-best form in the process following return to Willie Mullins; had struggled in four runs for Paul Nicholls (beaten favourite three times).

Sully D'Oc AA (Fr)

7 b g Konig Turf - Samarra D'Oc (Moon Madness)

Anthony Honeyball | John P McManus

PLACINGS: 15d1211/P/6256/1382-1 | RPR **147**+c

Starts	1st	2nd	3rd	4th	Win & Pl
17	6	4	1	1	£114,709

137	4/21	Punc	2m 123-150 Ch Hcap yield	£26,339
125	10/20	Asct	2m3f Cls3 Nov 120-132 Ch Hcap gd-sft	£9,747
	12/17	Pau	2m1¹/₂f Hdl 3yo v soft	£16,410
	12/17	Pau	2m¹/₂f Hdl 3yo soft	£12,308
	10/17	Toul	2m1¹/₂f Hdl 3yo good	£8,205
	8/17	Breh	1m3¹/₂f NHF 3yo	£4,274

Big improver in second season over fences last term and did particularly well in the spring, winning a big 2m handicap at Punchestown after a length second in the Red Rum at Aintree; worst runs in each of the last two seasons have both come at Cheltenham.

Summerville Boy (Ire)
9 b g Sandmason - Suny House (Carroll House)

Tom George | R S Brookhouse

PLACINGS: 311/474/61F125/1455- | RPR **159+**h

Starts	1st	2nd	3rd	4th	Win & Pl
19	6	3	1	3	£220,346

11/20	Aint	2m4f Cls2 Hdl gd-sft	£18,768
1/20	Chel	2m4¹/₂f Cls1 Gd2 Hdl soft	£28,475
11/19	Uttx	2m Cls3 Ch soft	£7,018
3/18	Chel	2m¹/₂f Cls1 Nov Gd1 Hdl heavy	£71,188
1/18	Sand	2m Cls1 Nov Gd1 Hdl heavy	£28,475
5/17	Klny	2m1f NHF 5-7yo soft	£5,265

Smart hurdler at around 2m4f, winning first time out over that trip at Aintree last season to add to victory in the 2020 Relkeel Hurdle; just came up short in stronger races, though, and hasn't proved the strongest stayer at 3m; won over fences in 2019 before chase career was aborted.

Tamaroc Du Mathan (Fr)
6 b g Poliglote - Thisbee Du Mathan (Turgeon)

Paul Nicholls | Mrs Johnny De La Hey

PLACINGS: 1/2057/121U- | RPR **154+**c

Starts	1st	2nd	3rd	4th	Win & Pl
9	3	2	-	-	£44,482

2/21	Kemp	2m4¹/₂f Cls1 Nov Gd2 Ch good	£13,668
131	11/20	Winc	1m7¹/₂f Cls3 Nov 115-134 Ch Hcap gd-sft	£7,310
4/18	Ange	1m7¹/₂f Hdl 3yo soft	£8,727

Flourished over fences last season, winning two of first three chases including a 2m4f Grade 2 novice at Kempton (second behind Shishkin at that track in between); well below par and already well beaten when unseating rider at Ayr on final run.

Tea Clipper (Ire)
6 b g Stowaway - A Plus Ma Puce (Turgeon)

Tom Lacey | Jerry Hinds & Ashley Head

PLACINGS: 1/1112/1533- | RPR **142**h

Starts	1st	2nd	3rd	4th	Win & Pl
8	4	1	2	-	£62,453

134	10/20	Chep	2m3¹/₂f Cls1 Gd3 127-146 Hdl Hcap good	£22,780
127	12/19	Hntg	2m Cls3 115-128 Hdl Hcap gd-sft	£12,512
11/19	Kemp	2m Cls4 Nov Hdl good	£4,094
10/19	Wwck	2m Cls4 Nov Hdl good	£4,549

Won last season's Silver Trophy at Chepstow (fourth win out of five over hurdles at the time) and progressed again during the spring, finishing third in the Coral Cup at Cheltenham and on first run over 3m at Aintree; likely to go novice chasing.

Teahupoo (Fr)
4 b g Masked Marvel - Droit D'Aimer (Sassanian)

Gordon Elliott (Ire) | Robcour

PLACINGS: 1112- | RPR **138+**h

Starts	1st	2nd	3rd	4th	Win & Pl
4	3	1	-	-	£47,684

2/21	Fair	2m Gd3 Hdl 4yo soft	£14,487
1/21	Fair	2m Hdl 4yo heavy	£8,955
10/20	Autl	2m2f Hdl 3yo heavy	£18,305

Won first three juvenile hurdles last season, twice by wide margins following switch from France, including a Grade 3 at Fairyhouse; returned there in a higher grade at Easter rather than going to Cheltenham but beaten at odds-on by subsequent Grade 1 winner Jeff Kidder.

Telmesomethinggirl (Ire)
6 b m Stowaway - Wahiba Hall (Saddlers' Hall)

Henry de Bromhead (Ire) | Kenneth Alexander

PLACINGS: 1/350/131131-5 | RPR **143+**h

Starts	1st	2nd	3rd	4th	Win & Pl
10	4	2	3		£71,201

3/21	Chel	2m1f Cls1 Nov Gd2 Hdl gd-sft	£37,982
9/20	List	2m4f Hdl good	£9,250
8/20	Bell	2m4f Hdl soft	£5,750
6/20	Rosc	2m Mdn Hdl good	£5,000

Impressive winner of last season's Mares' Novices' Hurdle at the Cheltenham Festival; had progressed well the previous summer before not proving quite as effective on softer ground on return at Leopardstown; well beaten when taking on the boys at Punchestown.

The Big Bite (Ire)
8 b g Scorpion - Thanks Noel (Tel Quel)

Henry Oliver | N T Griffith & H M Haddock

PLACINGS: 10/11408/412/1236- | RPR **153+**c

Starts	1st	2nd	3rd	4th	Win & Pl
14	5	2	1	2	£48,319

139	11/20	Aint	2m Cls3 126-139 Ch Hcap gd-sft	£12,346
1/20	Donc	2m4¹/₂f Cls4 Ch soft	£4,289
12/18	Hayd	1m7¹/₂f Cls2 Hdl heavy	£12,660
11/18	Chep	2m Cls4 Mdn Hdl gd-sft	£4,094
12/17	Hntg	2m Cls6 NHF 4-6yo gd-sft	£1,949
3/17	Ling	2m Cls6 NHF 4-6yo stand	£1,560

Progressive 2m-2m4f handicap chaser; won well at Aintree last season and was placed in further good handicaps, notably the Greatwood Gold Cup at Newbury; disappointed when third favourite for the Silver Trophy at Cheltenham on final run.

The Big Breakaway (Ire)

6 ch g Getaway - Princess Mairead (Blueprint)

Colin Tizzard | Eric Jones, Geoff Nicholas & John Romans

PLACINGS: 1/114/1223d — RPR **152+**c

Starts		1st	2nd	3rd	4th	Win & Pl
8		3	2	1	1	£63,209
	11/20 Chel	3m¹/₂f Cls2 Nov Ch soft				£12,628
	12/19 Newb	2m4¹/₂f Cls4 Nov Hdl 4-6yo soft				£4,484
	11/19 Chep	2m3¹/₂f Cls5 Mdn Hdl soft				£2,794

Didn't quite build on impressive victory on chasing debut at Cheltenham last season, failing to win again; still far from disgraced when second and third in Grade 1 novice chases, including behind Monkfish at the festival, though pulled up on final run at Aintree.

The Big Dog (Ire)

8 b g Mahler - Saddlers Leader (Saddlers' Hall)

Peter Fahey (Ire) | Damien J Kelly & Colin Kelly

PLACINGS: 2/F41/4219/2/3U331- — RPR **145**c

Starts		1st	2nd	3rd	4th	Win & Pl
12		3	2	3	2	£78,904
136	2/21 Punc	3m4f 125-149 Ch Hcap soft				£42,143
	1/19 Gowr	2m4f Mdn Auct Hdl soft				£11,009
	1/18 Naas	2m3f NHF 5-7yo sft-hvy				£5,451

Lightly raced and progressive chaser who gradually found his feet after more than 18 months off the track last season and broke his duck in the valuable Irish Grand National Trial at Punchestown; missed the real thing due to preference for softer ground.

The Big Getaway (Ire)

7 b g Getaway - Saddlers Dawn (Saddlers' Hall)

Willie Mullins (Ire) | Mrs J Donnelly

PLACINGS: 1/2/21413/31- — RPR **157+**c

Starts		1st	2nd	3rd	4th	Win & Pl
8		3	2	2	1	£39,708
	12/20 Leop	2m5f Ch yield				£6,250
	1/20 Naas	2m3f Mdn Hdl yld-sft				£8,014
	11/19 Punc	2m¹/₂f NHF 4-7yo soft				£5,857

Grand chasing type who looked like taking high rank among last season's novices, hacking up in a Leopardstown beginners' chase, until rubbed off in the new year through injury; has thrived at around 2m4f (third in the 2020 Ballymore) but should get 3m.

The Bosses Oscar (Ire)

6 b g Oscar - Cuteasafox (Vinnie Roe)

Gordon Elliott (Ire) | Bective Stud

PLACINGS: 3/212125/12226- — RPR **155**h

Starts		1st	2nd	3rd	4th	Win & Pl
10		3	5	-	-	£62,111
	10/20 Thur	2m6¹/₂f Hdl yield				£7,750
	12/19 Leop	2m4¹/₂f Mdn Hdl 4yo soft				£7,986
	10/19 Thur	2m NHF 4-7yo yld-yld				£5,324

Progressive staying hurdler last season who was unlucky not to land a good handicap, finishing

second three times in big fields, including the Pertemps Final at Cheltenham; should make a fine chaser.

The Glancing Queen (Ire)

7 b m Jeremy - Glancing (Kayf Tara)

Alan King | Dingwall, Farrell, Hornsey & Murray

PLACINGS: 1/1351/8/13125- — RPR **134**h

Starts		1st	2nd	3rd	4th	Win & Pl
10		4	1	2	-	£61,207
	1/21 Bang	2m¹/₂f Cls4 Nov Hdl heavy				£3,769
	11/20 Wwck	2m5f Cls4 Nov Hdl gd-sft				£3,769
	4/19 Aint	2m1f Cls1 Gd2 NHF 4-6yo soft				£25,322
	11/18 Chel	2m¹/₂f Cls1 List NHF 4-6yo good				£12,379

Won two novice hurdles last season, most impressively over 2m5f first time out, and pointed to a return to further when a strong-finishing fifth in the Mares' Novices' Hurdle at the Cheltenham Festival; had also filled that spot in the 2019 Champion Bumper; likely to go novice chasing.

The Jam Man (Ire)

8 br g Papal Bull - Kathy Jet (Singspiel)

Ronan McNally (Ire) | Ronan M P McNally

PLACINGS: 2F9P/071111429/P160- — RPR **153+**c

Starts		1st	2nd	3rd	4th	Win & Pl
34		10	3	1	1	£168,517
129	11/20 Navn	3m 126-147 Ch Hcap sft-hvy				£62,500
128	12/19 Navn	3m¹/₂f 122-150 Hdl Hcap soft				£42,523
122	7/19 NAbb	3m2¹/₂f Cls3 103-129 Hdl Hcap gd-fm				£6,583
121	6/19 Ctml	3m1¹/₂f Cls4 96-122 Ch Hcap good				£5,289
114	6/19 Sthl	3m Cls4 Nov 93-122 Ch Hcap good				£4,614
115	9/18 Sthl	2m4¹/₂f Cls4 100-115 Hdl Hcap good				£4,094
109	6/18 Hexm	2m7¹/₂f Cls3 92-117 Hdl Hcap good				£7,083
94	3/18 Sedg	2m4f Cls4 79-105 Hdl Hcap heavy				£4,094
87	3/18 Ayr	2m5¹/₂f Cls5 73-101 Hdl Hcap soft				£3,184
80	3/18 Catt	3m1¹/₂f Cls5 75-98 Hdl Hcap soft				£3,509

Smart and versatile stayer who had enjoyed most success over hurdles and on the Flat until exploiting a much lower chase mark with a remarkably easy win in last season's Troytown at Navan; twice struggled back over hurdles, including when sixth in a Grade 3 at Haydock.

The Shunter (Ire)

8 b g Stowaway - Tornado Lady (Gulland)

Emmet Mullins | John P McManus

PLACINGS: P/U494P/411413112-34 — RPR **155**c

Starts		1st	2nd	3rd	4th	Win & Pl
29		5	1	6	7	£198,204
140	3/21 Chel	2m4¹/₂f Cls1 Gd3 130-154 Ch Hcap gd-sft				£46,423
135	3/21 Kels	2m Cls2 124-150 Hdl Hcap gd-sft				£46,920
128	11/20 Chel	2m¹/₂f Cls1 Gd3 128-154 Hdl Hcap soft				£45,560
	9/20 Punc	2m5f Ch yld-sft				£6,250
	9/20 Dpat	2m3f Mdn Hdl good				£5,000

Made astonishing progress last season, starting as an 18-race maiden yet winning five times over hurdles and fences, most notably in the Plate at Cheltenham; finished second in a Grade 1 novice chase at Aintree and fourth in the Galway Plate this summer.

Thedevilscoachman (Ire)

5 br g Elusive Pimpernel - Hagawi (Selkirk)

Noel Meade (Ire) John P McManus

PLACINGS: 1/15117- RPR **145+**h

Starts	1st	2nd	3rd	4th	Win & Pl
6	4	-	-	-	£35,861
	2/21	Punc	2m¹/₂f Nov List Hdl soft		£14,487
	1/21	Navn	2m1¹/₂f Nov Hdl heavy		£8,429
	11/20	Cork	2m Mdn Hdl 4yo heavy		£6,000
	1/20	Naas	2m NHF 4yo gd-yld		£5,591

Won three novice hurdles last season, most notably a Listed race at Punchestown; seen as a Cheltenham candidate after that but waited for Fairyhouse only to disappoint when seventh in a Grade 2 (second failure in Graded company after fifth behind Appreciate It over Christmas).

Third Time Lucki (Ire)

6 br g Arcadio - Definite Valley (Definite Article)

Dan Skelton Mike & Eileen Newbould

PLACINGS: 2/3114/1121464- RPR **146+**h

Starts	1st	2nd	3rd	4th	Win & Pl
11	5	1	1	3	£40,439
	12/20	Kemp	2m Cls2 Nov Hdl gd-sft		£10,047
	10/20	Weth	2m Cls3 Nov Hdl gd-sft		£5,913
	10/20	Uttx	2m Cls4 Nov Hdl 4-6yo gd-sft		£3,769
	1/20	Hntg	2m Cls5 NHF 4-6yo soft		£2,274
	12/19	MRas	2m1¹/₂f Cls5 Mdn NHF 4-6yo soft		£2,274

Won three novice hurdles last season and unlucky not to add to that tally at Musselburgh (late blunder); ran another big race when a close sixth on handicap debut in the County Hurdle at Cheltenham (led in the straight) but below par when fourth in a Grade 1 at Aintree.

Third Wind

7 b/br g Shirocco - Act Three (Beat Hollow)

Hughie Morrison Mouse Hamilton-Fairley

PLACINGS: 30/1211/714/5251P- RPR **153+**h

Starts	1st	2nd	3rd	4th	Win & Pl
14	5	2	1	1	£107,335
	2/21	Hayd	3m¹/₂f Cls1 Gd2 Hdl soft		£17,085
	12/19	Winc	2m5¹/₂f Cls2 120-146 Hdl Hcap heavy		£11,574
	3/19	Sand	2m4f Cls1 Nov Gd3 123-138 Hdl 4-7yo Hcap soft		£42,203
	2/19	Tntn	2m3f Cls4 Nov Hdl soft		£5,133
	12/18	Plum	2m4¹/₂f Cls4 Mdn Hdl soft		£4,094

Won last season's Rendlesham Hurdle, making the most of a soft opening at that level (got 6lb from runner-up Lisnagar Oscar); came up short

in good handicaps and Graded races otherwise, finishing fifth in the Long Walk Hurdle and pulled up at Aintree.

Thomas Darby (Ire)

8 b g Beneficial - Silaoce (Nikos)

Olly Murphy Mrs Diana L Whateley

PLACINGS: 112312/2313/3303- RPR **157**h

Starts	1st	2nd	3rd	4th	Win & Pl
14	4	3	6	-	£111,297
151	1/20	Asct	2m3¹/₂f Cls1 Gd3 125-151 Hdl Hcap heavy		£28,475
	1/19	Tntn	2m¹/₂f Cls4 Nov Hdl gd-sft		£5,133
	10/18	Chel	2m¹/₂f Cls3 Mdn Hdl good		£9,285
	5/18	Hntg	2m Cls5 Am Mdn NHF 4-6yo good		£2,274

Has found winning hard since impressive victory in a handicap hurdle at Ascot in January 2020 forced him into Graded company; produced best run since then when stepped up to 3m in a Grade 1 at Aintree, seeing out the longer trip well; failed as a chaser two seasons ago.

Three Stripe Life (Ire)

5 br g Leading Light - Hirayna (Doyoun)

Gordon Elliott (Ire) K Haughey & Laura Haughey & Kieran T Byrne

PLACINGS: 14- RPR **129+**b

Starts	1st	2nd	3rd	4th	Win & Pl
2	1	-	-	1	£8,249
	1/21	Navn	2m NHF 4-7yo heavy		£5,268

Ran a fine race for one so inexperienced (unraced in point-to-points) when fourth in last season's Champion Bumper at Cheltenham; had won sole bumper by nine lengths at Navan; good prospect for novice hurdles.

Threeunderthrufive (Ire)

6 b g Shantou - Didinas (Kaldou Star)

Paul Nicholls McNeill Family

PLACINGS: 21/11161- RPR **143+**h

Starts	1st	2nd	3rd	4th	Win & Pl
7	5	1	-	-	£42,232
	4/21	Prth	3m Cls1 Nov List Hdl gd-sft		£11,960
	2/21	Muss	3m Cls2 Nov Hdl soft		£12,512
	11/20	Ludl	2m5f Cls2 Hdl good		£9,747
	10/20	Ling	2m3¹/₂f Cls4 Mdn Hdl soft		£3,769
	1/20	Chep	2m Cls5 NHF 4-6yo heavy		£2,274

Very useful novice hurdler last season; won four out of five races, with sole defeat coming when a creditable sixth in the Albert Bartlett at Cheltenham; bounced back when gaining biggest win in a Listed novice at Perth.

Thyme Hill

7 b g Kayf Tara - Rosita Bay (Hernando)

Philip Hobbs   The Englands & Heywoods

PLACINGS: 123/1114/121-   RPR **163+**h

Starts	1st	2nd	3rd	4th	Win & Pl
10	6	2	1	1	£215,453
	4/21	Aint	3m¹/₂f Cls1 Gd1 Hdl gd-sft		£84,195
	11/20	Newb	3m Cls1 Gd2 Hdl good		£28,475
	12/19	Newb	2m4¹/₂f Cls1 Nov Gd1 Hdl soft		£25,929
	11/19	Chel	2m5f Cls1 Nov Gd2 Hdl soft		£18,006
	10/19	Chep	2m3¹/₂f Cls1 Nov Gd2 Hdl gd-sft		£19,933
	10/18	Worc	2m Cls5 NHF 4-6yo good		£2,274

Arguably the leading British-trained staying hurdler last season, with sole defeat coming when mugged on the line by Paisley Park in the Long Walk Hurdle; missed the Stayers' Hurdle through injury but bounced back to gamely beat Roksana in a Grade 1 at Aintree.

Tiger Roll (Ire)

11 b g Authorized - Swiss Roll (Entrepreneur)

Gordon Elliott (Ire)   Gigginstown House Stud

PLACINGS: /2P511/4111/52/P614-   RPR **168+**c

Starts	1st	2nd	3rd	4th	Win & Pl
40	13	6	3	5	£1,417,686
	3/21	Chel	3m6f Cls2 Ch gd-sft		£30,246
159	4/19	Aint	4m2¹/₂f Cls1 Gd3 142-164 Ch Hcap gd-sft		£500,000
	3/19	Chel	3m6f Cls2 Ch soft		£40,235
	2/19	Navn	2m5f Gd2 Hdl yield		£23,919
150	4/18	Aint	4m2¹/₂f Cls1 Gd3 142-161 Ch Hcap heavy		£500,000
	3/18	Chel	3m6f Cls2 Ch soft		£40,261
	3/17	Chel	4m Cls1 Nov Gd2 Am Ch gd-sft		£71,952
138	10/16	Limk	3m 131-144 Ch Hcap yield		£43,382
	6/16	Kbgn	2m4f Nov Ch good		£6,331
	5/16	Baln	2m1f Ch good		£5,200
	10/14	Chel	2m¹/₂f Cls2 Hdl 4yo gd-sft		£18,768
	3/14	Chel	2m1f Cls1 Gd1 Hdl 4yo good		£68,340
	11/13	MRas	2m¹/₂f Cls4 Hdl 3yo soft		£3,899

Dual Grand National winner who controversially missed the race last term after a dispute over his handicap mark; had looked as good as ever when landing a fifth Cheltenham Festival win in the Cross Country Chase, though showed little in two runs over regulation obstacles either side of that.

Time To Get Up (Ire)

8 ch g Presenting - Gales Return (Bob's Return)

Jonjo O'Neill   John P McManus

PLACINGS: 2/42/3411-   RPR **148**c

Starts	1st	2nd	3rd	4th	Win & Pl
7	2	2	1	2	£83,794
138	3/21	Uttx	4m2f Cls1 List 132-154 Ch Hcap gd-sft		£67,524
130	2/21	Winc	3m1f Cls3 122-140 Ch Hcap heavy		£10,234

Made a big mark when sent chasing last season, improving as he went up in trip and winning the Midlands National at Uttoxeter (runner-up won the Scottish National next time); open to further improvement after just four runs over fences; likely Grand National type.

Tommy's Oscar (Ire)

6 b g Oscar - Glibin (Luso)

Ann Hamilton   Ian Hamilton

PLACINGS: F/56223/3121112613-   RPR **140+**h

Starts	1st	2nd	3rd	4th	Win & Pl
8	4	2	1	-	£38,841
132	3/21	Kels	2m Cls2 122-148 Hdl Hcap gd-sft		£15,432
124	1/21	Muss	1m7¹/₂f Cls2 104-130 Hdl Hcap soft		£6,238
	12/20	Newc	2m Cls4 Nov Hdl soft		£3,769
	12/20	Sedg	2m1f Cls4 Mdn Hdl gd-sft		£3,769

Chasing type who did really well to win four times over hurdles last season at around 2m, most notably in a handicap at Kelso off 132; ran another fine race when third in the Scottish Champion Hurdle at Ayr on final run; should stay further.

Topofthegame (Ire)

9 ch g Flemensfirth - Derry Vale (Mister Lord)

Paul Nicholls   Chris Giles & Mr & Mrs P K Barber

PLACINGS: 1/142/F412/2212/

Starts	1st	2nd	3rd	4th	Win & Pl
11	3	5	-	2	£240,041
	3/19	Chel	3m1¹/₂f Cls1 Nov Gd1 Ch soft		£98,473
142	2/18	Sand	2m7¹/₂f Cls3 123-147 Hdl Hcap soft		£56,270
	12/16	Asct	2m5¹/₂f Cls3 Mdn Hdl gd-sft		£7,798

Has missed the last two seasons through injury just as he looked to have developed into a top staying chase prospect; won what proved a red-hot RSA Chase in 2019 (Santini and Delta Work behind) and was second in two more Grade 1 novice chases either side of that; ruled out for season as guide went to press.

Tornado Flyer (Ire)

8 b g Flemensfirth - Mucho Macabi (Exceed And Excel)

Willie Mullins (Ire)   T F P

PLACINGS: 131/1P/411P35/22543-   RPR **166**c

Starts	1st	2nd	3rd	4th	Win & Pl
16	5	2	3	2	£180,578
	12/19	Navn	2m1f Nov Gd3 Ch soft		£19,932
	11/19	Naas	2m3f Ch sft-hvy		£7,720
	12/18	Punc	2m4f Mdn Hdl good		£7,087
	4/18	Punc	2m¹/₂f Gd1 NHF 4-7yo yield		£52,212
	1/18	Fair	2m NHF 5-7yo soft		£5,451

Grade 1 bumper winner who has largely operated in similar company over obstacles but is yet to strike in eight subsequent races at the top level; came closest when a length second to Min in last season's John Durkan Chase and also ran well when third in the Ryanair.

Torygraph (Ire)

6 b/br g Mahler - Oddly Presented (Presenting)

Gordon Elliott (Ire)   Gigginstown House Stud

PLACINGS: 245/32118-6   RPR **144+**h

Starts	1st	2nd	3rd	4th	Win & Pl
9	2	2	1	1	£18,652
	1/21	Thur	2m7f Nov Hdl sft-hvy		£7,112
	12/20	Fair	2m7¹/₂f Mdn Hdl sft-hvy		£5,000

Proved a revelation when stepped up in trip

in novice hurdles last season, twice winning impressively after an ordinary bumper career; sent off just 7-1 for the Albert Bartlett at Cheltenham but finished only eighth and fared even worse at Punchestown.

Tritonic
4 ch g Sea The Moon - Selenography (Selkirk)
Alan King   Mcneill Family & Ian Dale
PLACINGS: 115-   RPR **142+h**

Starts	1st	2nd	3rd	4th	Win & Pl
3	2	-	-	-	£21,480
	2/21	Kemp	2m Cls1 Gd2 Hdl 4yo good		£12,814
	1/21	Asct	1m7¹/₂f Cls3 Hdl 4yo soft		£6,173

Smart Flat performer who took really well to hurdles last season, showing an impressive turn of foot when running away with the Adonis at Kempton; disappointed in fifth when the leading British-trained contender for the Triumph Hurdle.

Truckers Lodge (Ire)
9 b g Westerner - Galeacord (Accordion)
Paul Nicholls   Gordon & Su Hall
PLACINGS: 2/1441221/24121/U77-   RPR **156c**

Starts	1st	2nd	3rd	4th	Win & Pl
18	6	5	-	4	£159,544
141	3/20	Uttx	4m2f Cls1 List 131-157 Ch Hcap heavy		£84,478
	10/19	Chep	2m7¹/₂f Cls3 Ch gd-sft		£7,018
	3/19	Extr	2m7f Cls4 Nov Hdl gd-sft		£4,224
123	12/18	Chep	2m7¹/₂f Cls3 110-129 Hdl Hcap heavy		£6,758
	5/18	Sthl	2m4¹/₂f Cls5 Mdn Hdl good		£3,444
	4/17	Chep	2m Cls6 NHF 4-6yo soft		£1,949

Thrived in top staying handicaps as a novice two seasons ago, easily winning the Midlands National having finished second in the Welsh National; raised 14lb for that win and could manage only seventh in those two races last term.

Two For Gold (Ire)
8 b g Gold Well - Two Of Each (Shernazar)
Kim Bailey   May We Never Be Found Out Partnership
PLACINGS: 61/4114/1112/2P313U-   RPR **157+c**

Starts	1st	2nd	3rd	4th	Win & Pl
17	8	2	2	2	£99,180
149	2/21	Wwck	2m4f Cls2 129-155 Ch Hcap soft		£21,896
	1/20	Wwck	3m Cls1 Nov Gd2 Ch soft		£19,933
	12/19	Kels	2m7¹/₂f Cls3 Nov Ch soft		£12,116
132	11/19	Carl	2m4f Cls3 Nov 117-135 Ch Hcap soft		£8,123
	1/19	Bang	2m7f Cls4 Nov Hdl soft		£4,094
	12/18	Weth	2m5¹/₂f Cls4 Nov Hdl soft		£4,224
	2/18	Donc	2m¹/₂f Cls5 NHF 4-6yo gd-sft		£2,599
	12/17	Sthl	1m7¹/₂f Cls5 Am NHF 4-6yo good		£2,599

Consistent handicap chaser who deserved his victory over 2m4f at Warwick last season having been placed in other good races at Wetherby and Kempton; pulled up when quietly fancied for the Ladbrokes Trophy, making mistakes and weakening from the home turn.

Umbrigado (Ire)
7 br g Stowaway - Dame O'Neill (Dr Massini)
David Pipe   John White & Anne Underhill
PLACINGS: 2/1116/560/221116-   RPR **152+c**

Starts	1st	2nd	3rd	4th	Win & Pl
13	6	2	-	-	£61,043
144	3/21	Newb	2m4f Cls1 Gd3 132-153 Ch Hcap good		£22,780
139	2/21	Weth	1m7f Cls3 114-139 Ch Hcap soft		£7,018
	1/21	Font	2m3¹/₂f Cls4 Nov Ch heavy		£4,761
	2/19	Extr	2m2¹/₂f Cls4 Nov Hdl gd-sft		£4,549
	12/18	Sthl	1m7¹/₂f Cls5 Mdn Hdl soft		£3,119
	11/18	Uttx	2m Cls5 NHF 4-6yo good		£2,274

Took really well to fences last season, taking on more experienced handicappers and completing a hat-trick in the Greatwood Gold Cup at Newbury; below-par sixth when stepped up to Grade 1 level at Aintree; won from 2m-2m4f and also has form over 3m as a hurdler.

Unexcepted (Fr)
7 br g Anzillero - Eaton Lass (Definite Article)
Willie Mullins (Ire)   John P McManus
PLACINGS: 3/12P/16-8P   RPR **155+c**

Starts	1st	2nd	3rd	4th	Win & Pl
8	2	1	2	-	£21,721
	10/20	Tipp	2m1f Ch sft-hvy		£5,500
	11/19	Fair	2m Mdn Hdl sft-hvy		£5,857

Made a big impression when winning first time over fences last season and showed promise despite drawing a blank after; struck into when favourite for a Grade 3 at Killarney after travelling best on handicap debut at Punchestown.

Vanillier (Fr)
6 gr g Martaline - Virgata (Turgeon)
Gavin Cromwell (Ire)   Mrs H M Keaveney
PLACINGS: P/1/21201-4   RPR **153+h**

Starts	1st	2nd	3rd	4th	Win & Pl
6	2	2	-	1	£73,266
	3/21	Chel	3m Cls1 Nov Gd1 Hdl gd-sft		£55,127
	11/20	Naas	2m3f Mdn Hdl sft-hvy		£7,000

Won last season's Albert Bartlett at Cheltenham by 11 lengths, benefiting from a prominent ride off a modest gallop but still impressing up the hill; won just one of five other races, although was sick after Leopardstown and perhaps over the top at Punchestown either side of festival win.

Vinndication (Ire)
8 b g Vinnie Roe - Pawnee Trail (Taipan)
Kim Bailey   Moremoneythan
PLACINGS: 1111/1135/14/2U60-   RPR **165+c**

Starts	1st	2nd	3rd	4th	Win & Pl
14	6	1	1	1	£152,349
151	11/19	Asct	3m Cls1 Gd3 137-163 Ch Hcap gd-sft		£56,950
	12/18	Asct	2m5f Cls5 Nov Ch soft		£19,933
	11/18	Carl	2m4f Cls3 Nov Ch soft		£7,473
	2/18	Hntg	2m3¹/₂f Cls1 Nov List Hdl soft		£17,085
	1/18	Asct	2m5¹/₂f Cls3 Nov Hdl 4-7yo soft		£6,758
	12/17	Leic	2m4¹/₂f Cls3 Nov Hdl soft		£6,498
	11/17	Ludl	2m Cls4 NHF 4-6yo good		£3,249

Classy stayer who finished second behind

Cyrname in last season's Charlie Hall Chase and was going well when unseating his rider in the Ladbrokes Trophy (joint-favourite); return to hurdles didn't work on last two runs.

Vintage Clouds (Ire)

11 gr g Cloudings - Rare Vintage (Germany)

Sue Smith — Trevor Hemmings

PLACINGS: 3/1P2F6/5P3158/7531- RPR **157+c**

Starts	1st	2nd	3rd	4th	Win & Pl
38	6	11	6	1	£262,938

143	3/21	Chel	3m1f Cls1 Gd3 132-158 Ch Hcap soft	£46,423
143	1/20	Hayd	3m1½f Cls1 Gd2 136-156 Ch Hcap heavy	£42,713
143	11/18	Hayd	3m1½f Cls2 130-144 Ch Hcap good	£31,714
132	10/17	Aint	3m1f Cls3 Nov 120-133 Ch Hcap gd-sft	£9,097
	11/15	Hayd	2m3f Cls3 Nov Hdl 4-7yo soft	£6,498
	1/15	Weth	2m Cls6 NHF 4-6yo soft	£1,643

Evergreen staying chaser who gained the biggest win of his career in the Ultima Handicap Chase at last season's Cheltenham Festival; last three wins have remarkably all come off 143 across two and a half years and never better than fifth off higher than 145 (now 150).

Voix Du Reve (Fr)

9 br g Voix Du Nord - Pommbelle (Apple Tree)

Iain Jardine — D & D Armstrong Ltd & L Westwood

PLACINGS: 13FU1/45436/042203-0 RPR **159c**

Starts	1st	2nd	3rd	4th	Win & Pl
35	7	5	5	3	£187,745

	4/19	Fair	2m4f Nov Gd1 Ch gd-yld	£53,153
	11/18	Punc	2m Nov Gd2 Ch good	£23,235
	10/18	Gway	2m2f Ch yield	£7,632
	7/18	Bell	2m4f Hdl gd-fm	£7,087
	5/18	Klny	2m4f Hdl good	£9,812
	11/15	Engh	2m1½f Hdl 3yo v soft	£17,860
	9/15	Nanc	2m1f Hdl 3yo v soft	£7,814

Grade 1 winner for Willie Mullins in 2019 but hasn't won during the last two seasons, though came close following switch to Iain Jardine last season, finishing second twice over hurdles at Musselburgh; good third when reverting to fences at Ayr.

Waiting Patiently (Ire)

10 b g Flemensfirth - Rossavon (Beneficial)

Christian Williams — Richard Collins

PLACINGS: 1/111/111/U23/3/23P- RPR **169+c**

Starts	1st	2nd	3rd	4th	Win & Pl
16	7	4	3	-	£292,855

	2/18	Asct	2m5f Cls1 Gd1 Ch soft	£85,827
	1/18	Kemp	2m4½f Cls1 List Ch gd-sft	£22,780
	11/17	Carl	2m4f Cls1 List Ch gd-sft	£17,085
	1/17	Hayd	2m4f Cls1 Nov Gd2 Ch soft	£18,546
	12/16	Newc	2m½f Cls3 Nov Ch soft	£6,498
123	11/16	Sedg	2m½f Cls3 Nov 115-130 Ch Hcap soft	£6,498
	1/16	Sedg	2m4f Cls4 Nov Hdl gd-sft	£3,798

Fragile chaser who has been very lightly raced in recent seasons but underlined his talent again last term, finishing second in the King George on his first run for more than a year; found 2m1f too sharp when third in the Clarence House before being pulled up in the Bowl at Aintree; has since left Ruth Jefferson.

Whatmore

9 b g Schiaparelli - Polymiss (Poliglote)

Henry Daly — Strachan, Lewis, Gabb, Graham & Inkin

PLACINGS: 681/31772/134344/22- RPR **149c**

Starts	1st	2nd	3rd	4th	Win & Pl
23	5	4	3	5	£85,093

	5/19	MRas	2m5½f Cls4 Nov Ch good	£4,952
135	11/18	Bang	2m3½f Cls2 121-144 Hdl Hcap gd-sft	£14,076
	3/18	Wwck	2m Cls4 Nov Hdl soft	£4,419
	10/17	Bang	2m½f Cls4 Nov Hdl good	£3,249
	5/17	Aint	2m1f Cls4 Nov Hdl good	£3,899

Hasn't won since May 2019 but has been knocking on the door in top handicap chases; finished fourth in the novice handicap at the Cheltenham Festival in 2020 and was second in both runs last season (favourite both times), just losing out to Yorkhill in the Rehearsal Chase.

Wilde About Oscar (Ire)

6 b g Oscar - Baie Barbara (Heron Island)

Dan Skelton — Mike & Eileen Newbould

PLACINGS: 214/11P110- RPR **150+h**

Starts	1st	2nd	3rd	4th	Win & Pl
9	5	1	-	1	£38,512

146	3/21	Uttx	2m4f Cls2 128-146 Hdl Hcap gd-sft	£17,023
	2/21	Extr	2m1f Cls1 Nov List Hdl heavy	£8,970
	11/20	Aint	2m4f Cls4 Nov Hdl 4-6yo gd-sft	£4,419
	10/20	Uttx	2m Cls4 Nov Hdl 4-6yo gd-sft	£3,769
	12/19	Wwck	2m Cls5 NHF 4-6yo soft	£2,599

Prolific novice hurdler last season, winning four times, most notably a Listed novice at Exeter and a handicap at Uttoxeter off top weight (mark of 146); flopped on both runs in a higher grade when pulled up in the Challow Hurdle and tailed off at Aintree.

Yala Enki (Fr)

11 b/br g Nickname - Cadiane (Cadoudal)

Paul Nicholls — Hills Of Ledbury

PLACINGS: 66/1357/0313/2F314U- RPR **165+c**

Starts	1st	2nd	3rd	4th	Win & Pl
46	11	6	8	6	£382,364

	1/21	Tntn	3m4½f Cls2 Ch soft	£11,711
	1/20	Tntn	3m4½f Cls2 Ch heavy	£31,714
150	11/18	Bang	3m Cls2 126-150 Ch Hcap gd-sft	£16,266
146	2/18	Hayd	3m4½f Cls1 Gd3 138-161 Ch Hcap heavy	£60,067
146	3/17	Kels	3m2f Cls2 125-147 Ch Hcap heavy	£17,545
139	12/16	Hayd	2m7f Cls2 120-139 Ch Hcap soft	£15,640
	2/16	Asct	2m3½f Cls2 Nov Hdl soft	£15,640
130	1/16	Kemp	2m5f Cls1 List 127-153 Hdl Hcap soft	£22,780
	11/15	Extr	2m5½f Cls3 Nov Hdl gd-sft	£5,523
	2/14	Fntb	2m2f Ch 4yo v soft	£9,600
	10/13	Pari	2m1f Ch 3yo gd-sft	£7,415

Very smart staying chaser who has run well in a string of gruelling tests of stamina in recent years, finishing third in the last three editions of the Welsh Grand National; has gained only two wins since 2018 at Taunton, though was also a short-head second at Cheltenham last season.

You Raised Me Up (Ire)

8 b g Presenting - Morning Supreme (Supreme Leader)

Martin Brassil (Ire)   Chiat Kwong Ching & S Mulryan

PLACINGS: 5/4/1/42253/110-   RPR **142**h

Starts	1st	2nd	3rd	4th	Win & Pl
11	3	2	1	2	£43,789
2/21	Naas	2m3f Nov Hdl soft			£10,536
9/20	List	2m Mdn Hdl soft			£6,000
8/18	Gway	2m2¹/₂f NHF 5-7yo soft			£9,267

Second-season novice hurdler last season and put experience to good use when winning in novice company at Listowel and Naas; very well backed when sent off favourite for the County Hurdle at Cheltenham but found to be lame after finishing only tenth.

Younevercall (Ire)

10 b g Yeats - Afarka (Kahyasi)

Kim Bailey   Youneverknow Partnership

PLACINGS: /1F61/17/2181/24P81-   RPR **157**h

Starts	1st	2nd	3rd	4th	Win & Pl
17	7	2	1	1	£98,385
4/21	Sand	2m5¹/₂f Cls1 Gd2 Hdl good			£23,919
4/19	Sand	2m5¹/₂f Cls1 Gd2 Hdl good			£31,323
144	11/18	Kemp	2m5f Cls2 122-145 Hdl Hcap good		£11,886
135	11/16	Kemp	2m5f Cls2 128-135 Hdl Hcap good		£11,886
4/16	Hntg	2m4¹/₂f Cls4 Nov Hdl gd-sft			£3,899
10/15	Uttx	2m Cls5 Mdn Hdl good			£2,599
8/15	Sthl	1m7¹/₂f Cls6 NHF 4-6yo good			£1,949

Talented but fragile hurdler who has won the last two runnings of the Grade 2 Select Hurdle at Sandown, albeit two years apart because of the pandemic; didn't quite appear to stay the longer 3m trip when fourth in the Long Walk and eighth in the Stayers' Hurdle last season.

Zambella (Fr)

6 b m Zambezi Sun - Visby (Irish Wells)

Nigel Twiston-Davies   Simon Munir & Isaac Souede

PLACINGS: 11/U44/71112F2-   RPR **147**c

Starts	1st	2nd	3rd	4th	Win & Pl
12	5	2	-	2	£85,112
1/21	Leic	2m Cls1 List Ch soft			£14,682
12/20	Wwck	2m4f Cls1 Nov List Ch soft			£11,746
11/20	Bang	2m1¹/₂f Cls1 Nov List Ch soft			£14,238
4/19	Comp	2m2f Hdl 4yo v soft			£19,459
3/19	Fntb	2m2f Hdl 4yo v soft			£8,649

Won her first three races over fences last season, all Listed mares' chases; shortest price of the British runners (albeit 28-1) in the Mares' Chase at Cheltenham and still in contention when falling three out but didn't stay 3m when beaten favourite at Perth on final run.

Zanahiyr (Ire)

4 ch g Nathaniel - Zariyna (Marju)

Gordon Elliott (Ire)   Noel & Valerie Moran

PLACINGS: 1114-2   RPR **148+**h

Starts	1st	2nd	3rd	4th	Win & Pl
5	3	1	-	1	£58,183
12/20	Leop	2m Gd2 Hdl 3yo soft			£17,500
11/20	Fair	2m Gd3 Hdl 3yo soft			£13,750
10/20	Baln	2m2f Mdn Hdl 3yo soft			£5,000

Sent off 11-8 favourite for last season's Triumph Hurdle after three impressive wins in late 2020 but didn't quite deliver in the spring; caught flat-footed when fourth at Cheltenham and just held when a strong-finishing second at Punchestown; could benefit from longer trips.

Zanza (Ire)

7 b g Arcadio - What A Bleu (Pistolet Bleu)

Philip Hobbs   Louisville Syndicate Elite

PLACINGS: 18101/P16F60/421FP6-   RPR **152+**c

Starts	1st	2nd	3rd	4th	Win & Pl
18					£51,519
138	11/20	Newb	2m¹/₂f Cls2 134-147 Ch Hcap good		£19,028
136	11/19	Newb	2m¹/₂f Cls3 120-136 Cond Hdl Hcap gd-sft		£6,433
131	3/19	Newb	2m¹/₂f Cls2 120-134 Hdl Hcap gd-sft		£9,747
12/18	Tntn	2m3f Cls4 Nov Hdl gd-sft			£5,133
11/18	Chep	2m Cls4 Nov Hdl soft			£4,094

Impressive winner of a good 2m handicap chase at Newbury last season on just his third run over fences but plagued by misfortune subsequently; going well when fell three out at Cheltenham next time and badly hampered by fallers at Cheltenham and Aintree in the spring.

INDEX OF HORSES

INDEX OF HORSES

INDEX OF HORSES